PLEASURE GROUNDS OF DEATH

PLEASURE GROUNDS OF DEATH

The Rural Cemetery in
Nineteenth-Century America

Joy M. Giguere

University of Michigan Press
Ann Arbor

For questions or permissions, please contact um.press.perms@umich.edu

Published in the United States of America by the
University of Michigan Press
Manufactured in the United States of America
Printed on acid-free paper
First published July 2024

A CIP catalog record for this book is available from the British Library.

Library of Congress Cataloging-in-Publication Data

Names: Giguere, Joy M., 1980– author.
Title: Pleasure grounds of death : the rural cemetery in nineteenth-century America /
    Joy M. Giguere.
Description: Ann Arbor : University of Michigan Press, 2024. | Includes bibliographical
    references and index.
Identifiers: LCCN 2024008396 (print) | LCCN 2024008397 (ebook) | ISBN 9780472076895
    (hardcover) | ISBN 9780472056897 (paperback) | ISBN 9780472221790 (ebook)
Subjects: LCSH: Cemeteries—Social aspects—United States—History—19th century. |
    Group identity—United States—History—19th century. | Country life—United States—
    History—19th century.
Classification: LCC GT3203 .G54   2024 (print) | LCC GT3203 (ebook) |
    DDC 363.7/50973091734—dc23/eng/20240328
LC record available at https://lccn.loc.gov/2024008396
LC ebook record available at https://lccn.loc.gov/2024008397

This book will be made open access within three years of publication thanks to Path to Open,
a program developed in partnership between JSTOR, the American Council of Learned
Societies (ACLS), University of Michigan Press, and The University of North Carolina Press
to bring about equitable access and impact for the entire scholarly community, including
authors, researchers, libraries, and university presses around the world. Learn more at
https://about.jstor.org/path-to-open/

Cover illustration: Laurel Hill Cemetery, Philadelphia.

FOR MY MOM, PATRICIA GIGUERE,
BECAUSE YOU READ ALL THE DRAFTS

Contents

CHAPTER 6

Digital materials related to this title can be found on
the Fulcrum platform via the following citable URL:
https://doi.org/10.3998/mpub.11614217

Illustrations

Acknowledgments

There are always many people and institutions to thank when publishing a book, and the first among these is Sara Cohen, my editor at the University of Michigan Press. She reached out to me in 2018 to talk about my research while I was at the annual meeting of the American Historical Association. During our conversation, Sara expressed great enthusiasm for my research on the rural cemetery movement of the nineteenth century, and I moved ahead with writing the proposal for *Pleasure Grounds of Death*. In 2019, I signed an advance contract with the Press, with an original projected completion date of December 2020. Then, of course, COVID-19 took over everything, we all went remote with teaching and learning, and like so many mothers in academia, my research and writing came to a full stop. Even when we went back to campus and the classroom, all of the new expectations and modifications that had to be made for teaching and learning during an active pandemic meant that I wrote virtually nothing for this book for well over a year. Thanks to Penn State University, which granted me my first sabbatical in the fall of 2022, I was able to take advantage of the time afforded to me to really knuckle down and finish the first draft of the manuscript, which I submitted to Sara for peer review in December 2022, two years after my original contractual deadline. Through everything, she has shown inexhaustible patience and given me the grace that I often refused to give myself when I had neither the time nor the energy to write. Sara, thank you so much for your patience and your faith in me and this project.

I would also like to extend many thanks to the following institutions and individuals who assisted with my research on rural cemeteries in some way over the last decade: Meg Winslow and Mount Auburn Cemetery; the research staff at Laurel Hill Cemetery; the Filson Historical Society; the Kentucky Historical Society; the Virginia Historical Society; Jennie Benford with the Homewood Cemetery Historical Fund; Dr. Beth Roark and Allegheny

Cemetery; and Rachel Wolgemuth and West Laurel Hill Cemetery; thanks also to John Martine, Judy Juntunen, and Ed Snyder for taking photographs at cemeteries I couldn't visit myself.

To all those who read drafts of this manuscript, I would first and foremost like to extend thanks to my mother, Patricia Giguere, who has been my proofreader since I was in grade school. She's a person of great talent and creativity, and I can only hope that what I have written will give her pleasure. To my peer reviewers—Dr. Ryan K. Smith at Virginia Commonwealth University and Dr. Erik R. Seeman at the University of Buffalo—your insight and recommendations were immeasurably helpful. I would also like to offer gratitude to my friends and colleagues who read drafts of this and other manuscripts, portions of which ended up here: Dr. Jennifer Nesbitt and Dr. Noel Sloboda at Penn State York and Dr. David Turpie and Jennifer Shaffer Merry at the Arizona Historical Society. I must also thank the members, past and present, of the Penn State York faculty writing group (aka the research emotional support group): Dr. Jennifer Nesbitt, Dr. Sonia Molloy, Joel Burkholder, Suzanne Shaffer, Dr. Nicole Muscanell, and Dr. Stephen Foster.

Finally, I wish to thank friends and family who have always shown support and enthusiasm for my two-decades-long love affair with cemeteries—my parents, Patricia and Gerard Giguere; my grandparents, Raymond and Marie Siembab; my uncle Richard Siembab; my Association for Gravestone Studies family, which has become so wonderfully large over the years; and my dear friends, colleagues, and students at Penn State York. And, of course, I thank my husband, Ben Proud, and my sons, Charlie and Raymond—you always get me and you always let me bring you to cemeteries. We have so many more to visit.

I take full responsibility for any errors, factual or otherwise, that might appear in this manuscript.

Modified portions of the following previously published articles appear in this book:

"'Variety There Must Be': Eclecticism, Taste, and the Nineteenth-Century Rural Cemetery Landscape," *Markers XXXIII: The Annual Journal of the Association for Gravestone Studies* (2017): 82–104.

"'Too Mean to Live, and Certainly in No Fit Condition to Die': Vandalism, Public Misbehavior, and the Rural Cemetery Movement," *Journal of the Early Republic* 38, no. 2 (2018): 293–324.

"Localism and Nationalism in the City of the Dead: The Rural Cemetery Movement in the Antebellum South," *Journal of Southern History* 84, no. 4 (2018): 845–82.

"'Flaunting the Evidence of Treason in the Face of Loyalty': Funerals, Grave Decoration, and the Fashioning of Kentucky's Civil War Identity," *Ohio Valley History* 19, no. 4 (Winter 2019): 19–44.

Introduction

When I was a graduate student at the University of Maine at Orono in the early 2000s, it did not take long for me to discover the largest cemetery I had ever seen—Mount Hope Cemetery, located in nearby Bangor. I first encountered Mount Hope while working on my master's degree in historical archaeology but initially gave it little of my attention. This was because when I began my thesis fieldwork in 2004, I was immersed in finding and cataloging pre-1820 gravestones in the southern part of the state. My work at the time kept me occupied with the colonial-era burying grounds that contained rows of upright slate headstones and footstones bearing the popular emblems of the period—winged death's heads, cherubs, and urns and willows. Archaeologists James Deetz and Edwin Dethlefsen were at that time my role models for their research asserting that colonial gravestones were significant artifacts worthy of serious scholarly attention and that the iconographic emblems they bore reflected the cultural and religious ideologies and transformations of eighteenth-century New England.[1] When I drove by cemeteries like Mount Hope, dotted with obelisks, shafts, mausoleums, and marble as far as the eye could see, I would simply mutter, "too new," and continue on my way. Living near, and later in, Bangor, however, meant that I drove by Mount Hope on a regular basis.

Eventually, in my search for someplace quiet and outdoors that wasn't the woods, where I might be mistaken for a whitetail deer, I ventured to the cemetery. Going to Mount Hope became my regular escape from campus or my apartment. I felt I had recognized what was invisible to others around me—that this place was a treasure. For me, Mount Hope was like a secret garden of death about which only I and the intermittent joggers and dog walkers knew. Some days I would hike around and look at the monuments, of which there seemed to be an endless variety. Other days I would find a spot where I would sit and think, write in my journal—sometimes entries where I contemplated my own mortality, others where I pondered whether the special collections librarian I liked on campus liked me back (we've been married since 2009)—and sometimes write poetry. Really, *really* awful poetry. At some point during this time, I learned that portions of the film adaptation of Stephen King's *Pet Sematary* were filmed at Mount Hope (also that my apartment during my doctoral program years was just a couple of blocks away from King's house).

When I decided to remain at Orono and began my doctoral program in history in 2005, I knew that I would continue to focus my research on commemorative culture—cemeteries, grave markers, monuments and memorials, and public memory. It was only then, when I eventually settled on the Egyptian Revival as the topic for my dissertation, that I came to understand that Mount Hope was not just a really large local cemetery but also one of countless burying grounds across the country known as "rural cemeteries" established during the nineteenth century from the 1830s through the 1860s. Originally created in the decades before the establishment of large public parks, rural cemeteries doubled as parklike natural spaces to which the living could escape for an afternoon. It was within the precincts of the rural cemetery where visitors would ride their carriages, take walks, look at monuments, contemplate mortality, mourn the dead, and, at times, misbehave. I had, in the twenty-first century, gone to my local rural cemetery and unknowingly engaged in many of the very same activities that visitors had done within the city of the dead over a century and a half before.

As historians since the 1970s have rightfully acknowledged, "rural cemetery" is really a misnomer—the term refers to the aesthetics rather than the location of the burial place.[2] Meticulously landscaped to resemble untouched nature, rural cemeteries embodied the popular nineteenth-century aesthetic of the picturesque, which blended human artifice with preexisting nature. Twentieth-century architectural historian Caroll Louis Vanderslice Meeks (1907–66) articulated best the prevailing qualities of the picturesque in his 1950 article "Picturesque Eclecticism" for the *Art Bulletin*: as a reaction "against the restriction of classicism," the picturesque exhibited roughness, movement, irregularity, variety, and intricacy. Noted Meeks, "It signifies that the forms and their relationships are complex and not immediately discerned, that curiosity is aroused, that the beholder must make an effort to decipher them and that his interest will be provoked by his temporary perplexity."[3] The result within the context of the rural cemetery movement was the fashioning of burial landscapes that incorporated hills, ponds and lakes, footpaths and carriage paths, architectural features such as carriage gateways and chapels, and an inexhaustible array of trees, shrubs, and flowers. To all of that was added the great variety of tombs, monuments, and mausoleums by those who purchased lots for themselves and their loved ones, which they often further ornamented with even more flowers and greenery.

Albeit rural by design, the rural cemetery was an urban institution located on the fringes of development—thus really suburban in location—and intended to serve the burial needs of city dwellers who, by the 1820s and 1830s, were rapidly expanding in number due to immigration and the factory development of the first Industrial Revolution. For some historians, the development of these new burying grounds so dedicated to the cultivation of the seemingly natural environment into a picturesque whole signified efforts "to grant universal access to the kinds of environmental 'amenities' that were clearly being threatened by industrialization and urbanization."[4] In this understanding of rural cemeteries, they were democratic institutions driven by the egalitarian ideals of Jacksonian America, open and available to all ages, sexes, and classes in society so that Americans of every ilk might enjoy and benefit from their environmental charms and didactic monuments—as well as escape the degrading effects of urban overcrowding, noise, and pollution.

Yet other historians have regarded the rural cemeteries as reflective of the broader conservative reformist trends of antebellum America, through which middle-class Anglo-Americans endeavored to shape public behaviors and cultural patterns in efforts to fashion a national identity that contemporaries would regard as refined and civilized. As noted by Stanley French, "The rural cemetery through its intended capacity as cultivator of the finer emotions was another facet of the conservative cultural uplift movement during the Age of the Common Man."[5] Blanche Linden, in her groundbreaking book on Mount Auburn Cemetery, *Silent City on a Hill*, contended that the cemetery's founders "were attempting not just to solve [Boston's] burial problems but to develop an American culture, in all senses of the word."[6] More recently, Jeffrey Smith has argued that even as rural cemeteries were revolutionary in shaping how Americans viewed and engaged with burial landscapes and the relationship between the cemetery and the urban environment, there were inherent paradoxes to rural cemeteries—"they were 'rural' yet urban, sacred yet secular, burial places for the dead but used regularly by the living, natural yet manicured"—while James R. Cothran and

Erica Danylchak have ably examined the importance of rural cemeteries in influencing the development of public parks, the growth of garden suburbs, and the emergence of the profession of landscape architecture.[7]

The American rural cemetery movement was indeed groundbreaking and culturally complex in many ways, but it did not emerge out of a vacuum. Efforts had already been made to create reform cemeteries as communities grappled with burial overcrowding and epidemic disease during the late eighteenth century. The first of these was the New Burying Ground (later renamed Grove Street Cemetery) in New Haven, Connecticut, in 1796. Reflective of the desire for order and the popularity of neoclassical architecture and aesthetics, reform cemeteries were designed with rectilinear carriage paths separating family lots and incorporated rows of planted trees for shade. New Haven's New Burying Ground, as the first major reform cemetery, "showed visitors an idealized image of the systematically ordered city," in which the landscape of both the living and the dead existed in complementary harmony with each other, "unified by the cultivated, artificial refinement of landscape plantings."[8] Larger than churchyards and public burying grounds, reform cemeteries gained traction during the first third of the nineteenth century, only to be replaced in the public's estimation by the much grander rural cemeteries that emerged during the 1830s. Nevertheless, the reform cemeteries of the 1790s and early 1800s laid important groundwork for shaping how Americans regarded the cultural and aesthetic utility of burying grounds as more than strictly functional landscapes in which to dispose of the dead.

Mount Hope Cemetery, where I spent so much of my time during graduate school, was established in 1834, making it the second oldest rural cemetery in the United States; Mount Auburn Cemetery in Cambridge, Massachusetts, holds the distinction of being the first and the progenitor of an entire cultural phenomenon known as the rural cemetery movement. Established in 1831 by a group of civic-minded professional men in Boston, Mount Auburn, at seventy-two acres, was a revolutionary institution that built upon the principles of the reform cemetery model and further upended people's notions of what a burying ground should look like, how it might function, and how the living might engage with the dead, with each other, and with nature in such a space. It was simultaneously a burying ground, a public park, and an experimental garden, as the Massachusetts Horticultural Society played a major role in its creation. It afforded plenty of space for lot holders to purchase land where they could bury their dead and ornament the space as they saw fit with plantings and monuments, for each lot became the private property of the lot holder. Expansive in scope with footpaths and carriage paths, Mount Auburn was intended to serve the needs of the living just as much as those of the dead. Fashioned in an era when the forces of urbanization and industrialization were transforming the landscapes of the living and peeling back the natural world in the name of civilization and modern development, Mount Auburn further served as an oasis where visitors could convene with nature without the noise and distractions of the city. It was also during this period when Americans, still looking to prove themselves and their nation as modern, cultivated, and, most importantly, *civilized*, actively engaged in establishing cultural institutions that reflected such qualities—libraries, museums, learned societies, and colleges among them. Rural cemeteries, which were promoted as landscapes that exuded such qualities as taste and refinement—qualities that were regularly contested within the general public—became one of the most important such institutions during the nineteenth century and were major destinations for local visitors as well as tourists from abroad.

Due to the success and enormous popularity of Mount Auburn Cemetery, from the 1830s through the 1860s, it became a priority of every major city and of towns of varying sizes to establish their own rural cemetery. To fail to do so meant that a community was not keeping up with the times and that its inhabitants were not properly caring for their dead. As a cultural movement that became national in scope, rural cemeteries were thus simultaneously tied with national identity as well as local identity, for the presence of a rural cemetery reflected upon both the nation and the individual communities in which they were located. Because the cemeteries were local institutions established as part of a national cultural movement, however, each one was unique, as it not only had to be designed according to the landscape of which it was a part but also further reflected the qualities of the communities whose needs they served. To this end, rural cemeteries simultaneously reinforced and were at times the locus for conflicts over the social, racial, gendered, and religious dynamics of their communities. Albeit principally established as nonsectarian Protestant cemeteries, the picturesque rural cemetery became popular across different faiths. Jewish synagogues often purchased space within or adjacent to the local rural cemetery, establishing proximity with the Protestant dead as an assimilationist tactic, while some Catholic dioceses established their own rural cemeteries, such as New York City's Calvary Cemetery.

In reflecting the racial boundaries and dynamics of their living populations, rural cemeteries illustrated that matters of racism and segregation
were by no means driven by a simple North-South dichotomy, and each
community followed their own socially and legally prescribed rules for the
segregation (or integration) of the dead. In some cities, the rules even varied from cemetery to cemetery. For instance, in Richmond, Virginia, only
middle-class and elite whites could be buried at Hollywood Cemetery, but
at the municipally owned Oakwood Cemetery established several years
later, sections were reserved for the burial of paupers as well as free and
enslaved African Americans, as space for the burial of these populations
was an absolute necessity.[9] Many rural cemeteries, in both the North and
the South, either had nondiscriminatory burial policies—such as Mount
Auburn, Albany Rural Cemetery, and Allegheny Cemetery in Pittsburgh—or
had established segregated sections for the burial of African Americans—
such as Green-Wood in Brooklyn, Frankfort Cemetery in Kentucky, and
Elmwood Cemetery in Memphis. Free Black communities during the antebellum period in Philadelphia and Baltimore, barred altogether from interment within the local rural cemeteries, established their own new burying
grounds. Lebanon and Olive Cemeteries in Philadelphia and Laurel Cemetery in Baltimore embraced the rural cemetery style and also affirmed the
respectability of the free middle-class Black Americans who operated and
used these spaces.[10] Even as cemetery landscaping changed by the end of
the century, Black communities as late as the 1890s continued to fashion
cemeteries that embraced the ideals and aesthetics of the rural cemetery
movement.[11]

During the Civil War, rural cemeteries became major repositories for the
soldier dead and thus also critical sites for the formation of the public memory of the war. As they were many communities' largest burying grounds
with room to spare, rural cemeteries in the South set aside land for military
burials due to immediate need for space, while those in the North provided
land for the soldier dead as an act of patriotism. In the postwar period, those
rural cemeteries that contained the bodies of Union and Confederate soldiers became sites for the formation of public history and memory as communities raised funds for the erection of sizable soldier monuments, and in
cemeteries where soldiers from both sides of the conflict were buried, they
likewise became sites of contest over matters of loyalty and identity.

During the years encompassing the Civil War and Reconstruction, the
rural cemetery movement continued to influence burial reform and urban

development in midwestern and Pacific coastal communities, as towns and cities that exited the frontier stages of development sought to exhibit the patterns of taste and refinement already fashioned east of the Mississippi River. Nevertheless, even as the rural cemetery movement continued to expand in these years, public taste increasingly favored the new "landscape lawn" plan first introduced by Prussian landscape designer Adolph Strauch at Cincinnati's Spring Grove Cemetery in the 1850s. Focused more on creating artificially beautiful, rather than picturesque, landscapes that diminished lot holders' authority over care and decoration of their plots in favor of establishing a more unified visual effect, the landscape lawn plan increasingly became the dominant cemetery aesthetic during the 1870s. Preexisting rural cemeteries integrated the new landscape design along with launching construction projects to modernize their institutions and thus keep pace with the changing tastes of society, while new rural cemeteries integrated the landscape lawn plan either partially or wholly from the start. By the end of the century, new cemeteries, now managed by a class of professional superintendents who, along with newly professionalized funeral directors, dominated what was rapidly becoming a deathcare industry in which care for the dead by the living became an act of consumption that did not require family to be involved in the physical care of the deceased or even of their grave. Such transformations paved the way for the memorial park of the twentieth century, in which death and nature became practically invisible.

Pleasure Grounds of Death thus represents an effort to expand upon what has, in the last half century, developed into a rich historiography dedicated to the rural cemeteries, individually and collectively, of the nineteenth century.[12] In this book, I contend that the new landscapes of the dead were often just as fraught with conflicts over class, race, gender, identity, and even fractious medical debates about the cause of epidemic disease as were the landscapes of the living. Their founders articulated what rural cemeteries would ideally accomplish in terms of shaping the public's morals and taste, but as they opened and became accessible to the general public, matters concerning proper use, appropriate behavior, tasteful design, and the fashioning of personal and collective memory and identities were regularly open to interpretation. As previous scholars have noted, rural cemeteries were endeavors undertaken by professional middle-class and elite men who sought to exert their cultural influence over their communities in a shared desire to cultivate a modern, model civil society. The heterogeneity of American communities, and even the variety of tastes and preferences exhibited by middle-class and elite Americans as they ornamented their burial plots, often meant that the general public—which regarded the rural cemetery as a shared multipurpose space—undermined founders' and managers' desires for a uniform vision of refinement and shared values. During the 1860s, the rural cemeteries as sites for cultural contest became further complicated as these landscapes of the dead mirrored the political sectionalism of a nation torn asunder by war. The cemeteries then became center stage for the post-war conflicts that arose over memorialization of the war's dead and the fashioning of the public history and public memory of the Civil War. As these contests unfolded east of the Mississippi River during these years, the rural cemetery movement continued to expand westward, as communities striving to exit the frontier stage of development established institutions that residents regarded as foundational to claiming status as a modern, civilized town or city.

Even so, the rural cemetery was an evolving institution that, while driven by certain shared principles of landscaping aesthetics, had always been adapted to local circumstances and changing aesthetic preferences. By the 1870s, the landscaping and memorial ideals of the 1830s and 1840s were under fire as an increasing number of Victorian Americans favored the cleaner and more organized aesthetics of the landscape lawn cemetery, over-throwing the rugged naturalism of the picturesque for the artificially clean and manicured beautiful. By the end of the century, there were those who, ironically, charged the antebellum rural cemetery as reflecting chaos rather than refinement. In short, the rural cemetery of the nineteenth century was not a static burying ground or cultural institution. It was, as it remains today, a dynamic environment defined by human engagement and the contestation that often results when a heterogeneous community seeks to use and define the meaning of shared space. Albeit fashioned with a common set of principles vested in founders' beliefs in the importance of expansive spaces for the proper burial of the dead where the living could also benefit from convening with nature and melancholy reflection, the rural cemetery was an institution that was highly sensitive—and responsive—to the transformations experienced by communities and the nation itself during the nineteenth century.

In approaching such a study, I have sought to discuss a variety of rural cemeteries from across the country, but this is by no means a comprehensive catalog of every rural cemetery established during the nineteenth century, for there are hundreds nationwide. Some cemeteries, especially the larger or more culturally influential ones, such as Mount Auburn Cemetery, Laurel Hill Cemetery in Philadelphia, Green-Wood Cemetery in Brooklyn, Green Mount Cemetery in Baltimore, Cave Hill Cemetery in Louisville, and Hollywood Cemetery in Richmond, garner more attention than others. However, I have also combed through newspaper and periodical records to find lesser-known rural cemeteries in more out-of-the-way communities that merit discussion and illustrate that the impulses to create picturesque cemetery landscapes that could be enjoyed by the living were indeed universally shared across the country despite differences in local climate, flora, and topography and that the ways in which society engaged with these spaces were equally shared despite differences of religion, race, socioeconomic status, and geography. Albeit created during the mid-nineteenth century and reflective of the vast transformations then underway in American society and culture, the impact of the rural cemetery movement reverberates in the twenty-first century as many Americans continue to use these landscapes for burial, mourning, recreation, and green spaces in an increasingly busy and urbanized environment.

1

"Crowded Till They Are Full"

Burial Reform in the Early Republic

The history of the rural cemetery movement begins as a history of burial reform in America. That history originated not in Boston in the 1820s but in New Haven, Connecticut, three decades prior. By the 1790s, the American republican experiment had only just begun, but the coastal communities that blossomed throughout the Colonial Period had their origins in the seventeenth century, during which time British, Dutch, and German colonists had created churchyards and common burial grounds for the dead based upon Old World practices. Elite parishioners interred their dead in subterranean or semi-subterranean vaults built into the sides of urban churches, while the rank and file buried their dead in single burials marked with wooden, slate, sandstone, or other locally quarried stone in the open space of the churchyard or common burying ground usually located on the town green. With the exception of church vaults, such burial spaces were commons in the sense that they were available to the general public as a shared space.[1] Catholic and Jewish populations in the New World created their own denominational burying grounds associated with a church or synagogue, typically in close proximity to the relevant house of worship, similar to the Anglo-Protestant churchyard model.[2] As early as the 1750s, coastal communities in New England expanded their older common burying grounds, many of them established in the century prior, or added new ones to accommodate the increasing numbers of the dead.

The need for expansion derived from increased populations of the living—which subsequently resulted in expanding numbers of the dead—as well as from strains placed upon communities and their burial spaces by regularly occurring waves of epidemic disease. Yellow fever counted among the most feared diseases of the era, mainly because doctors could not agree on the nature of its spread—whether it derived from corrupted air, which they called miasmas, or was a contagious affliction; it was not until the research conducted in 1900 by the United States Army Yellow Fever Commission, led by Walter Reed, that the *Aedes aegypti* mosquito was identified as the vector for the disease.[3] Many who were stricken with yellow fever were lucky enough to only suffer the effects of the primary stage of the disease and then experience a remission. The poor souls who went on to succumb to the secondary hemorrhagic stage were a terrifying sight to onlookers, with bleeding from the eyes, nose, and mouth and the dreaded "black vomit," which signaled impending death—a foul mixture of blood that resembled coffee grounds or "chocolate coloured matter."[4] Even today, despite the availability of a vaccine, yellow fever remains without a cure and in its severe state has a 50 percent mortality rate; prior to the twentieth century, this was higher still.[5] The 1793 outbreak in Philadelphia, at that time the nation's capital, killed 10 percent of the population of fifty thousand while sickening far more, including Alexander Hamilton. With the fever causing mass panic, twenty thousand residents, including George Washington and Thomas Jefferson, fled the city and established the new national capital in Washington, DC. Less well known than the 1793 epidemic were the subsequent outbreaks of yellow fever and scarlet fever (commonly called throat distemper) the following year, which struck Hartford and New Haven in Connecticut.

It was in the aftermath of the 1794 epidemic in New Haven that the seeds for the rural cemetery movement were originally sown, where a new reform cemetery style inaugurated an era during which the town's new burying ground served as a model for what places of burial could be, how they might look in the Early Republic, and what kind of relationship the public would have with such spaces. The New Burying Ground, as it was originally called but later renamed the Grove Street Cemetery in the 1840s, established a new precedent for what urban cemeteries ought to be, so that by the time Mount Auburn Cemetery in Cambridge, Massachusetts, was dedicated in 1831, many Americans already understood that modern burial spaces would serve equally as sites for mourning, leisure, and interaction with nature. Here, grounds were arranged with specific social, religious, and racial categories in mind, which signaled a conscious rejection of the seemingly haphazard and egalitarian arrangement of burials and grave markers in the older church-yards and burying grounds. Further, the money and care devoted to its design and upkeep, the style of monuments erected within its boundaries, and the apparent liberality with which space was designated for both elites and non-elites (while maintaining clear delineations between these groups within the burial landscape) were all factors that transformed the cemetery into a cultural space of local, and even national, pride. For three decades, the reform cemetery model established in New Haven inspired Americans elsewhere to consider it as the best precedent for urban burial reform, as New York and Philadelphia endeavored to solve their churchyard problems in the 1820s. It was not until Mount Auburn's creation and dedication that burial reformers began to consider a more expansive option—not just for solving what they regarded as the urban burial crisis of the era but also for establishing a new institution that would help to define the emerging cul-tural idiom of the Early Republic and the changing relationship between the living, death, and the dead.

The residents of New Haven, who first settled the area in 1638, initially buried their dead between the town's church and the west side of the mar-ketplace in the space known as the town green. The site grew as need dic-tated, and twenty years after the town's founding, there were at least fifty graves with an estimated rate of growth of between five and ten interments per year. As local historian Henry Townshend noted in 1947 of these early burials, "Children pranked amongst them, young people galavanted, their elders indiscriminately walked over them, lounged amongst them and between Sabbath day services gossiped and ate their lunch; cattle roamed through them, dogs ran riot, and in the words of the old town records there was no 'comliness or safety from creaturs [sic] rooting up ye ground.'" In other words, much like the rural cemeteries established in later years, there was already a precedent for burial spaces doubling as landscapes for social engagement—the burying ground was a lived-in space, an integrated part of the built environment where the living traversed and engaged with each other over and around the dead. However, because the town green was right in the center of daily activities, including animals roaming promiscuously and generally contributing to the rapid deterioration of the conditions of graves and gravestones, security for the space of the dead became a matter of general concern. The selectmen voted in 1690 to erect a fence to protect the graves, but this never transpired.[6] Efforts were again made in the 1760s to erect a fence, to no avail, though one appears to have been built at some point before 1775. By the 1790s, the old burying ground was already considered overcrowded and in serious disrepair, and then tragedy in the form of a double epidemic struck the community. During the first half of the year in 1794, scarlet fever struck the town, killing 50, mostly children. Then, from June through October, 150 residents contracted yellow fever, among whom 63 perished. According to the Reverend Ezra Stiles, who served as Yale College's seventh president, in addition to the deaths from scarlet fever and yellow fever, another 51 people in New Haven died from "consumption" (tuberculosis) and other "lingering sickness," while 15 died from "other infirmities and diseases," bringing the total deaths for 1794 to 179. Stiles noted in his journal that the town census for 1791 put the population of New Haven at 3,471, which means a little over 5 percent of the town's population was buried at some point during the year.[7]

The overcrowded conditions of the old burying ground were already by some estimates considered "intolerable" by the early 1790s, with upwards of five thousand graves in an octagonal space measuring only seventy thousand square feet; the deaths wrought during the yellow fever epidemic merely served as the catalyst for burial reform. Such reform did not generate from the public at large, however. Rather, it was one man, James Hillhouse, a Revolutionary War veteran, treasurer of Yale College, and U.S. senator, who first proposed the establishment of a new burying ground in 1796 using land that he had acquired and owned since 1791. Having originally contemplated the creation of a private cemetery for his own family, Hillhouse instead offered "some seven acres" of land for the establishment of a new burying ground for the town. He then proceeded to form a "syndicate" with thirty-two prominent citizens—members of almost all of the old New Haven families—who each signed a written agreement to advance fourteen dollars to pay for the land as subscribers and thus make it a public burying ground. Following a successful petition to the Connecticut General Assembly for the creation of a corporation titled "The Proprietors of the New Burying Ground in New

Haven," the act of incorporation dated November 6, 1797, actually deeded ten acres rather than seven for the burying ground, which made it the largest space in the nation specifically dedicated to the burial of the dead.[8]

New Haven's New Burying Ground was innovative in a number of respects that made it a model for future reform cemeteries and, ultimately, the rural cemetery movement. For one, it was the first chartered cemetery in the country, operated on a corporate model. More significantly, it abandoned the ancient notion of burial space as a shared public utility, a common ground that everyone and no one within the community explicitly "owned," and instead was divided into family lots and lots explicitly designated for use by various religious, fraternal, racial, and socioeconomic bodies. Once the corporate charter for the New Burying Ground was granted, a standing committee organized the lots, and each lot consisted of six tiers. The northwest corner lot was made into the potter's field. The third tier of the first lot was set aside for the president and fellows of Yale College, while the first, second, and fourth tiers were designated for ecclesiastical societies, including the United Society, the Episcopal Society, and the First Society, each associated with the town's churches. The fifth tier of lot two remained available for strangers who might die in New Haven, while the fifth tier of lots three, five, and seven were for the poor of the town. The sixth tier of lot one was for the burial of people of color.[9] The remaining tiers were divided up into family lots available for purchase. Thus, the new cemetery, while still a public utility available for the burial of all of the city's dead, made clear delineations among the dead that mirrored the patterns of racial and socioeconomic stratification among the living.

The creation of the New Burying Ground was certainly prompted by the strains put upon the old burying ground by the yellow fever crisis of 1794, but it was also part of the broader spirit of reform and desire for the improvement of urban spaces, as citizens of the new republic sought to create a visual rhetoric of civilized refinement for their communities and nation. While upwardly mobile citizens constructed homes in the neoclassical style with porticoes and columns of the Doric and Ionic orders, and trees and other tasteful plantings lined streets and boulevards, so too did the proprietors of the New Burying Ground design the landscape so that it was an integrated extension of the city of the living. "The horticultural plans for the new burial ground" were a syncretic blend of several aesthetic influences, as noted by David Charles Sloane, and "combined elements of eighteenth-century English gardens, American domestic graveyards, and the flowering

View of monuments and family lots in Grove Street Cemetery (originally New Burying Ground), New Haven, Connecticut. (Photograph by the author)

orchards of the surrounding countryside."[10] Hillhouse and other city leaders planted elm trees along the main streets of New Haven, while they chose Lombardy poplars, "a species then being introduced as street trees in many American cities," in the cemetery's "alleys."[11] Trees, strategically planted as part of the built environment, conveyed refinement at this time; later, in the 1830s, they would be associated more with the wildness of nature in connection with popular romanticism. As noted by architectural historian Dell Upton, "Rather than positing culture-nature, city-suburb, or living-dead dichotomies, Hillhouse and his systematizing colleagues imagined the city and its cemetery as complementary aspects of urban life unified by the cultivated, artificial refinement of landscape plantings. The cemetery, separated and classified within itself, was in turn incorporated into the articulated landscape of the town, holding present and past generations in proper relationship, allowing appropriate commemoration while at the same time preventing the living and the dead from intruding on one another."[12]

The new cemetery was a success in attracting upwardly mobile and elite residents to purchase lots and erect monuments that reflected the emerging aesthetic tastes of the era. The very word "taste" was, according to historian Catherine E. Kelly, elastic during this era, as it referred to the value attributed to stimuli in the external world—consumer commodities such as books, magazines, and artwork, as well as institutions in which to observe and appreciate such products—while simultaneously being internalized by individuals; especially for educated and upwardly mobile Americans, taste "summoned gentility and moral character."[13] In 1811, Yale College president Timothy Dwight wrote glowingly of the cemetery and its progress in the fifteen years since Hillhouse first proposed its creation, and in his assessment he conveyed just how much the New Burying Ground reflected the increasing emphasis on the important role of the cemetery for residents in cultivating refinement and good taste. In describing the layout of the space, Dwight referred to the lots as "parallelograms, neatly railed and separated by alleys of sufficient breadth to permit carriages to pass each other." Dwight observed how trees had been set out in the alleys, that the name of each proprietor was marked on the railing of each family lot, and that each lot contained one or more monuments or markers over the burials.[14]

Grave marker styles had transformed considerably between the late eighteenth and early nineteenth centuries, as increasing numbers of wealthy Americans imported monuments carved from Italian marble while American marble quarries began operations and offered new opportunities for local sculptors and stone carvers to apply their craft. Historically, during the seventeenth and eighteenth centuries, grave markers across the New England landscape had been fashioned from wood, fieldstones, or locally quarried stone, such as slate, coarse granite, and sandstone (the Connecticut River Valley region is especially notable for its preponderance of distinctive red sandstone).[15] Throughout the Colonial Period, New England gravestone carvers crafted markers decorated with iconography that reflected the religious transitions from Puritanism to the evangelical revivals of the Great Awakening and eventually the greater materialism and secularistic humanism of the Revolutionary generation. Despite changes in iconographic patterns—from death's heads, to cherubs, to urns and willows—gravestones had remained relatively uniform in size and style, so that delineations between rich and poor were harder to readily identify in the older churchyards and common burial grounds.[16] By the beginning of the second decade of the nineteenth century, however, the variety and size of marker and monument styles had already become more diverse, a prelude to the explosion of memorial eclecticism that marked cemetery landscapes during the second half of the century (see chap. 3). Remarking upon the monuments in New Haven's New Burying Ground, Dwight noted that they were "almost universally of marble: in a few instances from Italy. . . . A considerable number are obelisks; others are tables; and others, slabs, placed at the head and foot of each grave."[17] Obelisks, while rightly part of the Egyptian Revival style of architecture, which increased in popularity throughout the nineteenth century, made their first appearance alongside such neoclassical decorative elements as columns and urns during the 1790s.[18] The obelisks in the New Haven cemetery, Dwight observed, "are arranged universally on the middle line of the lots, and thus stand in a line, successively, throughout each of the parallelograms."[19] By midcentury, the obelisk had arguably become the most popular cemetery monument style in the nation, its smooth, four-sided tapering shaft and Egyptianized pedestal just perfect for lengthy inscriptions recording the deeds of the illustrious and well-to-do dead. Indeed, obelisks and pyramidal monuments became so universally popular that Nehemiah Cleaveland, author of *Greenwood Illustrated* (1847), the history of and guidebook for Brooklyn's grand contribution to the rural cemetery movement, bemoaned, "We have seen a ground so full of pyramids and obelisks, that one could almost fancy it a gigantic cabinet of minerals, being all crystals set on end."[20] At the time when New Haven's New Burying Ground was still growing in popularity, however, the obelisk was still a relatively novel memorial form, one that many considered a simple and elegant monumental style that reflected a more subtly refined taste.

In its novelty as a new type of burial space in America, the New Burying Ground also inaugurated the era of the cemetery as both a tourist attraction and a source of local pride. As an extension of the city of the living, locals naturally continued to walk or take their carriages through the burying ground, but in creating a designed burial space containing plantings, family plots with monuments, and spacious paths for carriages, the residents of New Haven could point to their cemetery as a mark of the city's cultural development to outsiders. On this topic, Timothy Dwight remarked, "I have accompanied to it many foreigners, and many Americans, who have traveled extensively on the Eastern continent [Europe]; none of whom had ever seen, or heard, of anything of a similar nature." Such a distinction for New Haven was undoubtedly a source of enormous local pride, as Dwight continued, "An exquisite taste for propriety is discovered in every thing belonging to it; exhibiting a regard for the dead, reverential, but not ostentatious; and happily fitted to influence the feelings, and views, of succeeding generations. No spot of ground, within my knowledge, is equally solemn and impressive."[21] Several years later, from 1818 to 1819, Scotsman John Morison Duncan ventured to New Haven as part of his tour of the United States and Canada, where he made observations of the New Burying Ground that doubtless would have met with Dwight's approval. After noting the crumbling state of the remaining gravestones in the old burying ground that had not been relocated to the new cemetery (still called the New Burying Ground despite being in operation for twenty years by this time), Duncan stated approvingly, "In simplicity of arrangements and elegance of monumental decoration, [the new cemetery] leaves at a great distance all others I have any where seen."[22] The taste exhibited by the family monuments in the cemetery contrasted favorably, in Duncan's estimation, with those found in Glasgow, which, bearing "those quaint emblems of mortality and grief," exhibited "the bad taste of the proprietors." When compared to Westminster Abbey, which contained the "ashes of Monarchs, Barons, and Crusading Knights" and whose "damp of the long drawn aisles chilled me to the heart," Duncan asserted, "I doubt whether sympathy with my kindred dust were as strongly excited there, as in the burying ground at New Haven." Indeed, the only fault Duncan could find with New Haven's New Burying Ground was that "it is of too unvarying a level, the arrangement too precisely angular, and the numerous poplars too stiff and formal." In other words, the only real fault with the space was that it was *too refined* and, because it was flat and its alleys were all straight, perhaps a little boring. That being said, Duncan, not wanting to focus on what he considered minutiae, concluded, "There is so much to admire.... It is highly creditable to the taste and the feelings of the inhabitants of New Haven."[23] Despite social, religious, or racial differences and separation within the landscape, the exhibition of seemingly good taste across the entire cemetery thus established a sense of community pride as New Haven claimed its space within the cultural environment that placed increasing value on such a concept.

Efforts at burial reform in Europe began shortly after the establishment of the New Burying Ground in New Haven, beginning first with the creation of what would become the famed Père Lachaise Cemetery in Paris in 1804. Where New Haven's New Burying Ground served as the pattern for classical refinement in a burial landscape, Père Lachaise ushered in the notion that cemeteries could be "picturesque" in style—that is, that they could invoke nature as planned landscapes, with uneven and visually stimulating terrain that lacked the uniform arrangement that so defined the American reform cemetery. As noted by historian Blanche Linden, the French had grappled with the search for alternatives to the "old order" of burial, and by the 1780s, "theoretical plans for wooded cemeteries" derived from the English garden landscape "proliferated."[24] The Reign of Terror that followed the French Revolution, which spawned burial pits filled with guillotined bodies rather than new cemeteries, marked a rupture in the progress toward burial reform, but by 1799, plans were again put in motion for the creation of new, pastoral burying grounds. Père Lachaise marked a significant departure from the ancient churchyard tradition, for while it was named for the Jesuit from whose estate the land was purchased, it was a secular, nondenominational burial space that offered to the general public the dignity of single burials rather than burial in a common pit. Elite Parisians were slow, however, to embrace the new cemetery, and in its first four years in operation, only 72 monuments were erected. However, the Napoleonic Wars made death, once again, a "vivid reality" for the French, and, as such, the erection of private monuments "escalated annually from 51 in 1808 to 113 in 1812, 242 in 1813, 509 in 1814, and 635 in 1815, the year of Waterloo." By 1830, there were over 31,000 monuments in place at Père Lachaise, its original pastoral design obliterated by memorial architecture crammed together and "nearly touching like buildings on city streets."[25] It was in the years following the Napoleonic Wars but before the extreme overcrowding of the 1830s when travelers began to take greater notice of Père Lachaise as an important cultural landscape of the dead, a grand space noted for its picturesque beauty and the impressiveness of its monuments. One American visitor, Caroline Elizabeth Wilde Cushing, traveled to Paris in September 1829 and wrote of Père Lachaise, "This beautiful burial-place . . . is one of the most interesting spots I have ever seen. . . . These grounds, agreeably varied within hill and dale, present an almost infinite number of tombs of all descriptions and forms." The various plantings, which included the "mournful cypress and weeping willow," the shrubs, "flowers, and garlands," combined together with "the delicate whiteness of the marble monuments," presented for Cushing "a scene at once beautiful, solemn, and affecting."[26] Another American, the educator Emma Hart Willard, wrote of the cemetery in December 1830 to her students that it was a place "where the feeling of awe and solemn contemplation on human mortality, is wonderfully and sweetly tempered, by the emotions caused by its great beauty."[27] Père Lachaise thus provided an alternative model to the regimented, tastefully refined landscape embodied in the New Haven New Burying Ground, and worldly travelers found them-

Paris from Père Lachaise Cemetery (Rawlinson 536) proof engraving by William Miller after Turner, published in *The Miscellaneous Prose Works of Sir Walter Scott, Bart. Embellished with Portraits, Frontispieces, Vignette Titles and Maps* (London, 1836).

selves in the position to draw comparisons and choose what they considered to be the ideal landscape for the dead.

Such was indeed the case, for by the 1820s, as public discussions about burial reform and city burials became increasingly common in both Europe and America, travelers drew ready comparisons between the two major reform cemeteries on either side of the Atlantic. Scotsman James Stuart, who spent three years in North America and traveled through New Haven in April 1829, praised the New Burying Ground as "laid out with more care and attention, and better kept, than any other ground devoted to the same purpose in the United States. . . . In short, this is quite the *Pere la Chaise* of the United States."[28] In 1834, Theodore Dwight, nephew of Timothy Dwight, published *Things As They Are: Or, Notes of a Traveller through Some of the Middle and Northern States.* Having himself attended Yale College, the younger Dwight was well acquainted with the New Burying Ground and, having seen Père Lachaise, offered a critical appraisal and comparison of the two cemeteries. Of New Haven's cemetery, Dwight declared that it "has been too much praised, as it can lay no claims to an equality, as a mere object of taste, with that great and beautiful depository of the dead of Paris with which it has most frequently been compared." Whereas the cemetery in New Haven consisted of "a mere plain of limited size," Père Lachaise "occupies a great extent of irregular ground"; also, whereas New Haven's cemetery contained "small monuments, mingled with many upright slabs, planted in lines parallel with the straight poplars, which imperfectly shade them," Père Lachaise "presents a long succession of more costly and towering obelisks, pyramids, and fabrics of different styles, half surrounded by clusters of various trees and shrubs, occupying points favourable to effect." Despite the more picturesque layout of the landscape and the greater variety of costly monuments exhibited in the great Paris necropolis, however, Dwight ultimately determined that New Haven's—albeit *overly* praised by other writers—was still the superior cemetery. "I insist that more judgment, far higher taste has been shown in the New-Haven burying-ground," he concluded.[29] Of course, given that New Haven was his hometown, we cannot begrudge Dwight a certain degree of bias in this instance.

By the time Dwight published *Things As They Are* in 1834, Mount Auburn Cemetery in Cambridge, near Boston, had been in operation for three years, and while he praised the new aesthetic offered by the nation's first rural cemetery, his writing reflected a belief that the reform cemetery model offered by New Haven signaled the direction for American burying grounds albeit perhaps with the need for modifications involving more varied and undulating grounds to create a more picturesque, rather than rigidly classical, effect. After declaring New Haven's cemetery superior to Père Lachaise, Dwight effectively doubled down with his assertion, "In my view also the same might be said of every village burying-ground in our country, were it not for the too limited size generally allowed them, and the too common neglect with which they are treated. I speak from a deep sentiment of my heart when I say, that a secure enclosure, a few graveled walks, shaded by willows, enriched with flowering shrubs, and decently secluded from noise and dust, would furnish every village with a depository for the dead more appropriate, more truly beautiful, and for the living more instructive, than the boasted cemetery of the French metropolis."[30] The American model might be less visually stimulating but, when considering what was really necessary in a landscape for the dead, *should* cemeteries titillate the senses of the living? This and other questions—about where places of burial should be located, how large they ought to be, what kind of landscaping was necessary, and what their relationship to the spaces occupied by the living should be—were matters of significant concern throughout the 1820s as debates erupted in the major northeastern metropolises, particularly New York, Philadelphia, and Boston, over how to address burial reform.

The public health crises spawned by epidemic disease transformed the burial of the dead from a matter of everyday practice grounded in historical precedent to contested terrain as reformers challenged the wisdom of maintaining the status quo amid a rapidly changing society that was increasingly susceptible to waves of pestilence. At the heart of these arguments were questions over the source of infectious disease and the degree to which overcrowded churchyards and burying grounds were at fault. New York became the epicenter of debates over burial reform beginning in 1822, when a major epidemic of yellow fever struck the nation's largest city, which in the 1820 census counted nearly 124,000 residents.[31] In striking down somewhere between 2,400 and 2,500 victims, yellow fever accounted for the deaths of 2 percent of the city's population from August through October and placed major strains on the city's burying grounds, most of which had been in operation since the seventeenth century.[32] The area around Trinity Church and Churchyard was especially hard-hit by yellow fever, and so the churchyard rapidly became a central part of medical debates concerning the nature and spread of the disease, as well as the public health ramifications of ongoing city burials in appallingly overcrowded graveyards. Estimates indicate that by 1822, Trinity Churchyard, which spanned a mere two and a half acres, contained no fewer than 120,000 burials.[33] Other city churchyards and burying grounds were little better. The city's African Burial Ground (originally known as the Negroes' Burial Ground), in use from at least 1712 until the 1790s and consisting of six acres of land, was rediscovered by archaeologists who conducted excavations of the site from 1991 to 1992. While the remains of 400 individuals were excavated, it is possible that the cemetery ultimately held the remains of upwards of 10,000 people.[34] The city's potter's field, also established during the eighteenth century, likewise contained at least 10,000 bodies, which were buried three to four deep.[35] Even before the epidemic reached crisis proportions in July, a petition was laid out in March to terminate intramural (city) burials in both Trinity and St. Paul's Churchyards and to establish new "cemetries [sic] at a distance from the city."[36] Regarding Trinity Churchyard, one writer to the New York Spectator intoned, "It has long been impossible to inter one, without disinterring another. In consequence of this, during the Summer season, the effluvia arising . . . is not only offensive, but highly injurious to the health of the surrounding inhabitants."[37] What this writer described was the prevailing medical opinion since the late eighteenth century that disease, especially epidemic disease, resulted from corrupted air—"putrid miasmas"—that was produced by filth and decomposing animal (or human) matter.[38]

Facing the specter of a major public health crisis with the first appearances of yellow fever in July 1822, the New York City Board of Health, with Mayor Stephen Allen as president, convened to collect information on known cases of the disease and what might possibly be the cause for its spread. In August, Dr. Edward Miller submitted a report on behalf of a subcommittee appointed to examine the "influence of the grave yards" in the epidemic, in which he determined that "interments of dead bodies within the cities *ought to be prohibited*."[39] A resolution was then passed that, with respect to Trinity Churchyard in particular, "no grave be permitted to be opened or dug" for the foreseeable future under penalty of a $100 fine.[40] Public notice of the prohibition sparked a steady stream of letters and op-eds to the city's newspapers offering various proposals on alternatives to intramural burials in the churchyards or, alternately, defense of intramural burials, as well as arguments both for and against the churchyards as the source of disease. One writer to the *New-York American for the Country* explicitly pointed to New Haven as a model for how New York ought to reform its burial practices. After positing that city authorities ought to "select and purchase a suitable tract of ground—say twenty acres or more—that should be fitted for the purpose, laid out in regular form, and intersected by rectilinear paths and lanes and alleys," the writer then asserted, "Whoever has visited New-Haven, in Connecticut, must have witnessed with approbation the mode that has been adopted in that city." Interestingly, this writer noted that the "methodical arrangement" of the New Burying Ground in New Haven had been at times "a theme of ridicule," but it nevertheless offered a superior alternative to churchyard burials. In following the New Haven model, "families would be accommodated with distinct appropriations of ground; the cemeteries in the center of business might be devoted to the ordinary uses of life; the city would be exempted from the apprehension of its originating or contributing to spread a pestilence; and a place would be provided for the quiet slumbers of the dead, which, like Westminster Abbey, would be visited by the contemplative and the curious—by the philosopher and the Christian."[41]

As is often the case where proposals for change mean upending generations of tradition, there was, of course, opposition to the interdiction of churchyard burials and the proposal to establish new burying places. One defender of burying the dead in Trinity Churchyard, who signed their letter to the *New York Evening Post* as "A Member of the Trinity Church," invoked a variety of arguments in favor of preserving current practices; these included appeals to religious and community tradition, the positive effects the presence of a churchyard had on public morality, and the astute observation that "if the stench from Trinity Church yard be so offensive, and its effects so deleterious, how does it happen that they have never been found out until the present season? How can we account for what I am assured is the fact, that this stench has never been perceived by the grave diggers, the porters, the sexton or the clergy, and that they have never fallen victims to the deadly poison which is said to exhale from this putrid mass?"[42] Trinity Churchyard had been in operation for well over a century, and New York City had been free of yellow fever for nineteen years before the 1822 epidemic, so how could Trinity suddenly be the source for such a plague? In making such an argument, this defender of the traditional mode of interment struck at the heart of medical disagreements over the nature and spread of yellow fever— whether it was local in origin or imported via ships from the West Indies, whether it was contagious or arose from the putrefaction of animal or vegetable matter, or even if it was waterborne.[43]

Pamphlets published in 1822 and 1823, including Francis D. Allen's *Documents and Facts Showing the Fatal Effects of Interments in Populous Cities* and F. Pascalis-Ouvrière's *Exposition of the Dangers of Interments in Cities*, did much to convince city authorities that intramural burials were a positive evil in modern society and that the continuation of such practices would only escalate the number of public health crises involving epidemic disease.[44] One such advocate of Allen's assertions wrote to the *National Advocate* (New York) in November 1822 that "we are aware that in recommending the measure [closing the churchyards], we have to contend with settled prejudices, and the powerful influence of the church," and that even if "reason and common sense are not sufficient to allay prejudice and destroy superstition, the fear of contagion will do wonders." Accusing adherents to the churchyard burial tradition of being slaves governed by superstition who believed heavenly salvation could only be secured via such practice, the writer railed in conclusion, "We should throw off the yoke of superstition, and make everything bend to PUBLIC SAFETY."[45] The Common Council of the city concurred with this sentiment and voted in April 1823 to ban all burials south of Canal and Grand Streets, running from the North (Hudson) River to the East River—in short, the whole of the Lower East Side of Manhattan. Anyone caught interring a body in a churchyard in offence of the new ban faced the exorbitant penalty of $250 (the equivalent of a little over $6,000 today).[46] The resulting public outcry leveled against the Common Council derived in part from an adherence to tradition, though the arguments against barring further churchyard interments derived as well from the increasing numbers of medical men who countered Allen's and Pascalis-Ouvrière's pamphlets that churchyard burials, albeit olfactorily offensive on occasion, were *not* to blame for yellow fever.[47]

Even for those who did not ascribe to the notion that Trinity Churchyard was a source for yellow fever, advocates for closing the churchyards in Lower Manhattan argued that residents of the neighborhoods embracing the various churches ought to agree at least that the overcrowded conditions and "stench arising from that source" should be reason enough to pursue a new burial option for the city. One such proponent urged consideration of laying out "extensive grounds in the suburbs of the city which may be the great receptacle of the dead," where the grounds could be enclosed by "a handsome iron railing" and "surrounded with the weeping willow, and forest trees of an appropriate character." With lots laid out in squares and rows, "intersected with gravel walks," the whole space could be "planned and executed with taste."[48] While this writer did not explicitly invoke the name of New Haven's New Burying Ground, such a description for a proposed new place of interment was undoubtedly inspired by that reform cemetery. And so it was that the Common Council, when they voted in favor of closing the churchyards, also determined that a new municipal burying ground, called the City Burying Ground, would be established about three miles from City Hall on land that would eventually become Bryant Park. Encompassing about ten acres of land owned by the city, the Common Council directed the laying out of the City Burying Ground that included planting rows of willow and elm trees, constructing ten public burial vaults, and enclosing the site with a four-foot stone wall topped by a five-foot mortised fence. The hope was that, as in New Haven, the new nondenominational cemetery would prove popular among New Yorkers of all social classes. Such was never the case, however, and no middle-class or elite families purchased burial plots or any of the vaults. Instead, the land was used as a potter's field from 1823 until 1837, at which point the cemetery "was filled with the victims of three cholera epidemics, the Great Fire of 1835 and the hard times that preceded the panic of that year."[49] Critics of the Common Council believed that the governing body had taken undue liberties in banning churchyard burials as well as expending thousands of dollars for the preparation of the new cemetery. Another problem noted by critics of the City Burying Ground was its distance from the central areas of habitation. As one dissenter commented in 1823, while New Haven and Albany, New York, had established alternatives to their ancient and overcrowded burying grounds, these cities had not "removed its burying grounds to so remote and inconvenient a distance from the main seat of its population."[50] Designed with trees and other plantings to invoke the aesthetics of tasteful gardens, these were still nevertheless thoroughly urban burial spaces, constructed as part of the lived-in, built environment, surrounded on all sides by homes and businesses. Ironically, one of the notable features of the rural cemetery movement, and what made rural cemeteries so appealing to urban dwellers, was the decidedly suburban character of the new cemetery locations, typically between three and five miles away from the major city centers with which they were associated. The success of these ventures, in contrast with the failure of the City Burying Ground, and the willingness of mourners and tourists to travel what were in the 1820s considered unreasonable distances reflect the significant shift in cultural attitudes toward urban versus rural spaces as well as attitudes toward what were considered the most appropriate and reverential spaces in which to lay the dead to rest.

Burial reform may have floundered during the second half of the 1820s in New York, but in Philadelphia and Boston, civic-minded professional men labored almost simultaneously to establish new burial spaces to accommodate the needs of their religiously heterogeneous and rapidly expanding urban populations. As elsewhere across the Northeast, these cities by the 1820s were experiencing the strains that over a century of burials placed on their ancient common and churchyard burying grounds. However, efforts at burial reform resulted in two strikingly different paths: in Philadelphia, reformers were more business minded as they created mutual associations for the purpose of establishing urban private cemeteries and effectively competed with each other to secure purchasers of burial plots; in Boston, reformers from a myriad of backgrounds, including medicine, law, and mercantile, merged their common interest in establishing a new burying ground with the Massachusetts Horticultural Society in 1825 and designed the nation's first rural cemetery, Mount Auburn Cemetery in Cambridge, Massachusetts.

The efforts to achieve burial reform in Philadelphia met with mixed success until the establishment of Laurel Hill Cemetery in 1836, the city's first major contribution to the rural cemetery movement. Prior to this, six private cemeteries were established on the south side of Philadelphia between 1825 and 1827 following a city ordinance forbidding inner-city burials. These were the Mutual Association Burying Ground, Machpelah Cemetery, Philanthropic Cemetery, Union Burying Ground, La Fayette Cemetery, and Ronaldson's Cemetery (also known as the Philadelphia Cemetery). With the exception of Ronaldson's Cemetery, these were all created by mutual aid societies, which sold eight-by-ten-foot lots for ten dollars apiece.[51] James Ronaldson (1768–1841) distinguished his eponymous cemetery from the others established at this time by accepting for burial people of any or no religious affiliation, as well as actors and other undesirables "who were excluded from most churchyards on moral grounds."[52] Ronaldson likewise reserved burial lots for strangers and for members of the Scots' Thistle Society, an ethnic fraternity of which he was a member. However, despite these examples of relative liberalism in his burial policy, Ronaldson's Cemetery nevertheless forbade burial of African Americans and refused admittance to the coroner (who buried paupers).[53] Similar to the other private cemeteries established in South Philadelphia, Ronaldson organized burial space so that purchasers could obtain eight-by-ten-foot lots, priced between twenty-five and thirty dollars. In promoting his new cemetery, Ronaldson urged that "each lot should be owned by a separate family, and, also, where family connexions or friendships exist, that these friends should purchase lots adjoining each other."[54] Ronaldson's and the other private cemeteries continued to be places of interment until well after Philadelphia joined the rural cemetery movement, but, as time proved, where most of the larger cemeteries established beyond the limits of urban development survived and persisted through the twentieth and into the twenty-first centuries, these reform burial grounds in South Philadelphia eventually became defunct—in the best cases, they were formally shut down, their burials and gravestones relocated to other, larger cemeteries; in the worst circumstances, they were simply abandoned, left to be overgrown and forgotten, their monuments and memorials cast aside in the march of urban progress and development.[55]

It was clear to Philadelphians that the traditional mode of churchyard burial was no longer a reasonable option for many of the city's inhabitants, but they also did not necessarily agree with the direction that burial reform was taking during the 1820s. As one commentator, who signed their letter to the editor of the Philadelphia newspaper the *National Gazette* as "Censor," noted, religious burying grounds had "become crowded to excess" and anyone who wished for burial in a denominational churchyard but was not a member of that parish was charged exorbitant interment fees "at a rate beyond the reach of moderate means." A further problem was that "in consequence of the almost infinitesimal variety of sects and opinion which must necessarily be found in a populous city, there are many who belong to religious communities not sufficiently large to form congregations or deny the necessity of associating for worship," and lacking their own burying grounds, congregants of these minor religious sects faced paying high fees for burial in a churchyard whose denomination's tenets they might deny. Censor further denounced the emergence of private cemeteries as an antidote to the city's burial problems, leveling the charge that, in competing for purchasers of burial plots, the proprietors of such burying grounds were driven by avarice without concern for the perpetual care and protection of burials.[56]

Another writer to the *National Gazette* who identified themself as "A Citizen" concurred with Censor's assertions that the creation of private cemeteries would ultimately be a significant problem for the community, since, as they were restricted in space and operated for profit, there was no motivation by their proprietors to maintain the sanctity of preexisting burials in perpetuity once all of the spaces had been used. In conclusion, Citizen asserted, "The time must soon come, when of necessity other places of interment will be required than those now belonging to our religious communities." In their vision for what might be established, Citizen described what had, in essence, already been attempted in New York with the City Burying Ground and what would come to pass in Boston. "It is, moreover, desirable that the dead should be buried, either out of the city, or in places where the population is likely to continue thin. A public burial-ground" where rich and poor alike, regardless of religious affiliation, "may repose together in their common mother, earth." In other words, there needed to be a burial ground that emphasized the unity shared by the community of the dead. Making explicit the connection between the treatment of the dead and the reputation of the community, the writer concluded, "This would be consistent with the name of our city, and not less with the character and dispositions of her inhabitants."[57] However, the private cemetery model that manifested in 1820s Philadelphia carried through into the rural cemetery movement, as even Laurel Hill Cemetery would be established as a private space wherein undesirable occupants—mainly the poor and African Americans—were denied burial. It would not be until 1848 that the General Assembly of Pennsylvania passed an act to incorporate the Philadelphia Cemetery Company (not to be confused with Ronaldson's Cemetery), which operated as a public cemetery until its closure in the 1950s.[58]

Similar to its counterparts in southern New England and the mid-Atlantic states, Boston's major burying grounds dated back to the seventeenth century and by the early nineteenth century were sorely overcrowded and in disrepair. These included King's Chapel (1630), Copp's Hill (1660), and the Old Granary (1660). These graveyards had become so crowded by the 1730s that, according to Blanche Linden in Silent City on a Hill, "burials often had to be made four deep or in small, common trenches." The south end of Boston Common was opened up as a new graveyard in 1756, becoming a major site during the Revolutionary War for burials of common British soldiers, as well as the city's first burying ground used by African Americans. A further graveyard, the South Burying Ground, was established in 1810 on the Shawmut Peninsula Neck, but this addition could not alleviate the growing need for burial space. The city's population tripled in the half century following independence, and the meager five acres allotted for burial purposes across the entire city did not suffice.[59] Boston had experienced intermittent outbreaks of yellow fever since the first recorded introduction of the disease to the colonies in 1693, but compared to Philadelphia and New York, epidemics in Boston resulted in dozens, rather than hundreds or thousands, of deaths, and the last major appearance of the disease in the northern port city dated to 1805.[60] There were, certainly, concerns about public health and epidemic disease that informed the burial reform movement as it developed in Boston, but during the 1820s when a major movement developed in that direction, reformers placed much greater emphasis on the embarrassingly poor conditions of burying grounds then in use and how such disrepair reflected poorly on the reputation of the city and its inhabitants' care for the dead. As one observer noted in 1829, "The burial grounds of New England . . . present to the curious traveler, an ugly collection of slate slabs, of weeds, and rank or dried grass."[61]

Bostonians were well aware of the 1822 yellow fever epidemic in New York and of the subsequent battle over Trinity Churchyard and burials in city churchyards more generally. Following on the heels of Allen's and Pascalis-Ouvrière's pamphlets urging an end to intramural burials, the aptly named Boston physician John Gorham Coffin (1769–1829) anonymously published an essay in 1823 to the same effect titled Remarks on the Dangers and Duties of

Old Granary Burying Ground showing Franklin Cenotaph, ca. 1898.
(Courtesy Boston Public Library)

Sepulture: On Security for the Living, with Respect and Repose for the Dead. With-
holding his name from the publication, signing it simply as authored by "A
Fellow of the Massachusetts Medical Society," Coffin was partly inspired by
the Trinity Churchyard controversy but more immediately by the approval
in 1823 by Boston's City Council of a petition made by Saint Paul's Church
to install burial crypts in its basement, thus making the space a "public
cemetery."[62] Citing the absence of major epidemics in Boston despite overcrowded burying grounds, Coffin opened his essay with the assertion that
burial reform ought to be considered a prudent preventive measure, that
the city should not wait for a medical catastrophe before taking action. Coffin further reinforced prevailing miasmatic and anti-contagionist theories
of disease by citing examples from Europe—particularly France—where, in
various instances, proximity of the living to "the effluvia arising from the
putrid remains of *animal matters*" (e.g., corpses) and the stench thrown
off from overcrowded or opened graves had caused illness and death. As a
result of long experience with burial overcrowding, Coffin argued, "it is now

admitted in many parts of Europe, that city and church burials are capable of destroying the purity of the surrounding air and water; and of producing not only single deaths, but of originating infectious endemics. Better humanity and better science have at length triumphed in France; and since the year 1775, all burying in cities and churches has been prohibited."[63] Curiously, Coffin had no words to offer on Père Lachaise in Paris and whether it had improved public health in the city to any degree.

Despite emerging skepticism on the extent to which "putrid miasmas" arising out of burying grounds caused epidemic disease, Coffin's colorful language describing the conditions of New York's Trinity Churchyard exhibited his wholehearted endorsement for such a theory, even though Boston's experience (or lack thereof) with severe outbreaks of yellow fever proved otherwise. At the time of the yellow fever epidemic, Trinity was, as he claimed, "saturated with dissolved semi-liquid human flesh, oozing from every pore, and the incumbent atmosphere filled with noxious effluvia, concurring with the air of the city, contaminated by unexampled quantities of smoking filth, of fermenting, offensive animal and vegetable substances." With such conditions arising from the overcrowded burying ground, New Yorkers had no reason to wonder why their city was struck by such a terrible disease. Coffin himself acknowledged "that sickness and death have never yet arisen from domestic interments in Boston" but warned readers that the city was effectively tempting fate by not developing a plan for burial reform. In order to prevent the inevitable occurrence of such an outbreak in Boston, Coffin urged an end to "domestic interments"—burying in cities, in churches, or anywhere near the residences of the living—a practice that he could only attribute to long-standing "superstition, pride, and avarice."[64] Further advocating the abandonment of vault burials, which in his view promoted the spread of harmful miasmas, and even the use of coffins, which slowed the process of decomposition, Coffin proposed the creation of a new burial place "*without* and *beyond* the living city."[65] To this end, he cited New Haven's New Burying Ground as a model "to be improved by any amendments which genius or experience can suggest."[66] Quoting Timothy Dwight's essay on New Haven's cemetery at length, Coffin concluded, "A cemetery like this, in our vicinity, would probably prevent the inducement to bury any longer in our city and churches, and prepare the way for a removal of the contents of those tombs, which are already sending forth no equivocal admonitions into some of our temples," and expressed the hope that at some point in the future all remaining human remains and monuments would be relocated to "an ultimate, an uninterrupted, and an unoffending repository,—where the dead would indeed be at rest."[67]

It took another two years before anyone stepped forth to make a serious effort at burial reform in Boston. In November 1825, thirty-eight-year-old Boston physician and Harvard professor Dr. Jacob Bigelow (1789–1879), whose attention had been "drawn to some gross abuses in the rites of sepulture as they then existed under churches and in other receptacles of the dead in the city of Boston," invited several influential friends—fellow Harvard graduates and members of the Boston "Brahmin" class—to his home to discuss the creation of a new extramural burial space. The men who convened at Bigelow's home not only were active in cultural endeavors but also counted among the city's economic and intellectual elite, including John Lowell, William Sturgis, George Bond, Thomas W. Ward, John Tappan, Samuel P. Gardiner, and Nathan Hale. While these men involved themselves in the formation of new cultural organizations, such as the Boston Athenaeum and the Bunker Hill Monument Association, Bigelow was himself arguably the model for the nineteenth-century "Renaissance man."[68] Having earned his undergraduate degree from Harvard University in 1806, he completed his MD in 1810 at the University of Pennsylvania and became Harvard's first Rumford Professor at the new medical school in 1816. There he taught botany and "materia medica" (an early term for pharmacology), as well as a course on "the useful arts" from 1816 to 1827, resulting in the publication of his lectures in 1829, *The Elements of Technology*—thus popularizing the term "technology" in American discourse.[69] While Bigelow later assisted General Henry Dearborn in his landscape design for Mount Auburn, he alone was responsible for designing the cemetery's Egyptian Revival carriage gateway, the Gothic Revival chapel, the Norman-style round tower at the summit of the mount (dubbed Washington Tower, completed in 1857), and, in the wake of the Civil War, the monumental Egypto-American sphinx dedicated in 1872 to the Union soldiers that faces the chapel.[70] At this initial meeting, Bigelow presented his plan for a new cemetery, "composed of family burial lots, separated and interspersed with trees, shrubs, and flowers, in a wood or landscape garden," which was "received with approval by the persons present." Bigelow then charged Bond and Tappan with the responsibility to find a potential site for a new burying ground, but their efforts to find a suitable piece of purchasable land floundered, and it was not until 1830 that Bigelow successfully offered purchase through subscription of the land known as "Sweet Auburn," a property owned by wealthy merchant George Watson

Studio portrait of Dr. Jacob Bigelow, ca. 1860/61. (Courtesy Historic New England, Cartes-de-visite photographic collection)

Brimmer (1784–1838) and traditionally used as a place of resort, particularly for students at Harvard University.[71]

Concerns over public health and burial overcrowding may have driven early discussions concerning burial reform in Boston as elsewhere, but it quickly became clear that Bigelow's intentions for a new cemetery were that it would be as much a cultural institution reflective of the progressive learned spirit of the city as a solution to burial overcrowding. It was also an early intention that the new burying ground would be more than just a necropolis akin to New Haven's New Burying Ground, another gridded reform cemetery that functioned as an extension of the built urban environment. No, as the city's elites sought to transform Boston into the "Athens of America" through the formation of new institutions, they envisaged a multipurpose landscape used in part for burials that, by its function as well as its design, would reflect the city's progressive qualities, progressive not just in terms of business, education, and technological innovation but also with regard to placing a higher value on nature in the midst of industry and urbanization. As noted by historian Aaron Sachs, "Ambitious Americans, everywhere conquering nature and driving it out of their lives as if it were irrelevant, as if the Revolution had rendered them independent of the land itself, needed to be reminded of the moral and reposeful value of all things natural, of the services provided by the environments: Mount Auburn was meant to have shade as well as shades."[72] Erik Seeman further regards this embrace of nature as linked with the antebellum cult of the dead, in which rural cemeteries were "open-air cathedrals" that "sustained relationships between heaven and earth."[73] Prior to the purchase of Sweet Auburn, the establishment of the Massachusetts Horticultural Society by Bigelow, General Henry Dearborn (1783–1851), businessman John Lowell (1768–1840), and others signaled the emergence of this movement to place a higher value on cultivating the products of the natural world. Chartered by the state legislature in 1829 "to develop the quality and diversity of plants grown in New England," the new Horticultural Society reflected Dearborn's and Lowell's views that horticulture was not just a hobby but rather "the most distinguished of the fine arts."[74]

When Bigelow secured from Brimmer the agreement for the purchase of the Sweet Auburn property at a cost of $6,000 through the subscription of one hundred lots at $60 apiece, the new cemetery then being conceived would in fact be combined with an experimental garden operated by the Horticultural Society. In his 1831 report of the society, Dearborn, who served as president, wrote in language that conveyed the ideals of what they hoped the cemetery would be and how it would reflect upon their society: "With the Experimental Garden, it is recommended to unite a Rural Cemetery." Echoing the language from Coffin's 1823 essay, Dearborn asserted, "For the period is not distant, when all the burial grounds within the city will be closed, and others must be formed in the country,—the primitive and only proper location. There the dead may repose undisturbed, through countless ages." In Dearborn's estimation, the new cemetery would do far more than just serve as a new repository for the dead; it would also function as a common space in which the treasured dead of the city and nation could be gathered and properly memorialized in perpetuity. "There can be formed a public place of sepulcher, where monuments can be erected to our illustrious men, whose remains, thus far, have unfortunately been consigned to obscure and isolated tombs, instead of being collected within one common depository, where their great deeds might be perpetuated and their memories cherished by succeeding generations. Though dead, they would be eternal admonitors to the living,—teaching them the way, which leads to national glory and individual renown."[75] Described in this way, the intention from the start was made manifest that the new cemetery, albeit remote in location from the city, would be an object of public attention and resort, a space for the living wherein they could be instructed and inspired by the dead. Containing the remains of the illustrious dead, the rural cemetery would also bolster the reputation of the city and be a source of civic pride.

The Horticultural Society formed a committee whose responsibility it was to raise the subscriptions for the cemetery. At seventy-two acres, it was the largest cemetery ever established in the country's history, and the task of getting enough people to pay for lots was daunting; by contrast, New Haven's New Burying Ground, which many considered large, was still only eighteen acres, even after having been expanded in 1814 to accommodate the ongoing demands for burial space.[76] The individuals who made up the committee numbered among the city's most distinguished public figures. Charged with the responsibility of ensuring the venture's success, committee members included Chief Justice Joseph Story; statesmen Daniel Webster and Edward and Alexander Everett; Unitarian ministers Charles Lowell and John Pierpont; merchants George Brimmer and Samuel Appleton; astronomer George Bond; businessmen Abbot Lawrence and Joseph P. Bradlee; lawyers Franklin Dexter, James T. Austin, and Charles P. Curtis; insurance broker Zebedee Cook; author and antiquarian Lucius M. Sargent; and bookseller Charles Tappan. Included among the benefits for those who paid the subscription fee of sixty dollars was the choice of any available lot measuring three hundred square feet within the cemetery grounds and lifetime membership in the Horticultural Society.[77]

Part of what made the venture somewhat risky was that the establishment of a rural cemetery, comprising a vast expanse of land and located at a distance from the urban population, was entirely experimental. Thirty years of reform cemeteries built on the New Haven model had generated a certain level of public comfort with this type of burying ground, despite conflicts over the closing of churchyards. Detractors in Boston responded similarly to those in New York when presented with the proposed City Burying Ground—that, situated as it was outside the city in Cambridge, it was unreasonably distant for both mourners and the casual visitor. Embedded within these critiques were concerns about increasing socioeconomic stratification and the separation between the rich and poor. Reflecting such anxieties, one concerned citizen, who identified himself as "A Working Man," wrote to the *Boston Traveler*,

Mr. Editor—Will you allow me to inquire why it is, the Cemetery, now offered to subscribers in Boston, should be located at such a distance in Cambridge, when there are so many beautiful places within half the distance, which would not be subjected to toll bridges? How few will ever be able to visit it, unless they *own* or hire a conveyance? Will it not be inaccessible in all the storms and blocking snows of winter? And lastly, why is it made *free* to all the members of *one rich* Institution *in Cambridge* [Harvard University], whose parents are the most *wealthy* in the community; to the exclusion of *all others in Boston*, whose members are from all parts of the country, and equally meritorious except in *parentage* and *wealth*? I have wanted to become a subscriber to some institution of this kind, but must decline this until these questions are answered.[78]

These were certainly legitimate concerns, although the cemetery's original trustees expressed egalitarian intentions and sought to make Mount Auburn as open an institution as possible to all classes. The cost of sixty dollars for a private lot may have excluded many from within the laboring classes, so public lots for single interments were available at a cost of ten dollars.

In an address reprinted by the city's newspapers, Edward Everett attempted to allay such concerns and reinforce the idea that *anyone* could be buried at Mount Auburn: "Here it will be in the power of every one, who may wish it, at an expense considerably less than that of a common tomb, or a vault beneath a church, to deposit the mortal remains of his friends, and to provide a place of burial for himself, which, while living, he may contemplate without dread or disgust."[79] That may have been true, but there were significant differences between burial in a private lot and burial in the public lot. For those who purchased a three-hundred-square-foot lot for sixty dollars, they not only became members of the Horticultural Society but were considered "proprietors" of the cemetery; as such, they were encouraged to decorate their lots as they would their own garden, with flowers and bushes, ornamental fences, and monuments of their choosing. Individuals who paid for a single interment could pay an additional fifty cents so that a numbered stone corresponding to their name in the burial register would be put in place, but "no slab, monument, or fence shall be erected upon or around said graves without the approval of the Committee on Lots."[80] As a result of these restrictions, while people of varied economic status *could* be buried at Mount Auburn, the passage of time and subsequent filling of the landscape with innumerable monuments reflective of the status of the area's most wealthy and influential families reaffirmed the continuation of class distinctions even after death. This was a development that stood in stark contrast with the older burying grounds and churchyards that were filled with near-identical headstones made of slate or sandstone that bore similar inscriptions and iconography. New techniques for stone quarrying and cutting by the mid-1820s meant an increase in the popularity of headstones and monuments of varying materials, styles, and sizes—abandoning the slate headstones of the Colonial and Federal periods, Bostonians could now expand dramatically upon the memorial idiom. New Haven residents had, by the early nineteenth century, begun to embrace the obelisk as a newly popular monumental form; Mount Auburn quickly became home to monuments of marble and granite in the form of headstones, sculptures, obelisks, columns, and sarcophagi, all with decorative elements ranging from flowers and birds to angels and portraiture of the deceased.[81] Added to all of this was the availability of wrought-iron and cast-iron fencing and stone coping to demarcate family lots within the cemetery.[82] Such transformations meant the age-old aphorism "Death is the great equalizer" became significantly less applicable, as increasing numbers of people opted for burial in the rural cemetery and erected monuments of diverse sizes and styles to reflect their tastes and pocketbooks.

Restrictions on single interments and any reservations that working-class Bostonians may have had about the new cemetery venture were moot, for by August 1831 enough wealthy individuals had purchased the necessary one hundred subscriptions to pay for the cost of the land; the Horticultural Society then agreed upon holding a formal religious consecration ceremony on September 24. Unitarian minister John Pierpont gave the introductory prayer and composed an original hymn sung by everyone in attendance, while Joseph Story delivered the dedicatory address to a crowd of about two thousand.[83] In language reflective of the era's burgeoning romanticism in the arts, Story reflected upon the universal interest of people in the subject of death and care for the dead. To this end he declared, "If there are any feelings of our nature, not bounded by earth, and yet stopping short of the skies, which are more strong and more universal than all others, they will be found in our solicitude as to the time and place and manner of our death; in the desire to die in the arms of our friends; to have the last sad offices to our remains performed by their affection; to repose in the land of our nativity; to be gathered to the sepulchers of our fathers. It is almost impossible for us to feel, nay, even to feign, indifference on such a subject."[84] Twentieth-century

Americans, for whom death and dying became taboo subjects to be avoided, to the point of denying human mortality as an everyday occurrence, may have regarded Story's address as foreign and even morbid.[85] By contrast, for twenty-first-century Americans, who have had to face widespread premature death due to pandemic disease and the almost everyday occurrence of gun violence, Story's words likely have greater resonance as people have sought in the digital age to care for the dead in increasingly meaningful and personal ways.[86] For those in attendance, he merely spoke the truth of nineteenth-century Americans' everyday reality. Even among the wealthier classes, families grappled with exceedingly high infant and child mortality rates, the deaths of young mothers from pregnancy and delivery complications, and epidemics of countless infectious diseases, not just yellow fever, not to mention everyday dangers of workplace accidents, overturned carriages, and the occasional murder.[87] Death remained too ever-present in the lives of nineteenth-century Americans for the memento mori culture of the Puritans to completely pass away; rather, it had transformed and become more elaborate with time.

High mortality rates had not changed significantly since the Colonial era, but one of the significant transformations that occurred was, in contrast to the Puritans of the 1630s who regarded the physical remains of the deceased as little more than an empty husk to be disposed of from the sight of the living, the far greater importance Americans of the 1830s gave to the tender treatment of those remains.[88] "It is to the living mourner," declared Story, "to the parent, weeping over his dear dead child—to the husband, dwelling in his own solitary desolation—to the widow, whose heart is broken by untimely sorrow—to the friend, who misses at every turn the presence of some kindred spirit:—it is to these, that the repositories of the dead bring home thoughts full of admonition, of instruction, and, slowly but surely, of consolation also." In Story's estimation, the ability to travel to a beautiful burial space, away from the realms of business and industry, allowed the mourner to commune with the dead, both physically and spiritually. "As we sit down by their graves, we seem to hear the tones of their affection, whispering in our ears. We listen to the voice of their wisdom, speaking in the depths of our souls."[89] In a place such as Mount Auburn, the terrors of Death itself would be muted so that the mourner might better contend with their grief while also maintaining a relationship with the deceased. Only a rural retreat away from the city offered that possibility, in contrast to the urban churchyards and burying grounds, "crowded on all sides by the overhanging habitations of the living, [which] are walled in only to preserve them from violation," and even in "our country towns [where] they are left in a sad, neglected state, exposed to every sort of intrusion, with scarcely a tree to shelter their barrenness, or a shrub to spread a grateful shade over the new-made hillock."[90]

While he declared that with its consecration "Mount Auburn, in the noblest sense, belongs no longer to the living, but to the dead," Story concluded his remarks by firmly situating the importance of the cemetery's beneficial influence upon the living who would traverse its landscape. "The votary of learning and science will here learn to elevate his genius by the holiest of studies. The devout will here offer up the silent tribute of pity, or the prayer of gratitude. The rivalries of the world will here drop from the heart; the spirit of forgiveness will gather new impulses; the selfishness of avarice will be checked; the restlessness of ambition will be rebuked; vanity will let fall its plumes; and pride . . . will acknowledge the value of virtue as far, immeasurably far, beyond that of fame."[91] The cemetery would provide mourners and visitors alike an environment that by its very design would instill introspective contemplation, virtue, and morality. Regardless of age, sex, class, or occupation, the living and the dead would benefit from the new place of sepulture. The dead could now rest in a picturesque, inviolable place of repose, while the living could experience the beauties of the landscape— its trees, flowers, shrubs, hills, and monuments—and engage in beneficial self-reflection while maintaining an intimacy with the dead.

While the founders of Mount Auburn Cemetery set their venture apart as something altogether new in American burial practice—combining a place of sepulture with an experimental garden, which incorporated detailed landscaping meant to imitate untouched nature—the new rural cemetery in reality grew from the reform cemetery tradition that dated back to New Haven's New Burying Ground when it was established in 1796. James Hillhouse and his co-proprietors of the New Haven cemetery introduced the notion that the place of burial could be organized in such a way as to preserve familial relationships and distinctions of class and status and that the landscape could be explicitly designed with living visitors in mind. Further, New Haven's New Burying Ground expanded upon older, preexisting traditions of burial spaces as landscapes used as much by the living as by the dead. With the cemetery as an extension of the built urban environment, New Haven residents and visitors were expected to traverse its wide alleys, view the monuments, appreciate the refinement exhibited by the plantings, and generally take a bit of respite from daily life. The founders of Mount Auburn built upon the success of the reform cemetery model developed in New Haven and elaborated upon its core principles to fashion a magnificent, nondenominational suburban landscape that could function equally as an escape for the living from the rapidly expanding urban environment as well as a picturesque, uncrowded, and secure resting place for the dead. Just as reform cemeteries like those in New Haven and Philadelphia emphasized the importance of family lots, so too did Mount Auburn Cemetery, while also reflecting the more egalitarian tendencies of Jacksonian America by stressing the ability of people with varied economic means to have a space for eternal rest. The partnership with the Massachusetts Horticultural Society, which was but one of the experimental features of the Mount Auburn venture, did not last, but its dual function as cemetery and public park, its emphasis on an elaborate landscape design intended to evoke untamed nature, and the urging by its trustees that lot holders should improve their lots with plantings and shrubbery as they would their private homes and gardens were innovations that stuck. At the time of its consecration, however, it was not yet inevitable that Mount Auburn Cemetery would spawn an entire nationwide cultural movement. It was, in September 1831, another reform cemetery, far bigger and more elaborate than its predecessors, to be sure, but it was also in that moment the next step in a tradition that dated from the 1790s. It did not take long for visitors and critics to recognize that Mount Auburn was the final step in the reform cemetery tradition and the first step of an altogether new cultural idiom, the rural cemetery movement.

2

"The Hand of Taste"

The Success of Mount Auburn
and the Beginning of a Movement

The consecration of Mount Auburn Cemetery had an immediate and profound impact on the American cultural imagination. From its founding, Mount Auburn challenged Americans to reconsider their notions of not only what a burying ground could be but also what it *should* be, for both the living and the dead. It spawned a national movement based upon the novel idea of the "rural cemetery" not just as a model for burial alone but also as a space for urban dwellers to convene with the natural world, to seek moral and spiritual uplift, and to derive inspiration for such burgeoning modes of cultural expression as romanticism, sentimentalism, and the picturesque. The landscaping and monuments erected in Mount Auburn and its successors reflected the widespread softening in American attitudes toward death and dying, a phenomenon that stood in stark contrast with colonial New England's memento mori culture, with its emphasis on the inevitability of death and the corporeality of the body.[1] Mount Auburn's promoters were successful in whetting the public's appetite for a new burying ground that would double as a rural retreat for the living, and the praise lavished upon the cemetery by the press propelled Americans elsewhere to consider the potential benefits of embracing this new phase of burial reform. Even as editors and journalists urged replication of the rural cemetery model offered by Mount Auburn in cities across the country, travelers from both America and abroad expounded upon the beauties of the new city of the dead in accounts that found ready publication in newspapers, magazines, and published travel journals.

New Haven's New Burying Ground, while it had inspired other communities to follow its model, had failed to spawn a national reform cemetery movement in any true sense that captured the imagination of Americans, whereas the success of Mount Auburn was immediate and inspired imitation from coast to coast. The influence of the press as a shaper of middle-class taste and values within the context of the rural cemetery movement cannot here be understated. Leading among the voices touting the benefits of the rural cemetery for improving the reputation of individual towns and cities, and of the nation more generally, was the *North American Review*. Shortly before Mount Auburn's consecration ceremony, the magazine argued that since the example set by New Haven had not universally taken hold, "the burying-place continues to be the most neglected spot in all the region, distinguished from other fields only by its leaning stones and the meanness of its enclosure, without a tree or shrub to take from it the air of utter desolation. We cannot but hope that the cemetery about to be established will put our cities and villages to shame, and spread a better taste and feeling in this respect throughout the whole country."[2] Communities across the Northeast heeded its call, and the first string of rural cemeteries following Mount Auburn's precedent were Mount Hope Cemetery established in 1834 in Bangor, Maine, followed by Mount Pleasant Cemetery in Taunton, Massachusetts, and Philadelphia's Laurel Hill Cemetery, both established in 1836. By the end of the decade, the United States boasted eleven rural cemeteries scattered across and just beyond the Northeast, which, in addition to the four earliest, included the New Bedford Rural Cemetery (1837) and Worcester Rural Cemetery (1838) in Massachusetts; Brooklyn's massive Green-Wood Cemetery (1838) and Mount Hope Cemetery in Rochester (1838) in New York; Monument Cemetery (1838) in Philadelphia; Green Mount Cemetery (1839) in Baltimore; and Glendale Cemetery (1839) in Akron, Ohio.

The 1830s was a decade of rupture and transformation on a tremendous scale for Americans nationwide, as it witnessed the violence of the Nat Turner Rebellion, the radical turn of the abolitionist movement, and the concerted efforts of proslavery white southerners to reinforce their power over the enslaved; the failed efforts of the nation's southeastern tribes to retain their autonomy in the face of President Andrew Jackson's Indian Removal Act; the massive intensification of textile manufacturing and expansion of industrialization more generally; and the beginning of railroad expansion, which would fundamentally alter how Americans would move, settle, and consume.[3] Cultural developments both influenced and were influenced by the rural cemetery movement during this period, including an expanding romanticism associated with death and the commemoration of the dead; increased pressure nationwide to exhibit the trappings of "civilized" behavior, which included observing proper care and disposal of the dead; the establishment of cultural institutions that would validate the United States as a modern, respectable nation; an intensified need by all social classes for open, "natural" spaces to which they could escape from the increasingly crowded urban industrial landscapes; and, building upon developments already in place during the 1790s, a marked increase in the desire, especially by the urban industrial middle class, to exhibit refinement and "good taste" in every material undertaking, which extended to the decoration of cemetery burial plots with flowers and the erection of increasingly elaborate sepulchral monuments. The rural cemetery met the needs of expanding communities in the urban industrial Northeast, and the success of the movement by decade's end affirmed for Americans as well as travelers from abroad that the communities that had embraced this movement were actively engaged in transforming the United States into a modern nation.

In the wake of its consecration on September 24, 1831, Mount Auburn Cemetery captivated Americans both near and far, and by the end of the year it had become a national cultural phenomenon. Both the local and the national press wrote glowingly of the new place of sepulture as inaugurating a new age of respect for the dead, while weekly and monthly periodicals of every stripe, from literary to mechanics' magazines, reprinted Joseph Story's consecration address well into the following year. Urging progressive-minded citizens to undertake the establishment of a similarly styled burial space in their own communities, one such periodical exhorted "prominent citizens" to take inspiration from Story's words and "step forward and give the weight of their influence to a similar measure."[4] What many writers found most striking about Mount Auburn was the novelty of its design, which created a seemingly "natural" environment through the efforts of human artifice and which in turn gave visitors an experience that was altogether divorced from their daily urban travails. Thomas Green Fessenden, author and editor of the *New England Farmer*, expressed his enthusiasm for the new burying ground immediately following its consecration and declared that within a few years, "when the hand of taste shall have passed over the luxuriance of nature, we may challenge the rivalry of the world to produce another such residence for the spirit of beauty."[5] In his report for the annual meeting of the Massachusetts Horticultural Society in 1833, General Henry Dearborn, president of the society as well as principal landscape designer for Mount Auburn, concluded, "The whole establishment is in a most flourishing condition, and continues to receive the most encouraging attention and patronage." He further declared with certainty that cemeteries like Mount Auburn "will soon be established in the vicinity of all large cities."[6]

Mount Auburn Cemetery was novel in a number of ways, but what initially made it such an experimental new institution was its creation as an endeavor executed not by a cemetery corporation or association but rather by the Massachusetts Horticultural Society to function as both an experimental garden *and* a burying ground. When Dr. Jacob Bigelow first proposed the establishment of a suburban cemetery in 1825, the Horticultural Society did not yet exist, but Bigelow's initial meeting had included the very same men who would go on to serve in leadership positions following the society's incorporation by the Massachusetts State Legislature in 1829—including General Henry Dearborn, Zebedee Cook, and, unsurprisingly, Bigelow himself. The partnership between the cemetery and the Horticultural Society dissolved in 1835 with the subsequent incorporation by the state legislature of the Mount Auburn Corporation, but the Horticultural Society's original influence nevertheless had a lasting impact on rural cemetery aesthetics in subsequent decades.[7]

Having distinguished itself from the reform cemetery model at New Haven, the new burial space that emerged as the result of the Horticultural Society's interests yielded the creation of a burial landscape with an equal focus on landscaping and beauty and on adequately expansive space for the burial of the dead. The New Haven cemetery's novelty had been defined by its adherence to the neoclassical grid pattern that urban developers embraced during the 1790s and early 1800s, with the inclusion of individual, family, and associational lots as well as a smattering of well-regulated plantings that lined the carriage paths.[8] Père Lachaise Cemetery near Paris, which had become an international phenomenon by the 1820s and was, for many visitors and critics, the standard by which all other cemeteries must be measured, was in its design very similar to New Haven's burying ground, albeit on a much grander scale. By the time Mount Auburn was consecrated, Père Lachaise was a true city of the dead, packed with tombs and sepulchral monuments with nary any space between burial plots.[9] In its design, Mount Auburn diverged significantly from these precedents. Indeed, the genius of Henry Dearborn's design for Mount Auburn rested upon his ability to shape a preexisting wild landscape into one that was at once artificial but also seemingly the embodiment of the natural and romantic picturesque to anyone who visited. Marked by hills, ponds, a variety of footpaths and carriage paths named for various flora, and a great variety of trees, shrubs, and other plantings, not to mention the mount for which it was named, the cemetery embodied what many considered to be the ideal balance between human artifice and untouched nature. Doubling as an "experimental garden" in its first few years of operation, by May 1833, the cemetery gardener had already planted "four hundred and fifty varieties" of seeds for trees and other "ornamental plants" that had been sent to the Horticultural Society from Europe, Asia, and South America.[10] For visitors, then, the landscape offered not only picturesque vistas but also an element of the exotic in introducing Americans to hitherto foreign and rare plantings.

In its design, Mount Auburn's landscape further reflected a definitive shift away in popular aesthetics from the neoclassical grid ideal of the Federal period of the 1790s, retaining only from that era of burial reform the division of the landscape into well-defined family burial lots measuring three-hundred-square-feet (sold for sixty dollars per lot) as well as single interments marked for the availability of the general public at a cost of only ten dollars.[11] In the pricing for burial lots, Mount Auburn embodied the egalitarian and democratic ideals of its elite founders, who envisioned the cemetery as a space where anyone, regardless of class, could afford a decent burial. In establishing the cemetery as nonsectarian, Mount Auburn's founders further embraced a spirit of welcoming regardless of religious faith or denomination, and they likewise made no prohibitions or restrictions for lot purchasers based upon race or ethnicity. Such considerations were evident when statesman Edward Everett declared in one address that the cemetery "presents an opportunity for all, who wish to enjoy it, of providing a place of burial for those, for whom it is their duty to make such provision.

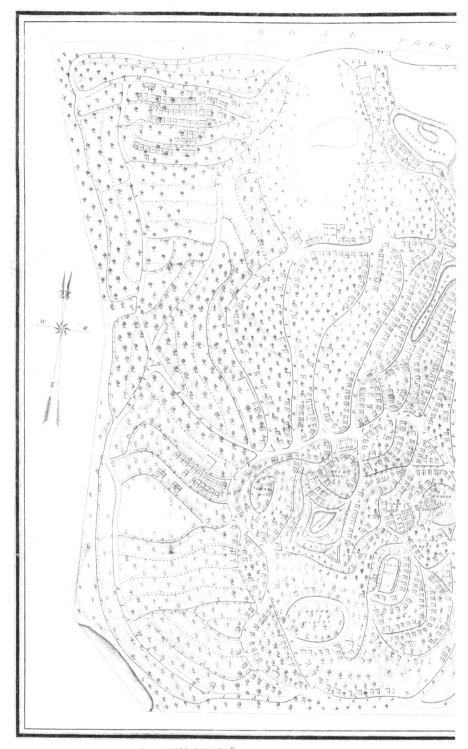

Map of Mount Auburn Cemetery by Alexander Wadsworth, 1841.
(Courtesy Digital Commons Commonwealth)

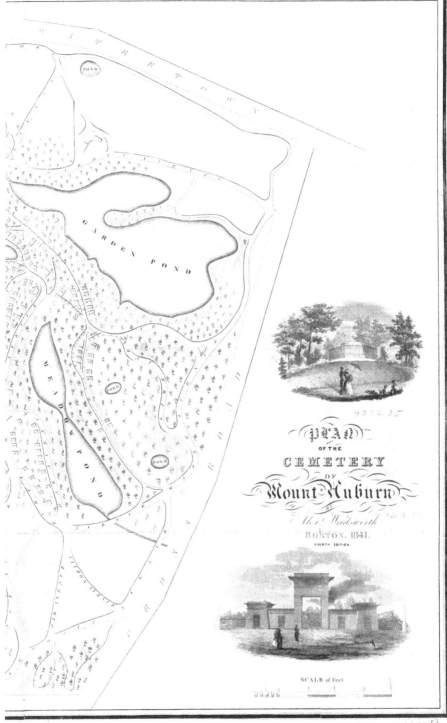

PLAN
OF THE
CEMETERY
OF
Mount Auburn

Alex. Wadsworth
BOSTON, 1841.
FOURTH EDITION.

SCALE of Feet

The space is ample, affording room for as large a number of lots, as may be required for a considerable length of time; and the price at which they are now to be purchased, it is believed, is considerably less than that of tombs."[12] The price for a family lot was not beyond the reaches of Boston's artisans and craftsmen, and in fulfillment of Everett's assertions, carpenters, engravers, and sailmakers, as well as members of the expanding professional middle class, purchased family lots soon after the cemetery's consecration.[13]

The relationship between the cemetery and the Horticultural Society dissolved in 1835, but this early partnership nevertheless shaped the planning for Mount Auburn and all subsequent cemeteries so that landscape design and the incorporation of many species of flora were part and parcel to what made a rural cemetery a rural cemetery. Shaped and manipulated as the cemetery was, however, the purpose behind such landscape design was to evoke a sense of untamed nature without the space *actually* being wild. Such was the ideal of one of the core facets of romanticism—the *picturesque*. Dating back to the eighteenth century, the picturesque as well as the sublime and the beautiful (or pastoral) were part of a unifying theory of aesthetics developed by the English. Whereas the sublime embodied "nature in all its wildness, completely outside the control of civilization," the picturesque struck a balance between art and nature, while the beautiful or pastoral involved the subordination of nature to civilization.[14] Upon the new cemetery's consecration, Fessenden's *New England Farmer* described its picturesque nature as it gushed, "The natural features of Mount Auburn are incomparable for the purpose to which it is now sacred. There is not in all the untrodden valleys of the West, a more secluded, more natural or more appropriate spot for the religious exercises of the living; we may be allowed to add our doubts whether the most opulent neighborhood of Europe furnishes a spot so singularly appropriate for a 'Garden of Graves.'"[15] This sense of seclusion from the land of the living was a persistent theme in visitors' accounts to the cemetery, for while it was only a few miles from the center of Boston, many writers were struck by the illusion of remoteness—not just from the land of the living but also from civilization itself. One visitor in 1835 thus described it: "Mount Auburn seems like a wilderness before you enter it. In truth, much of it is still very much *like* a wilderness. . . . Never in my life did I see a spot of no more than about 100 acres, for which Nature had done so much; to say nothing of what has been done by art. . . . The whole of Mount Auburn is diversified with hills, vales, ponds, trees, and shrubs; and intersected with paths," most of which were footpaths. Such variety within the landscape, with trees and bushes, sharp hills and gentle undulations, contrasted sharply with Boston Common, which resembled "a rich meadow, with rows of trees upon it and a few scattered over it."[16]

The men in charge of the design and forward progress of Mount Auburn Cemetery further envisioned that the aesthetics of the new space of burial would enable it to become for the living a place of moral uplift where one could engage in inward reflection away from the vicissitudes of the city. Joseph Story articulated this principle in his consecration address, as he explained, "Our cemeteries rightly selected, may be made subservient to some of the highest purposes of religion and human duty. They may preach lessons, to which none may refuse to listen, and which all, that live, must hear. Truths may be there felt and taught in the silence of our own meditations, more persuasive, and more enduring, than ever flowed from human lips." Story saw in the grave a place that was not merely a repository for the dead but a space with the capacity to arrest the attention of the living and be a silent exhortation to those still aboveground to improve their thoughts and actions:

> The grave hath a voice of eloquence, nay, of superhuman eloquence, which speaks at once to the thoughtlessness of the rash, and the devotion of the good; which addresses all times, and all ages, and all sexes; which tells of wisdom to the wise and comfort to the afflicted; which warns us of our follies and our dangers; which whispers to us in accents of peace, and alarms us in tones of terror; which steals with a healing balm into the stricken heart, and lifts up and supports the broken spirit; which awakens a new enthusiasm for virtue, and disciplines us for its severer trials and duties; which calls up the images of the illustrious dead, with an animating presence for our example and glory; and which demands of us, as men, as patriots, as Christians, as immortals, that the powers given by God should be devoted to his service, and the minds created by his love, should return to him with larger capacities for virtuous enjoyment, and with more spiritual and intellectual brightness.[17]

In short, Story believed that the new cemetery landscape had the capacity to make the men and women who went there become better versions of themselves, that it could draw forth from anyone who visited it feelings that are universal to the human condition and instill a greater ability to engage in healing introspection that otherwise had become difficult if not impossible within the noisy realm of the living.

Jacob Bigelow echoed Story's sentiments in an address he delivered in 1831 before the Boston Society for the Promotion of Useful Knowledge. While his words mainly focused on the ancient and modern practices of disposing of the dead, Bigelow concluded with his own reflections upon the new cemetery of Mount Auburn as a solution to the modern challenges of properly mourning the dead and reflecting upon one's own mortality. "The history of mankind, in all ages, shows that the human heart clings to the grave of its disappointed wishes, that it seeks consolation in rearing emblems and monuments, and in collecting images of beauty over the disappearing relics of humanity. This can be fitly done," he continued, "not in the tumultuous and harassing din of cities, not in the gloomy and almost unapproachable vaults of charnel houses;—but amidst the quiet verdure of the field, under the broad and cheerful light of heaven,—where the harmonious and ever changing face of nature reminds us, by its resuscitating influences, that to die is but to live again."[18] As a physician, Bigelow had been an early promoter of the rural cemetery idea on the supposition that the removal of the dead outside the urban center was necessary for the general health and well-being of the public, but he was also not beyond appealing to listeners' hearts and minds with images of religious and moral uplift, not to mention reinforcing the notion that to bury the dead in a suburban retreat was far more appropriate and respectful.

Story's and Bigelow's words were anticipatory and had yet to be proven at the time of the cemetery's consecration in September, but the idea that the rural cemetery would inspire moral reflection and elevated feelings in its visitors rapidly became a common theme in periodicals that extolled the virtues of the new burying space. In its October 1831 issue, the *North American Review* declared, "The burial-place is the retreat of the thoughtful. . . . It has a good effect upon the feelings; it makes the unfortunate more reconciled to this world, and the gay more thoughtful of another."[19] But these influences would not be reserved to the bereaved alone. Indeed, from the very beginning, the cemetery's planners anticipated its value as an institution for both the living and the dead, and among the living, both the mourner *and* the casual visitor. In an address delivered to the Massachusetts Horticultural Society in 1832, naturalist Thaddeus William Harris predicted that Mount Auburn would quickly become "one of the most instructive, magnificent,

Thomas Chambers, *Mount Auburn Cemetery*, oil on canvas. (Courtesy National Gallery of Art)

and pleasant promenades in our country" as well as "a place of healthful, refreshing, and agreeable resort."[20] His words were indeed prescient, for it was not long before crowds regularly ventured out to the cemetery for reasons other than mourning, and the press continued to reinforce the image of the rural cemetery as having a tangible effect on visitors' moral well-being.

Hoping to deter visitors from engaging in unseemly (or even sinful) behavior in Mount Auburn (for more on this, see chap. 3), the *American Quarterly Observer* offered a dramatic rebuke to those who would use the cemetery as "a scene of Sabbath breaking, and of thoughtless mirth," and, invoking the view of death as but an impermanent state of sleep or rest, warned that they would rue their behavior on the day of resurrection and judgment. Instead, "whenever we enter the consecrated cemetery, let us remember that it is one day to be to us, if we sleep there, the scene of unutterable emotions, and that we are now forming the character with which we shall awake at the morning of the resurrection, and which will make our tomb the threshold of an eternity of joy or sorrow."[21] Other writers acknowledged the inclination of an increasing number of visitors to venture to the cemetery for reasons other than bereavement or moral uplift, but rather than focus on the dire consequences to their immortal souls, the authors instead reasserted the power of Mount Auburn to pacify even the most jolly and raucous traveler. Reporting on the variety of visitors and their carefree gaiety upon arrival to the cemetery, George Ticknor Curtis, writing for the *New England Magazine* in 1834, described the immediate effect of Mount Auburn to sober and subdue "as soon as they have passed under those gathering shades." Such an effect should not be considered unpleasant, however, as Curtis continued, "Still, the influence of the place is not a melancholy or a saddening influence; it is better—it is expansive and soothing, filling the mind with the beauties of nature, and thus breaking the force of any passionate expressions of affliction, which may be ready to burst forth, and uniting the great idea of death in general, with images and objects which are not shadowy and hard to grasp, but before us, around us, and familiar."[22] In short, the cemetery would connect the visitor to the natural world, of which death is only a part.

As inheritors of the European memento mori tradition that emerged in full force during the Renaissance in the wake of the Black Death, colonial New Englanders had long regarded Death as the "King of Terrors." The evidence for this view can be seen today on the surviving slate headstones dating from the seventeenth and eighteenth centuries across the region, which bear easily recognizable mortality symbols, included among them winged skulls, crossbones, hourglasses and bells, and epitaphs that reminded the viewer of the inevitability of death and the corporeality of the body.[23] One of the most commonly inscribed epitaphs of the colonial period was derived from the late Medieval tale "The Three Living and the Three Dead," in which the dead address the living on the inevitability of death. Variations on this tale spread across continental Europe and the British Isles during the Renaissance.[24] On colonial gravestones, the sentiment of the story appears as the verse "Stranger, stop and cast an eye / As you are now, so once was I / As I am now, so you shall be / Prepare for death and follow me." *The American Quarterly* reflected upon this traditional view of death by declaring, "We frequently meet with the impression that death is to be looked upon as a great calamity, and since it is unavoidable, that we must endeavor to meet it with fortitude."[25] The reality for Puritans, as noted by David Stannard, was more complicated. Regarding death as both a "blessing" and a punishment for Original Sin, "Puritans were gripped individually and collectively by an intense and unremitting fear of death, while simultaneously clinging to the traditional Christian rhetoric of viewing death as a release and relief for the earth-bound soul."[26] For nineteenth-century Americans influenced by new religious movements, especially the radical evangelicalism of the Second Great Awakening, which rejected the doctrine of predestination embraced by New England Puritans, Mount Auburn's very design would "assist many in loosing [sic] those apprehensions of death."[27] Gravestones bearing mortality symbols had already fallen out of favor by the time of Mount Auburn's consecration, but beyond that, the landscape design itself would soften the horrors associated with death and bodily decay, in essence beautifying death in a picturesque landscape and providing a proper resting place in anticipation of the final resurrection.

Curtis reinforced the notion that Mount Auburn and subsequent such rural cemeteries had the power to break the horrors associated with death: "In these beautiful pleasure-grounds of Death, there is every thing needful to rob it of its terrors."[28] Stripped of its capacity to horrify the living, death became transformed in the mid-nineteenth century into something beautiful. The rural cemetery ably illustrated this transition in attitudes toward death, which was further supported by softening Christian doctrine on human mortality and the fate of the soul as a result of the popularization of evangelical theology during the Second Great Awakening. Added to this was the expanding popularity of consolation literature, which emphasized the importance of heavenly family reunion through death.[29] Even popular literature, poetry, and music (especially opera) reflected and magnified these transformations, as authors and composers romanticized the deaths of their main characters, particularly those suffering from consumption (tuberculosis), a disease that because of industrialization and urbanization was becoming one of the most common causes of death in nineteenth-century America.[30]

As diverse visitors, from mill girls to European elites, poured into the cemetery's precincts during its first years in operation, accounts of their experiences and their opinions of the new burial space varied widely, though most were overwhelmingly positive and reflected the kinds of feelings Mount Auburn's promoters had hoped it would provoke. One local Bostonian, William A. Brewer, visited Mount Auburn for the first time in Autumn 1832 at the behest of a visiting friend from Alabama, "who had an intense desire to see a place of which so much had been said and written." In writing of the divergent views held by himself and his friend prior to visiting the cemetery, Brewer in his account is illustrative of how, undoubtedly, many locals had to overcome prior associations of the space from when it was simply "Sweet Auburn," a genuinely wild and untouched landscape frequented for fun and leisure by children as well as "Harvardinians" (faculty and students from nearby Harvard University). Whereas Brewer's friend was motivated to visit Boston specifically to see Mount Auburn, envisioning it as "a 'city of the dead,' equalling in funereal splendor the far-famed 'Père la Chaise,' at Paris," Brewer, on the other hand, "was not in the practice of considering it as a place of solemn thought and profitable reflection; but rather as a lovely spot, where, if perchance reflection ever came, it came as to a secret haunt of those who stole there to pour their eloquence on the still winds, that they might be the better practiced for the meed [*sic*] of a feverish ambition."[31] However, Brewer's arrival to the cemetery with his friend immediately altered his estimation of the place, for upon seeing the massive Egyptian Revival gateway designed by Jacob Bigelow—erected in wood and painted to appear as granite—he fancied, "I almost imagined myself withdrawn from my father-land, and suddenly transported to those scenes in Egypt, made familiar to us by the accounts of [Giovanni] Belzoni, and [John] Martin's inimitable mezzotinto of the 'Departure of the Israelites.'" Combined with the inscription on top of the central portal, "*Then shall the dust return to the earth as it was; and the spirit shall return unto God who gave it,*" the whole scene before even entering the cemetery landscape conveyed a sense of solemnity. "How appropriate!" Brewer wrote of the effect.[32]

If Story and Bigelow had hoped the cemetery would encourage the idle visitor to think more keenly on mortality, then Brewer's account is illustrative of their success. Brewer described how, in the course of their exploration within the burying ground, he and his friend "indulged in a free interchange of thoughts and opinions respecting death—such as seemed naturally to flow from the conviction that we were treading upon soil consecrated to the sepulture of those whose spirits are breathed into them by the great Author of the universe."[33] By this time, there were as yet few monuments erected in the cemetery, though the two men paid homage to Mount Auburn's first resident, Hannah Adams, where Brewer's friend took the opportunity to acquire for himself a souvenir from the burial site—"he gathered a few fragments of the Sienite that had been hewn from the wall-stones of the tomb, and carefully wrapped them in paper, to be deposited in his collection of geological specimens—not so much as curiosities, as to serve as a talisman of a cherished reverence for the spot and its associations."[34] This account reflected exactly the kinds of feelings the cemetery's promoters had hoped to evoke from travelers—excluding, of course, the theft of stones from the tomb, which would have appalled the cemetery trustees—and Brewer went on in his narrative to urge anyone and everyone to venture to the cemetery and experience the place for themselves. So moved was he by his first exploration that Brewer headed back to Mount Auburn a few days later to "meditate" near the monument to Hannah Adams, and it was here that he experienced a "melancholy pleasure" that could not be entirely explained but had to be experienced for oneself. "Reader!" he implored, "go there now, and sit where I sat. Give up yourself to the purifying reflections which will naturally arise from the scenes there presented."[35]

A Lowell mill girl identified as Zillah conveyed her thoughts in the first issue of the worker-published journal the *Lowell Offering* in October 1840 following her visit to Mount Auburn, and her reflections, written in a most romantic prose, illustrate the success of the cemetery founders' hopes that its landscape could appeal to the higher sensibilities of all classes of people. Reflecting upon how Americans cared for their dead, Zillah declared, "However indifferent persons may pretend to feel on this point, if they will but wander through the calm, quiet shades of Mount Auburn, they cannot but choose between a place of so much beauty, and the bleak, barren spots which are usually selected for the last repose of the dead." Appreciative of the birdsong she could hear and the flowers as she "rambled through its many lovely and shaded paths," Zillah further noted the melancholy yet beautiful lessons to be taken from the monuments—one a tomb for an infant, another a "stately monument erected by a husband to the memory of his wife and children."[36] Published for the benefit of her fellow mill girls, Zillah's prose is similar to that which appeared in periodicals intended for consumption by the middle class, yet hers was written strictly for a female working-class audience who would have likewise made the cemetery a destination for when they had time off of work.

As an alternative to the rigid neoclassicism and rectilinearity embodied by New Haven's New Burying Ground and its imitators—such as Mound Cemetery in Marietta, Ohio; Ronaldson's Cemetery in Philadelphia; and Shockoe Hill Cemetery in Richmond, Virginia—Mount Auburn's picturesque landscape proved within a short time to be wildly successful, both in attracting visitors and in securing lot owners. In its report to the Massachusetts Horticultural Society in 1834, the Garden and Cemetery Committee rightly observed, "Mount Auburn has already become a place of general resort and interest, as well to strangers as to citizens; and its shades and paths, ornamented with monumental structures, of various beauty and elegance, have already given solace and tranquilizing reflections to many an afflicted heart, and awakened a deep moral sensibility in many a pious bosom. The Committee look forward, with increasing confidence, to a steady public patronage, which shall supply all the means necessary for the accomplishment of all the interesting objects of the establishment."[37] As both a cultural institution and a business model, with its emphasis on horticulture as well as access to a proper burial space for the dead, the rural cemetery aesthetic almost immediately replaced the older reform cemetery model, as urban industrial and commercial centers of the Northeast labored to provide new burying grounds for their expanding populations.

The residents of Bangor, Maine, were the first to follow Mount Auburn Cemetery's lead and established the nation's second nonsectarian rural cemetery. Located thirty miles from Penobscot Bay, Bangor was incorporated as a city in 1834 and was by that time a trade and shipping hub, as well as the "Lumber Capital of the World."[38] By the time of the city's incorporation, most of Bangor's older burying grounds either had been abandoned or were in disarray, their remaining graveyards overcrowded and bearing a "soul-chilling appearance" according to the city's mayor, Edward Kent.[39] Similar to the Massachusetts Horticultural Society's role in securing the establishment of Mount Auburn Cemetery and influencing its design and original function as both an experimental garden and a burying ground, the Bangor Horticultural Society was incorporated in the same year as the city, 1834, and soon thereafter negotiated with Joseph Treat for the purchase of fifty acres of elevated land adjacent to the Penobscot River. After the purchase, the Bangor Horticultural Society reincorporated as the Mount Hope Cemetery Corporation and hired Charles G. Bryant (1803–50), regarded as Maine's "first architect," to improve the grounds.[40] At the beginning of July 1836, corporation secretary John Barstow published a notice in the *Bangor (ME) Daily Whig & Courier* that lots in Mount Hope Cemetery were ready for sale at the price of twenty dollars per lot, a cost that, as at Mount Auburn, reflected the proprietors' desire that burial at Mount Hope should be accessible to the general public.[41] On the day before the cemetery's scheduled dedication later in the month, a writer to the newspaper who signed their editorial simply as "A"—who may very well have been the corporation's president, Amos Patton—invoked the influence of Mount Auburn by asking readers, "Who would not prefer a resting place among the hallowed and consecrated groves of Mount Auburn, to a solitary spot in the desert?" Like "A," other rural cemetery proponents would use language that diminished the value of other types of burying grounds as inferior, either because of the grounds' isolation and sense of abandonment from society or because of their too near proximity, overcrowded and boxed-in by urban development. Noting the importance of trees and flowers to make the space of burial beautiful and attractive, "A" further exhorted, "Let us then do what we can to make Mount Hope *worthy* of Bangor and her enterprising citizens. It is to be the Public Burial place of our City, as well as that of private individuals. Let us then make it a *garden*—let us have the winding stream, the shady mount, and the beautiful glen—and if nature has not been beneficent enough, let art triumph in her skill."[42] Such language, describing what Mount Hope *ought* to be for the citizens of Bangor, would become increasingly common as the rural cemetery movement expanded over the next few decades. That is, the rural cemetery itself would be a reflection of the community in which it was situated, an institution that provided evidence to the elevated sentiments, industriousness, and cultivated tastes of the living who dwelled beyond its borders.

Following the publication of this editorial, the cemetery was formally dedicated two days later on July 22—delayed from its scheduled dedication day of July 21 due to a rain shower that "thoroughly drenched . . . very many of our fair ladies." The crowds had scattered in the face of rain on that Thursday but swelled once again on Friday, when the men and women in attendance "manifested the true Bangor energy." Mayor Edward Kent presided over the dedication where he declared in language similar to Joseph Story at Mount Auburn, "the beauties of nature scattered on every hand was calculated to give a chastened and holy calm to the mind, and to lead the thoughts to study nature in her works, and to God as the great author."[43] Like its predecessor, Mount Hope quickly attracted visitors as well as lot holders, and it also appears to have been among the first rural cemeteries (if not the first one) to become a repository for the relocation of grave markers and human remains from the area's older graveyards. After only a few months in operation, in October 1836, the board of aldermen ordered the city's undertaker to remove "all the remains of persons buried in the old burying place near the Penobscot bridge" and relocate them to Mount Hope.[44] Such efforts established a precedent of binding a community's ancestors with present and future generations, allowing the older burying spaces in prime urban real estate to disappear without making the dead within those spaces face the

View at Mount Hope Cemetery, Bangor, Maine. (Photograph by the author)

ignominy of neglect and ultimate oblivion. Relocated to the rural cemetery, the city's dead of past generations would be remembered, their graves protected from urban development.[45]

Whereas it took two years from the time of the establishment of Mount Hope in Bangor to its dedication in July 1836, the rural cemetery in Taunton, Massachusetts—ultimately named Mount Pleasant Cemetery—was incorporated in March of that year and dedicated just a few weeks before Mount Hope, on the Fourth of July.[46] The Taunton *Whig and Reporter* related the day's events and reflected the same local pride of place as the news out of Boston and Bangor. Attendance at the cemetery's dedication was estimated at about one thousand, and the "audience—and we have never seen one more brilliant and beautiful—was arranged tier above tier, upon the gentle slope which nearly surrounded the stage, and entirely protected from the sun by the thick foliage of the trees." Similar to other consecration ceremonies, the one held in Taunton included the singing of choral music, an introductory prayer, and the performance of an original hymn, in this case written by "Miss Mary W. Hale" of that town and which alluded to the natural beauty of the place having the power to dispel fears of death in exchange for faith in eternal heavenly glory. This was followed by the principal oration for the day, a consecrating prayer, and another original hymn, sung to the tune of "Old Hundred" by all in attendance.[47] Compared to its contemporaries, Mount Pleasant Cemetery received far less attention from critics and travelers, but even so, it was clearly not without its merits for those who turned their gaze in the direction of Taunton. In *A Gazetteer of the United States of America*, published in 1854, author John Hayward wrote of Mount Pleasant that, "laid out on the plan of Mount Auburn," it was "among the most pleasing of our rural cemeteries." The town dated back to 1639, when Elisabeth Poole, "the pious Puritan lady[,] . . . conceived the bold design of planting a church among the Indians in this part of the wilderness" and purchased a large tract of land from Massasoit for the town's establishment. The "ladies of Taunton," in honor of their town's foundress, erected a statue to Poole by the cemetery's gates and so tied the town's rural cemetery with its deep ties to Puritan New England history.[48]

While the first five years of the rural cemetery movement witnessed the establishment of only two successors to Mount Auburn, both in northern New England, by the end of the movement's first decade, eighteen rural cemeteries that spanned from Maine to Ohio to Maryland were open to the public. Almost exactly one decade following the consecration of Mount Auburn, the *North American Review* again weighed in on the subject of rural cemeteries and wrote approvingly, "A better feeling has begun to prevail amongst us in regard to the burial of the dead. And from these facts we indulge the hope that a great public interest is henceforth to receive that care which it imperiously demands, and which will serve, in some measure, to do away that reproach, to which our neglect and indifference to it have, hitherto, justly subjected us."[49] Highlighting what it considered to be some of the most important contributions to the movement thus far, the article discussed Harmony Grove in Salem, Massachusetts, Laurel Hill in Philadelphia, Green-Wood in Brooklyn, and Green Mount in Baltimore, in addition to Mount Auburn. The proprietors of newly established rural cemeteries across the Northeast had all adhered to the basic principles of the picturesque aesthetic and endeavored to use landscape design as a means of dispelling the older horrors of death from the place of burial. All of the rural cemeteries established since Mount Auburn were likewise suburban institutions, located anywhere from one and a half miles, in the case of Baltimore's Green Mount Cemetery, to four miles, in the case of Laurel Hill

Cemetery, away from the urban core of the cities with which they were associated. In these respects, rural cemeteries were united together as part of a burgeoning national cultural movement. As the *North American Review* made plain, however, there was great variety to be found in the landscapes and architectural aesthetics, while the operational policies and intentions of cemetery founders and trustees often diverged significantly from the universalist tone established by Mount Auburn and its northern New England successors.[50]

The first rural cemetery that broke the mold in several respects was Philadelphia's Laurel Hill Cemetery, incorporated in 1836 with its first burial in October of that year (but not fully opened to the public until 1837). Elite Philadelphia Quaker John Jay Smith purchased the thirty-two-acre plot of land on the Schuylkill River that would become Laurel Hill. Instead of an untouched woodland, Laurel Hill had once been part of a grand family estate and thus was already partially landscaped at the time of the purchase. Its situation one hundred feet above the river immediately lent an air of the picturesque to the scene. The state legislature approved the establishment of the Laurel Hill Cemetery Company in 1837, whose members included Smith, Nathan Dunn, Benjamin W. Richards, Frederick Brown, William M. Meredith, Edward Coleman, George N. Baker, Henry Toland, and Nicholas Biddle. Like the men who founded Mount Auburn, the early leadership of Laurel Hill Cemetery was composed of local elites with varied business and cultural interests. Smith, for example, was a businessman as well as director of the Philadelphia Library Company, editor of Andrew Jackson Downing's *Horticulturalist* journal, and treasurer of the Athenian Institute.[51] Nathan Dunn made his business as a merchant in China and, after amassing an enormous collection of ten thousand Chinese collectibles and artifacts, opened the Chinese Museum in Philadelphia in 1838.[52] Edward Coleman and Benjamin W. Richards were both lawyers, and Richards was also a onetime mayor of Philadelphia. Frederick Brown was a druggist and one of the original founders of the Philadelphia College of Pharmacy.[53] George N. Baker was a state politician, and Nicholas Biddle was president of the Second Bank of the United States as well as a state politician, while Henry Toland distinguished himself as a wealthy merchant who served on a number of occasions as a purchasing agent for President Andrew Jackson, was a director of the Bank of the United States, and was a member of the Philadelphia Hibernian Society, a fraternal organization for Irish Americans.[54] Collectively, these men were akin to those from Boston as socioeconomic

General view of Laurel Hill Cemetery, lithograph by E. J. Pinkerton, 1844.
(Courtesy World Digital Library)

elites who expressed a strong compulsion simultaneously to engage with
and to enrich the civic and cultural environment of their city.

Unlike their New England counterparts, however, the men who managed Laurel Hill Cemetery envisioned the new burying ground as an elite
for-profit institution and eschewed the egalitarian policies established farther north. Whereas Mount Auburn, Mount Hope, and Mount Pleasant
Cemeteries had no regulations that barred burial for particular segments
of the population, Laurel Hill prohibited burials for the poor and African
Americans. For their part, Black Philadelphians established their own privately operated Lebanon Cemetery in 1849, designed according to the rural
cemetery model.[55] Such exclusions went unremarked by the press, and
instead Laurel Hill earned praise for its nonsectarian policy (found also in
the New England rural cemeteries). As the *National Gazette* (Philadelphia)
noted approvingly, "There is no intrusion *here* of that wretched spirit of sec-
tarianism, which in life makes one half mankind an enemy to the other . . .
which sometimes . . . separates the mouldering remains of husband and
wife—or father and child, if they happened during life, however conscien-
tiously, to worship the same God at different shrines. *Here*, at least, this evil
spirit is rebuked. *Here*, all the ground is alike holy."[56] The absence of religious distinction in the rural cemeteries became a hallmark of the institution nationwide, though certain faiths, such as Judaism and Catholicism,

required burial within their own consecrated grounds. So popular did the rural cemetery movement become, though, that in many communities, synagogues purchased land within or adjacent to their local rural cemeteries, while a number of Catholic and Jewish cemeteries also embraced the rural cemetery aesthetic.[57] Despite the religious liberalism found at Laurel Hill and elsewhere, however, the choices made by its managers encouraged classism and potentially exacerbated class tensions, for despite creating "a handsome stranger's ground" where individuals could be buried "at a moderate cost" in contrast to the sizable and more expensive family plots, the working class was not altogether welcome, whether alive or dead.[58] At a distance of four miles from the city, Laurel Hill was far more onerous to access for anyone without a horse, carriage, or fare for a public omnibus—in short, a workingman or workingwoman could not simply take a casual afternoon stroll to visit the cemetery. Nor could they attempt to visit the cemetery on Sundays when they likely were not working, for the cemetery was closed to all but funeral attendees and lot holders, who were issued tickets of admission.[59] This inaccessibility to anyone other than the middle class and elites thus provided an opportunity for other rural cemeteries established in the vicinity of Philadelphia to promote community and accessibility as part of their business model. For example, when Laurel Hill's counterpart, Monument Cemetery, was established only a mile and a half northeast of the city in 1838, one of its great selling points to the public was that "it is at so convenient a proximity as to be easily reached by the pedestrian without experiencing a sense of fatigue."[60] Similarly, the Woodlands Cemetery, established in 1840 on the western bank of the Schuylkill River, was located only a mile southwest of the city.[61]

Laurel Hill's managers further distinguished their cemetery by incorporating something altogether new as part of the landscape—a sculptural group by a distinguished artist that did not mark a grave but rather symbolized the cemetery's founders' desire to make theirs a *permanent* burying ground. The group of sculptures, executed by noted Scottish sculptor James Thom (1802–50), consisted of author Sir Walter Scott along with Old Mortality and his pony.[62] As described by the periodical *Atkinson's Casket* in 1837, "The figure of Old Mortality reclining on a grave stone, which he has been chiselling [*sic*] and cleaning to preserve it from losing its inscription, is one of the most expressive specimens of the art we have ever seen; he is holding the celebrated conversation with Sir Walter Scott, detailed in the beautiful

Sir Walter Scott and Old Mortality, Laurel Hill Cemetery. (Photograph by the author)

introduction to the novel. Sir Walter is represented of full size, and it is the only full length statue of him in existence." The grouping would make Philadelphia stand out among the cities participating in the rural cemetery movement, for "it is something for Philadelphia to boast of, that she possesses the only stone resemblance of this great author and good man."[63] The following decade, the *Guide to Laurel Hill Cemetery* described the figures and made explicit the sculptures' major purpose—"The Managers of the Cemetery, in placing these figures on the grounds, had in view the possibility of embodying the idea that Laurel Hill is to be permanent; as Old Mortality loved to repair defaced tombstones, so the originators of the plan of the Cemetery hope it may be the study of their successors to keep the place in perpetual repair, and to transmit it undefaced to a distant date."[64] With Old Mortality in place, Laurel Hill would also be more than a cemetery; it would be an open-air art museum. Indeed, developments in sepulchral art in subsequent decades would only enhance this association, as elites increasingly erected sculptural figures by American and European artists over their lots. With sepulchral art becoming more costly, artistic, and elaborate, rural cemeteries further entrenched industrial-era class divisions by providing clear visual markers that maintained class distinctions even after death.[65]

The figures of Sir Walter Scott and Old Mortality were unique to Laurel Hill Cemetery, but the desire for permanence and security for the dead within the walls of the burying ground was not; indeed, the hope for these cemeteries to serve their communities in perpetuity was a prevailing feature as the rural cemetery movement expanded across the country. Cities that embraced the idea of establishing suburban rural cemeteries did so, at least in part, due to concerns that older public burial grounds and churchyards were rapidly decaying and/or becoming overcrowded, that they were being overtaken by urban development, and, worst of all, that they were subject to vandalism and grave robbing. Rural cemetery promoters amplified these sentiments while promoting the permanence of their new institutions. The new cemeteries needed to fulfill what many perceived as a need for more space and security, and the men who created these landscapes also vested them with rhetorical and visual markers that reinforced the idea to the public that the rural cemeteries would last forever while displacing, or at the very least improving upon, traditional burial patterns.

One way to evoke permanence was through the rhetoric of rural cemetery consecration addresses. Orators often discussed how the cultures of antiquity buried their dead outside of cities in "natural" spaces, thus linking the American endeavor to an extended chronology of civilizational development. The survival of many burial spaces, tombs, and monuments throughout history, even as civilizations rose and fell, implied that by following ancient precedent in establishing rural cemeteries, these American burying grounds would likewise stand the test of time. At Mount Auburn, Joseph Story thus described the precedent for rural cemeteries in antiquity:

> The Greeks . . . discouraged interments within the limits of their cities; and consigned their relics to shady groves, in the neighborhood of murmuring streams and mossy fountains . . . and called them, with the elegant expressiveness of their own beautiful language, CEMETERIES, or "Places of Repose." The Romans, faithful to the example of Greece, erected the monument to the dead in the suburbs of the eternal city. . . . And the Moslem Successors of the emperors, indifferent as they may be to the ordinary exhibitions of the fine arts, place their burying-grounds in rural retreats, and embellish them with studious taste as a religious duty.[66]

In consecrating Mount Hope Cemetery in Rochester, New York, in 1838, the Reverend Pharcellus Church invoked the example set by the ancient Egyptians, whose cemeteries were "surrounded by trees and intersected by canals, to render it, as its name imported, a literal elysium." Referencing popular contemporary views of Egypt, Church stated that "a provision for their dead occupied more of their attention than that of the living; and while every vestige of their abodes in life has yielded to the oblivious wave of time, their mausoleums, catacombs and massive pyramids still peer aloft in their primeval glory, showing the hoary marks of more than forty centuries."[67] At the consecration of Worcester Rural Cemetery in Massachusetts in 1838, speaker Levi Lincoln drew upon examples from both the East and the West to support his assertion that "rural Cemeteries are not the suggestions of artificial taste, or the work of modern innovation. They come from the moving impulses of the heart, and are common to all times and to all people." Like other speakers before him, Lincoln invoked the examples set by the ancient Egyptians, Greeks, and Romans, as well as Europeans from "the days of chivalry." Drawing upon more distant and exotic examples, Lincoln described the Chinese, who, "to this day, erect their tombs without their cities 'upon hills covered with pines and cypress.'" Further, "the beauty of the Mohammedan burial grounds is said to excite the admiration of every traveller," while "the Afghans call their cemeteries 'the cities of the silent,' and hang garlands on the tombs, and burn incense before them, because they believe that the ghosts of the departed dwell there, and sit, each at the end of his own grave, enjoying the fragrance of these offerings."[68] Yet other speakers recalled examples from the Bible, as in the case of the Honorable John McLean at the dedication of Spring Grove Cemetery in Cincinnati in 1845. Opening his remarks with the story of Abraham burying his wife, Sarah, McLean intoned, "In all ages of the world, the living have felt solicitude about the place of their interment."[69] Despite Anglo-American burial practices having been derived from the English churchyard tradition dating as far back as the eighth century, the efforts made in these speeches were to link the American rural cemetery with more ancient and global patterns of caring for the dead in rural environments.[70]

Another rhetorical device in the consecration addresses involved simply declaring that these new cemeteries were meant to last forever. Toward the end of his consecration address, Joseph Story asserted, "We are here to consecrate this spot. . . . And I stand here by the order and in behalf of this [Horticultural] Society, to declare that, by these services, it is to be deemed henceforth and forever so dedicated. Mount Auburn, in the noblest sense, belongs no longer to the living, but to the dead. It is a sacred, it is an eternal trust. It is consecrated ground. May it remain forever inviolate!"[71] At Mount Hope in Rochester, in language that foreshadowed the emergence of perpetual care contracts that cemeteries would begin to offer later in the century, Church declared, "Here, our dead may repose without danger of being invaded by the dwellings of the living. . . . The lots here sold will be secured to the purchasers forever, under such circumstances too, as to afford every assurance, that, should their families remove to the ends of the earth or become extinct, the graves of their friends will be respected and will share in the general improvements which the grounds may be expected to receive."[72] This allusion to encroachment by the living appeared more explicitly in Levi Lincoln's dedication address for Worcester Rural Cemetery, as Lincoln detailed how earlier burial grounds, even the one established as recently as 1828 in Worcester, had become "objectionably exposed and common," because "of the Rail-road, which passes directly through it."[73] The new cemetery, on the other hand, had the benefit of "the approval of the Representatives of the people, and the protection of the law, [so that] the land has been prepared, and with this day's solemnities, is forever devoted to its sacred uses, in receiving the remains, and perpetuating the memory of the dead."[74] In some cases, one is struck by the demonstrative nature of the language employed by the speaker. In Cincinnati at Spring Grove, for instance, McLean exhorted, "This territory lies on the confines of eternity. . . . And I now—in the presence of you all—DEDICATE THIS GROUND—not to the living—BUT TO THE DEAD! The trust shall endure, until time shall be no longer."[75] Perpetuity was the watchword of the day at these and other consecration ceremonies, but development and the march of time would nevertheless eventually lead some of these "permanent" cemeteries to oblivion.

Despite often being published and made available to the public, consecration address rhetoric was ultimately fleeting and meaningful only for those who attended the consecration event or bothered to read the published addresses; cemetery architecture in the form of carriage gateways, on the other hand, was a permanent fixture on the landscape that offered a visual reinforcement of the intentions of those who founded and managed the cemeteries. Mount Auburn set the precedent for imposing gateways with the erection in 1832 of a massive Egyptian Revival portal designed by Jacob Bigelow. Bigelow had studied the illustrations of Egyptian ruins from Vivant Denon's *Description de l'Egypte* (1809–25) and sought to achieve archaeological verisimilitude in his design, modeling it from "some of the best examples in Dendereh and Karnac."[76] In his published Harvard lectures, *Elements of Technology* (1829) and *The Useful Arts* (1840), Bigelow had made his admiration for ancient Egyptian construction, especially the seemingly permanent quality of their architecture, clear. In *Elements of Technology*, he described the Egyptian style of building as "more massive and substantial than any which has succeeded it."[77] In *The Useful Arts*, comparing the Egyptian with Greek and Roman architecture, he argued, "Many of the other structures of antiquity now extant owe their preservation to accident; those of Egypt have the principle of their preservation within themselves."[78] The *North American Review* echoed this sentiment: "The *early* Egyptians built neither for beauty nor for use, but for eternity."[79] Greek architecture might possess beauty and grace, but the Egyptians, the great caretakers of the dead in the history of Western civilization, built their temples, tombs, and monuments with permanence in mind. When the rural cemetery movement began, then, it is unsurprising that the Egyptian Revival, at a time when architectural eclecticism was becoming increasingly common, would be popular for the new cemetery landscapes. Constructed initially of wood and painted to resemble stone, the gateway was rebuilt in 1843 in granite according to the original design and dimensions. Reflecting upon the construction of the more permanent gateway in stone, Bigelow wrote in his *History of the Cemetery of Mount Auburn* that its size, design, and quality of construction would "entitle it to a stability of a thousand years."[80]

Other cemeteries followed suit in erecting imposing carriage gateways to mark their principal entrances, and by the 1840s, a number of solid stone entrances were also constructed as part of the revitalization of older burying grounds. New Haven's New Burying Ground, renamed the Grove Street Cemetery in 1848, had a large red sandstone Egyptian Revival portal surmounted with the words "The Dead Shall Be Raised," designed and constructed by architect Henry Austin from 1845 to 1848.

Architect Isaiah Rogers designed two copies of an Egyptian Revival portal that were constructed at the Old Granary Burying Ground in Boston in 1840 and then at the Jewish Touro Cemetery in Newport, Rhode Island, in 1843.[81] Like Mount Auburn, Rochester's Mount Hope Cemetery, established in 1838, and Forest Hills Cemetery, established in 1848 in Roxbury, Massachusetts, near Boston, originally had Egyptian Revival gateways constructed in wood, but these were later torn down and replaced with stone entrances in the increasingly popular Gothic Revival. Such changes were testament to

Entrance to the New Haven Cemetery, ca. 1850. (Henry Austin Papers, courtesy Yale University Library)

the fact that, as popular as the Egyptian Revival was for cemetery gateways (and, subsequently, sepulchral monuments), it nevertheless had to compete with other architectural revival styles. Architects William Strickland and Thomas Ustick Walter submitted Egyptian Revival designs in 1836 for the entrance to Laurel Hill Cemetery, but the cemetery managers ultimately opted for a neoclassical portal.[82] Robert Cary Long Jr. initially designed an Egyptian Revival entrance for Baltimore's Green Mount Cemetery, but the cemetery trustees there opted instead for his alternative Tudor/Gothic Revival entrance design, constructed from 1840 to 1846.[83] Green-Wood Cemetery in Brooklyn, Allegheny Cemetery in Pittsburgh, and Cave Hill Cemetery in Louisville all erected Gothic Revival stone entrances.

As cemetery trustees and managers sought to construct gateways that would communicate stability and permanence to visitors, this competition between popular architectural revivalist styles for the cemetery landscape often centered on concerns about how appropriate the Egyptian style was for a Christian context, whereas Gothic architecture was simultaneously Christian and—albeit nowhere near as old as Egyptian architecture—vested with the weight of history with origins dating back to the twelfth century. Architect James Gallier, writing for the *North American Review* in 1836, reflected this tension in an essay in which he expressed preference for "the sublime, the glorious Gothic," while rejecting most other forms of architectural revivalism.[84] Gallier was generally appalled by his countrymen's predilection for architectural eclecticism and reserved his most caustic disapprobation for the Egyptian style. He regarded its use in predominantly Christian American cemeteries as wholly inappropriate: "Egyptian architecture reminds us of the religion which called it into being, the most degraded and revolting paganism which ever existed. It is the architecture of embalmed cats and deified crocodiles; solid, stupendous, and time-defying we allow, but associated in our minds with all that is disgusting and absurd in superstition."[85] Nevertheless, the Egyptian Revival became one of the most popular styles for sepulchral monuments—the Egyptian obelisk was arguably the most pervasive memorial form to appear in nineteenth-century cemeteries across the country. Ultimately, the choice for gateway designs boiled down to the aesthetic preferences of those who managed the cemeteries and their finances. Further, regardless of whichever style was employed, solid stone entrances accompanied by perimeter walls and/or fences provided the sense of security and permanence that cemetery founders and the general public hoped for in their new burial landscapes.

These themes of permanence through landscape and architecture established in the first years of the rural cemetery movement became among the preeminent features of burial reform ideology through the end of the 1830s and beyond. Arguably no other rural cemetery established during this first decade embodied such ideals more than the grandiose Green-Wood Cemetery established in Brooklyn. Chartered in 1838 and formally established with the purchase of land in 1839, Green-Wood Cemetery represented a culmination of all of the major trends that had developed during the 1830s. New Yorkers had, since the ban on intramural burials during the yellow fever outbreak of 1822, sought to find an alternative to city burials to no avail. Proposals for suburban cemeteries had come and gone for over a decade when one of the future proprietors of Green-Wood, Henry E. Pierrepont (1808–88), visited Mount Auburn Cemetery in 1832 and returned to New York with the idea of establishing a similar rural cemetery on land in the Gowanus Hills of Brooklyn. It was not until the Depression of 1837 that real estate prices dropped sufficiently enough that the purchase of a sizable plot of land could

Tudor-style gateway and Gothic Revival chapel tower, Allegheny Cemetery, 1848, Pittsburgh. (Photograph by the author)

be accomplished, and in 1838, the cemetery's founders purchased close to two hundred acres for a little more than $134,000 (the equivalent of about $4.25 million today).[86] The largest of the rural cemeteries established at that point, Brooklyn's Green-Wood Cemetery stands out during the first decade of the rural cemetery movement for going above and beyond in offering to the public of New York City and surrounding areas a burial institution that, its trustees hoped, would be unmatched for size and beauty anywhere else in the country. The land encompassed "former tracts of farmland and pastureland, six ponds, and stands of both hardwood and evergreen trees." Its lowest points came within twenty feet of sea level, while its highest hills were over two hundred feet, including the site known as Mount Washington. The highest points offered "panoramic vistas encompassing Jamaica Bay, New York Harbor, the East River, and the Atlantic Ocean, as well as New York City, Brooklyn, Staten Island, New Jersey, and small towns and villages in every direction." In developing the layout of the grounds, civil engineer Major David Bates Douglass (1790–1849) first constructed a four-and-a-half-mile avenue for visitors—this would later be expanded and formally labeled "The Tour."[87]

Like Mount Auburn, Green-Wood was operated as a nonprofit institution with the intention that all money accrued from the sale of lots would go directly into improvements to the grounds, especially those that would reaffirm the permanence of the new cemetery and heighten its reputation as an important cultural center. In 1839, David Douglass, who was also president of the board of trustees, authored a pamphlet outlining the history of choosing the land, the process of receiving a charter from the legislature, and plans for the landscaping design and its improvement. Regarding the trustees' plans for the land, Douglass wrote,

> ALL the proceeds are thenceforth to be expended in the preservation and embellishment of the premises,—for the erection of substantial and permanent improvements, such as inclosure and terrace-walls of masonry round the entire precinct; a porter's lodge, gate-way, and flag tower; a Chapel; one or more distinctive monuments; and eventually, without doubt, a succession of monuments commemorative of the distinguished characters and events of national history. It will be recollected that the Trustees in addition to their own resources, for these objects, are empowered under their charter, to hold and apply any endowments which may be committed to them for the erection of monuments, &c., and may become, therefore, not only a Cemetery corporation, but virtually a National Monument Association.[88]

The cemetery trustees clearly intended their rural cemetery to have all the architectural markers of permanence already in existence or under construction at other rural cemeteries, but like the managers of Laurel Hill Cemetery in Philadelphia, they also desired to go above and beyond such structures with the erection of monuments unassociated with specific graves. The trustees did not merely envision Green-Wood as a cemetery or space to be used and enjoyed by the public—in the same pamphlet, they offered encouragement to visitors to come and view the grounds—but also imagined it to become a manner of outdoor museum. Hearkening to the language of permanence in other cemeteries' consecration addresses, the trustees of Green-Wood further argued that no person could rightfully regard any locale as permanently their "home" if their accompanying burial ground was not permanent, and so the importance of this rural cemetery as they saw it lay

Greenwood, the most beautiful of American cemeteries, Brooklyn, New York.
(Stereoview, International View Co., 1899, courtesy Library of Congress Prints and
Photographs Division)

in helping to cement the ties between the living within New York City and
its environs and the dead. "One of the most sacred and enduring of human
ties, is that by which the hearts of men are bound to the burial places of their
departed friends; and no residence can be permanently regarded as HOME,
which is not also identified, prospectively or actually, with the memory of
those we love."[89]

Despite numerous false starts since the 1820s to implement burial
reform in New York City, the public response to Green-Wood Cemetery
from its founding was overwhelmingly positive, and even before there were
many burials in the cemetery, it was a popular destination for the living. The
Long-Island Star (Brooklyn) reported in 1840 that "on some days, more than
a hundred carriages have passed through" the grounds and anticipated that
the "time is not far distant when the Green-wood will become famous as
the most 'gorgeous sepulchre' on the face of the earth."[90] In its assessment
of the rural cemeteries a decade after the consecration of Mount Auburn,
the *North American Review* observed of Green-Wood that it "has become one
of frequent resort during the summer months, and this circumstance alone
has done much to recommend it to public favor.... There can be little doubt
of the ultimate and entire success of the enterprise."[91] Another correspondent for the *Brooklyn Daily Eagle* wrote in 1844 that with the improvements
that had taken shape in recent years, Green-Wood was "a lovely and inviting

place for interments," and while it could use "a greater number of flowering shrubs and plants" such as those found at Mount Auburn, as well as benches upon which visitors on foot could take a rest, the cemetery nevertheless "surpasses many of the so-called rural cemeteries; and as it goes on improving, with the lapse of time, it will rival the *Pere la Chaise* after which it was modeled."[92] Such was the case with virtually all rural cemeteries, however, as cemetery founders, dedication orators, and the local press often repeated variations on the same claim, that *theirs* would stand apart as the loveliest, the most picturesque, the most impressive of burial spaces that could only reflect positively on the cultural development of their community and the residents within it.

By the end of the following decade, landscape designer and the nation's de facto tastemaker, Andrew Jackson Downing, wrote approvingly in 1849, "One of the most remarkable illustrations of the popular taste, in this country, is to be found in the rise and progress of our rural cemeteries." Noting that the precedent set by Mount Auburn "took the public mind by storm," Downing observed that nearly twenty years since its consecration, "there is scarcely a city of note in the whole country that has not its rural cemetery." Despite the numerous examples of rural cemeteries by this time across the Northeast and into the Midwest, Downing enumerated Boston, Philadelphia, and New York City as the "three leading cities" in the movement with Mount Auburn, Laurel Hill, and Green-Wood, respectively, as the most outstanding examples, followed by communities elsewhere.[93] Mount Auburn was so distinguished because it was the progenitor of the rural cemetery movement and it was "richly picturesque"; Laurel Hill, in Downing's estimation, was distinctive as "a charming *pleasure-ground*, filled with beautiful and rare shrubs and flowers"; and Green-Wood, by size alone, was the most "grand, dignified, and park-like" of all rural cemeteries established thus far.[94] Indeed, these three by the end of the 1830s had become the holy trinity of rural cemeteries from which all others established during subsequent decades drew inspiration and comparison. Revealingly, Levi Lincoln alluded to the influence of these three locations in his consecration address for Worcester Rural Cemetery in 1839: "New York has now her suburban burial places. Philadelphia has planted, on Laurel Hill, her 'Field of Peace;'—and near our own metropolis, in solemn order, but unrivalled beauty, stands lovely Mount Auburn,—'GARDEN OF GRAVES'! Many of our principal towns are following these salutary examples, and we trust, the time is not far distant, when regard to health, and a cultivated sentiment of propriety will give to *all* our burial places the retired situation, and tasteful arrangement, of a *rural cemetery*."[95] As the rural cemetery movement continued into the 1840s and 1850s, expanding beyond the confines of the Northeast, writers and travelers inevitably made comparisons between the newer burying grounds established in the Midwest and the urban South and at least one of these three, significant among the first phase of rural cemeteries. Such comparisons necessarily revealed shifting patterns of taste as well as pride of place, as the rural cemetery movement, while national in scope, increasingly reflected local and regional cultural values and ideals.

Even as the founders of the rural cemeteries envisioned their landscapes to encompass multiple roles—burying ground, experimental garden, public park, outdoor museum—and to reflect the development of American civilization to a higher standard of cultural refinement and taste, those very same men who established their cemeteries with these ideals in mind nevertheless had to contend with the reality of how the general public as well as lot holders would actually engage with these landscapes. While much was made on paper of how the rural cemeteries would inspire visitors to cultivate their elevated feelings and moral development, in truth, when confronted with vast, picturesque landscapes designed equally to serve as public parks and as sacred spaces for the burial of the dead, many Americans of the Early Republic quite frankly did not know exactly how to comport themselves in the ways that cemetery trustees and managers hoped. Additionally, as the beginning of the first Industrial Revolution enriched an increasing number of families who could afford to erect monuments sculpted from marble and tombs with granite facades, questions over matters of taste in the embellishment of the cemetery landscapes became increasingly complex. Cemetery proprietors who purchased family plots *owned* that bit of cemetery land and were thus encouraged to decorate those plots as they saw fit, with flowers, shrubs, monuments, and anything else that struck their fancy. However, within such an environment where there developed the freedom of choice limited only by financial means, conflicts necessarily arose over what constituted good *taste* within the cemetery landscape—much the same way architectural critics clashed over the styles employed for cemetery gateways. And so, as writers, orators, and those who created the first wave of rural cemeteries lauded the great possibilities of what they could be for the American public and what they could represent as an altogether new cultural institution, they were ultimately in for a rude awakening once the cemeteries became fully operational and the reality set in as to the diversity of tastes and behaviors that would be exhibited within their precincts.

"People Seem to Go There to Enjoy Themselves"

Experimentation in the Cemetery Landscape

The founders of the cemeteries established during the first decade of the rural cemetery movement had very definite ideas about how their new burying grounds would serve the public as multifunctional spaces for both the living and the dead. Ideally, with their picturesque landscaping and removal from urban development, the cemeteries would be for the living a space for melancholy reflection and moral uplift, while for the dead they would offer a beautiful, respectful, and uncrowded space in which to rest for eternity. But they were to be more than that as well. In an era when the expanding middle class was increasingly focused on cultivating expressions of taste and refinement, the rural cemetery offered an environment where families could decorate their future final resting places with flowers and shrubs like those in their gardens at home and erect monuments befitting their aesthetic preferences and socioeconomic status. In the absence of large public parks, the rural cemeteries were likewise intended to serve as spaces for public recreation, including the elite and middle-class pastime of the promenade, in which the well-to-do and upwardly mobile went out in public to see and be seen.[1] As Henry Dearborn expressed in his 1831 report to the Massachusetts

Horticultural Society, Mount Auburn would be "a holy and pleasant resort for the living" that would become "one of the most instructive, magnificent, and pleasant promenades in our country . . . a place of healthful, refreshing, and agreeable resort."[2] Mount Auburn Cemetery was the testing ground for exactly how the living would ultimately engage with the rural cemetery as an altogether new cultural institution, and implicit in Dearborn's language was the assumption that the rules of the promenade would simply transfer to the new landscape, and as such, visitors would implicitly know what was expected of them in terms of behavior.

When it came to matters of taste and public behavior within the cemetery landscape, however, the reality proved to be far more complex and often irksome for those in charge of managing the new cities of the dead. What constituted taste in a sepulchral monument was a constant source of debate, especially since Americans, with the exception of the wealthy, could for the first time begin purchasing something more substantial than a simple headstone beginning in the 1830s. There were no explicitly defined rules for sepulchral art and architecture, so for those who purchased a monument or contracted to have a family tomb built, individuals opted for styles according to personal preference and what their pocketbooks would allow. The increasing variety of disparate monument styles quickly led to public debates within the nation's major periodicals and among architects on what constituted "good taste" and what was ultimately most appropriate for a memorial setting. Further complicating the cultural dynamics of the rural cemetery, matters related to public behavior within the rural cemeteries quickly proved to be a source of ongoing consternation through much of the nineteenth century for cemetery trustees and purveyors of middle-class taste, fashion, and respectability. At the time of Mount Auburn's dedication, the cemetery's trustees assumed the public would implicitly understand how they were to behave in a consecrated space for the burial of the dead. But as it was intended to likewise function as a public park, and as there were no clearly defined regulations for visitors at the time of the cemetery's consecration, it was left to the visitors themselves to decide how they should engage with the cemetery's environment. Indeed, throughout the antebellum period, the dynamics of behavior in public spaces, including theaters, restaurants, and later parks and even waterfalls, were constantly evolving sources of contest over who had the right not only to use but to define the "proper" use of space.[3]

Within a year of the cemetery's consecration, the trustees' faith in the public's ability and willingness to comport themselves respectably was shaken, and as such they established firm regulations for visitors. However, the creation of rules governing how cemetery proprietors (lot holders) and the general public could access and use the landscape was a matter of trial and error that reflected larger issues pertaining to accessibility and exclusion within the public sphere. Mount Auburn Cemetery functioned as the initial social laboratory for how cemetery trustees chose to police the rural cemetery landscape, and subsequent cemetery founders took their cue from their counterparts in Boston while further modifying their rules for lot ownership and public access according to local or regional social values and expectations. The result of these developments was that nineteenth-century rural cemeteries, as institutions presumably freely open and available to all, were often the locus for contests over matters of taste, respectability, and accessibility during an era in which the American middle class increasingly sought to exert its authority over the nation's social life and cultural institutions.

Creating a tasteful environment with monuments and plantings and attracting the living to what were envisioned to become magnificent cities of the dead were preeminent aims in the minds of the men who founded the nation's rural cemeteries. As Jacob Bigelow predicted in 1831, "In a few years, when the hand of taste shall have scattered among the trees, as it has already begun to do, enduring memorials of marble and granite, a landscape of the most picturesque character will be created. No place in the environs of our city will possess stronger attractions to the visitor."[4] Several months following the cemetery's consecration, the *New England Magazine* decried "the utter destitution of taste" that had been exhibited in New England's graveyards and expressed the hope that Mount Auburn "will have a most beneficial and decided effect."[5] Echoing the writings of Mount Auburn's founders, Theodore Dwight urged in 1834 that cemeteries "should be planned with reference to the living as well as the dead; and should at once be convenient and pleasant to visiters [*sic*], guarded from injury and every thing like disrespect," and he cautioned that they ought not "be placed in the centre of a village." Situated too close to everyday activities, rural cemeteries would become like the older graveyards, "regarded with too much indifference," with the ground "made a thoroughfare and even a place of sport by children."[6] For most visitors, it was necessary to reach Mount Auburn and subsequent rural cemeteries by carriage or horseback, and so there was ever the implication that there must be some effort involved to head out to the cemetery for an afternoon. As such, a visit to the rural cemetery involved far more than just a casual stroll—for many visitors, it was an event. Writers from within and beyond the United States urged travelers to make their way to the nation's rural cemeteries, such as Gideon Miner Davison, who in 1834 wrote, "Every traveller of taste should visit the new cemetery at Mount Auburn," declaring it "the *Pere la chaise* of this country." Describing the cemetery's extensive carriage and pedestrian paths, Davison noted how "interments as yet have been very few."[7] In these early years, the cemetery resembled a park far more than a burying ground, which increased its early appeal as a place of resort.

Visitors from near and far besieged Mount Auburn, and the experience of a couple of years taught the cemetery's trustees that it would be necessary to make certain restrictions to rein in visitors' enthusiasm for the place. Jacob Bigelow would later reflect in his history of Mount Auburn published in 1859 that the subject of admission had, "at different times, been a source of perplexity to the Trustees." Reflecting the spirit of inclusivity of its founders, during the cemetery's first year of operation, "promiscuous admittance was allowed to persons on foot, on horseback, and in carriages. But, in short time, great inconvenience was felt from the number of persons, in pursuit of pleasure, who rode or drove recklessly through the grounds, to the detriment of the paths and the annoyance of other visitors."[8] Repeated complaints of noise and reckless driving ultimately led the trustees to make a blanket prohibition on both carriages and horses in April 1833. At this point there were only nine "monuments of marble or granite," with "several others . . . in preparation here and in Europe," and so the major issue at hand was raucous behavior rather than vandalism.[9] Nevertheless, as the trustees soon learned, regulating admission and public behavior was itself an experimental venture necessitating trial and error, and they ultimately had to make adjustments and accommodations.

In light of the carriage and horse prohibition, abolitionist William Lloyd Garrison's *Liberator* (Boston) reported, "There are some objections to this arrangement, as the paths and avenues are so extensive, and some of the lands so elevated, that many persons, the aged or infirm, will be prevented from visiting them, on account of the fatigue to which they will be exposed."[10] Never before had accessibility for the aged and physically disabled been a concern when it came to burial grounds, since the second largest cemetery in the nation, New Haven's New Burying Ground, was but a fraction of the size of Mount Auburn and completely flat. The trustees were responsive to these concerns, and Joseph Story, as chair of the committee in charge of the care of the cemetery grounds, reported in September that "in consequence of the abuses that followed the free admission of visitors," no one on horseback would be allowed entrance into the cemetery, while lot holders would be issued special tickets of admission that would allow them to drive their carriages freely within the cemetery grounds (any transfer of such tickets was prohibited), and anyone on foot would still be allowed entry without the need for tickets.[11] The trustees added further restrictions regarding the speed at which carriages could be driven—no faster than a walk—and recommendations as to the proper "fastening of horses."[12]

The following year, local papers reported that vandalism against the cemetery's landscape had increasingly become a problem, especially "the injury done the trees, by inconsiderate visitors."[13] The challenge when it came to matters of vandalism, however, was that what constituted vandalism and misuse of the property for cemetery trustees and managers of other important cultural sites was, for the general public, an expression of their own love and enthusiasm. In some cases, destructive behavior connoted the public's view of their collective ownership of a particularly important or popular site. Such was the case at George Washington's estate (and grave) at Mount Vernon, which suffered regular depredations in the form of people taking pieces of the natural and built environment as relics or, conversely, leaving their mark by carving their names or initials on the trees and buildings.[14]

Given the high volume of traffic experienced at Mount Auburn on Sundays, the trustees determined in July 1834 that the gates would thenceforth remain closed to all but proprietors and their guests on the Sabbath, a decision that prompted the *Saturday Morning Transcript* (Boston) to scold:

> It is a subject of regret that in this country nothing is sacred, nothing protected from the hands and *whips* of rude unthinking boys, youths, and even adults where they have access. . . . On Sundays, and other days of leisure, the Cemetery is thronged by those who have *no personal interest* to preserve the monuments, &c., from depredation, and the consequences have been very injurious.[15]

Without commenting on specific acts of misbehavior, the *American Quarterly Observer* noted with concern the fate of the souls of those "who make this place a scene of Sabbath breaking, and of thoughtless mirth; wasting here that time in sin."[16] Limiting Sunday admissions to lot holders would have curtailed the number of working-class visitors who were likely considered at this time to be the main culprits of these depredations. However, the unseemly behavior of visitors thus lamented in the press likely resulted in far more than just broken branches, and clearly not only members of the working class were committing transgressions, for the list of regulations expanded dramatically in the ensuing months.

New rules included a prohibition on anyone carrying refreshments into the cemetery—in other words, no picnics. In Boston, at least, there was precedent for picnicking within the realm of the dead. The Old Granary Burying Ground, the city's third oldest burial place, abutted the homes on Park Street, an elite neighborhood located near the Common. There were few new burials after the turn of the nineteenth century, and Dr. J. Collins Warren described living near the burying ground as a child:

> It afforded far from a mournful prospect to the occupants of the Park Street dwellings, and served as a playground for the children of the family. In the summer-time the foliage was most luxuriant; and before the advent of horse-cars on Tremont Street, the enclosure afforded to the inhabitants of Park Street all the advantages of private grounds; giving protection from the noises of city life, and providing a much enjoyed breathing space in the very heart of the metropolis. . . . Many were the adventures in the 'Old Granary,' as it was called. Members of my family can still tell of picnics and other festivals held upon the quaint old table-like structures covering the graves of families with historic names.[17]

Families such as Warren's likely thought nothing of picnicking in the enclosure when Mount Auburn opened to the public in 1831.

In addition to barring food, the trustees established specific expectations for personal comportment. As stated in the cemetery's "Regulations Concerning Visitors," "All persons who shall be found within the grounds making unseemly noises, or otherwise conducting themselves unsuitably to the purposes to which the grounds are devoted, will be required instantly to leave the grounds, and upon refusal will be compelled to do so; such persons will also be prosecuted." Specific regulations for the protection of everything contained within the cemetery grounds were especially detailed and included prohibitions against picking flowers, "EITHER WILD OR CULTIVATED," damaging shrubs or trees, or damaging or defacing monuments. Offenders would face legal prosecution. Such was the growing concern over vandalism against plantings that anyone found within the cemetery in possession of flowers or shrubs "will be deemed to have unlawfully taken them"—therefore, anyone *bringing* flowers or plants to the cemetery needed to check in with the gatekeeper upon entry so as to avoid prosecution. Since the land that made up Mount Auburn had originally been a genuinely wild space where hunting undoubtedly took place, the trustees felt it further necessary to prohibit the discharge of any firearms in the cemetery. Trespassers or anyone who broke any of the rules were liable to prosecution and payment of a fine up to $50, while those who gave information to the gatekeeper or superintendent of anyone who broke the rules would receive a $20 reward.[18] In modern currency, this works out to a hefty $1,576.49 fine and a $630.60 reward.[19] As Bigelow would note, because of the ongoing influx of "improper persons" despite the adopted regulations, the trustees ultimately required every visitor—even those on foot—to obtain a ticket of admission, and thus ended the era of "promiscuous admission."[20]

By September 1834, the Garden and Cemetery Committee of the Massachusetts Horticultural Society was able to happily report that the new regulations, especially concerning Sunday visitors, had "been highly beneficial" and had "put a stop to many of the depredations which thoughtless and mischievous persons had been too apt to indulge in." The committee also remarked that the opening and closing of the gates at sunrise and sunset had been "indispensable to the due security" of the cemetery and that while all of the new regulations "allow a free access to the grounds to all visitors at reasonable times, and in a reasonable manner," they helped to prevent "secret misconduct."[21] Without providing specific examples in their report, it remains that what constituted secret misconduct can only be left to the imagination. The new restrictions, though numerous, by no means diminished the popularity of Mount Auburn as a destination either for locals or for tourists from afar. Englishwoman Harriet Martineau, who visited Boston in the 1830s, wrote glowingly of her trip to the cemetery. Escorted personally by Joseph Story, she noted, "Several carriages were at the gate; for the place is a favorite resort on other accounts besides its being a 'place of sleep.'"[22] George Ticknor Curtis, in describing Mount Auburn and its European counterparts as "beautiful pleasure-grounds of Death" for readers of the *New England Magazine*, also alluded to the great variety of visitors who traveled to the city of the dead. One might expect to see "a gay party, just stepping into their vehicles or mounting their horses," "the *ennuyée*" looking to pass the time, or the husband and wife heading out at sunset "to strew a few flowers" upon their child's grave. Curtis invited his readers to go along, too, but admonished, "Let us walk, nor drive up in dusty splendor to the crowded gate-way, tossing our reins to the keeper as we would to the ostler of a tavern."[23] Regulations may have been in place, but writers recognized that since Mount Auburn was a popular tourist destination and leisure space, visitors needed to be reminded that it was, above all, a place for the burial of the dead and that rather than act according to their own personal whims, their behaviors should reflect the solemnity and sacred quality of the precincts they traversed.

Its early years of operation proved that Mount Auburn Cemetery was undeniably a social laboratory for testing how a geographically expansive burying ground might be used and abused by the public. As the rural cemetery model caught hold and expanded across the Northeast during the 1830s and thence to the urban South and the Midwest by the 1840s, the trustees of subsequent rural cemeteries looked to Mount Auburn as a model not just for its size and landscape aesthetics but also for guidance on how to police their burying grounds without the growing pains that Mount Auburn's trustees had to endure. In other words, new cemeteries had firm regulations in place *before* their gates opened to the public. Virtually all rules and regulations established by later rural cemeteries contained provisions similar to Mount Auburn's, such as banning picnicking, horse racing, unattended children, and any kind of flower picking or vandalism of gravestones and other sepulchral monuments. A number of cemeteries prohibited other specific behaviors, such as smoking, using firearms, using obscene language, or being too loud or generally too jolly and raucous. Some specifically prohibited dogs. Many employed a prohibition on some variation of the phrase "improper persons," whom gatekeepers or superintendents could turn away at will—such a general description implies that any number of individuals could be barred admission, and one is left to imagine that this could have included people of color, prostitutes (or women presumed to be "unladylike"), drunkards, teenagers, or really anyone the gatekeeper did not like the looks of. Mount Auburn was certainly a model in many respects for other rural cemeteries, but in fashioning regulations to restrict admission and to police their boundaries, trustees elsewhere clearly did not wholly embrace the relatively inclusive model and egalitarian principles exhibited by the men of Boston.

For instance, the wealthy Quaker John Jay Smith, who established Philadelphia's Laurel Hill Cemetery in 1836, set forth a vision that Laurel Hill would be an elite white burying ground where burials for the poor and people of color were prohibited. The manner in which cemeteries encoded prohibitions on the sale of lots to non-whites varied across time and space, with some cemeteries more or less explicitly stating such exclusions in their bylaws. The language in Laurel Hill's regulations published in 1837 could easily be missed by the casual reader. Hidden in the section titled "Lots Not Transferable," the regulations state, "The managers beg to inform persons who may wish to obtain lots in the cemetery, that they will have the ground they purchase secured to them, and their families and heirs, for a burial place for ever; and for the burial *of such other white persons as they may choose to admit* [emphasis added], provided, such admission is free of charge, and without any compensation."[24] Nowhere else in the Laurel Hill bylaws does it explicitly state that the sale of lots was reserved strictly for white people, yet that fact is made clear in this section.

Regarding visitation at Laurel Hill, as at Mount Auburn, lot holders alone could ride their carriages within the grounds, but even they were required to go on foot on Sundays. The greater distance—roughly four miles outside downtown Philadelphia—along with more stringent carriage restrictions implies that Laurel Hill's trustees were less concerned over matters of physical accessibility than were their counterparts in Boston. Such a distance from downtown Philadelphia and the pains that needed to be taken to reach the cemetery by no means diminished its attraction to visitors. Indeed, the beauty of its landscaping, views overlooking the Schuylkill River, and exclusivity of the space made it one of Philadelphia's must-see attractions. As noted by one writer, for strangers to the city, Laurel Hill ought to be "one of the first places they should visit while sojourning among us."[25] The matter over distance and exclusivity further helped Philadelphia's other reform and rural cemeteries distinguish themselves from Laurel Hill. Monument Cemetery, for instance, could be set apart from its more elite counterpart specifically because it was not an onerous undertaking to access this rural cemetery, which boasted many of the same landscaping and aesthetic features as Laurel Hill. Originally called "The American Pere La Chaise," Monument Cemetery, located on Broad Street, was situated only one and a half miles from the city center. Like many Americans of the 1830s who could neither fathom nor foresee the extent of urban sprawl that would occur later in the century, one observer wrote that this distance was "sufficiently remote to prevent the apprehension that it may ever be encroached upon by our growing population, while, at the same time, it is at so convenient a proximity as to be easily reached by the pedestrian without experiencing a sense of fatigue."[26] Later, in the 1850s, Philadelphia became home to two more rural cemeteries—Mount Moriah Cemetery (est. 1855) located in southwest Philadelphia, which measures two hundred acres and contains 150,000 burials, and Mount Vernon Cemetery (est. 1856), which encompasses twenty-seven acres and is situated directly across the street from Laurel Hill Cemetery. The case of Philadelphia thus illustrates that over time many of the nation's larger cities established not one but multiple rural cemeteries that could cater to the interests (not to mention physical and financial abilities) of their diverse urban populations as well as visitors from away.

Green-Wood Cemetery's regulations highlighted the early lack of uniformity in cemetery policies as well as their enforcement across the Northeast. It was Green-Wood that introduced the prohibition on smoking in its rules concerning visitors adopted in 1839 (Baltimore's Green Mount Cemetery was even more specific in banning the smoking of cigars, the wording of which implies that pipes were acceptable).[27] Further, while as at other cemeteries porters at the gate reserved the right to turn away any "improper persons," even if they bore a ticket of admission, they were also at liberty to admit strangers without tickets by their own discretion.[28] An account of just such an exception appeared in the New York *Evening Mirror* in 1845, in which the newspaper described an Englishman who made his case to the porter for entry by pleading that he did not want to leave the country without seeing the nation's largest rural cemetery. Upon the man's pledge that should he find a spot he liked, he would buy the plot and have his body buried there, the porter relented and let him in.[29]

There was also lack of uniformity with regard to the racial dynamics within these northeastern rural cemeteries. In contrast to Laurel Hill, where Black burials were prohibited, and Mount Auburn, where there were no burial restrictions based upon race, Brooklyn's Green-Wood Cemetery maintained a "colored section" consisting of a group of seven lots in the northwest corner. In 2017, a group of interns were tasked with documenting, restoring, and proposing interpretations for these lots, which had, over the course of time, fallen into disrepair and were largely forgotten. These lots, "previously known as the 'Colored Lots,' were specifically designated for 'Colored Children' or 'Colored Adults,'" according to the cemetery's records. One of the lots was purchased in 1849 by the Association for the Benefit of Colored Orphans. In rehabilitating this section of Green-Wood, the interns renamed the section the "Freedom Lots" to bring a greater sense of dignity to those interred within this area.[30] By maintaining a relatively obscure, segregated section of Green-Wood for people of color, it is therefore a matter of historical irony that one of the cemetery's biggest attractions for nineteenth-century visitors was the grave and marker within the main part of the cemetery for eighteen-year-old Do-Hum-Me of the Sac Indians. Nehemiah Cleaveland, who wrote the popular guidebook to the cemetery, *Green Wood Illustrated*, published in 1847, devoted five pages to Do-Hum-Me's grave on "Indian Mound," with romanticized descriptions of her fortitude in suffering through her final illness, and what an exceptional example of her race the young Native American was.[31] Such a description was rooted in the noble savage stereotype first popularized during the eighteenth century, while Cleaveland's attention to Do-Hum-Me's suffering is reflective of the kind of sentimental fictional narratives involving the drawn-out deaths of sympathetic characters that had become widely popular by midcentury.[32] As for Do-Hum-Me's grave, as though it were an exhibit from P. T. Barnum's museum of curiosities, it was situated firmly within the main part of the cemetery and yet singled out for its novelty within a landscape saturated with the burials of middle-class and elite Anglo-Protestants and was an attraction to be ogled by visitors, an indigenous oddity in a sea of whiteness.[33]

As more rural cemeteries were established within and beyond the borders of the Northeast from the late 1830s into the 1840s, they took a cue from Mount Auburn, Laurel Hill, and Green-Wood Cemeteries and instituted regulations for visitors at the time of their founding. Mindful of Mount Auburn's early struggles with reckless drivers, subsequent rural cemeteries prohibited riders on horseback (Louisville's Cave Hill Cemetery allowed such riders only if they were accompanied by a lady, presumably to keep their behavior in check), required that only ticket-bearing lot holders could drive their carriages within the cemetery grounds, and added provisions regarding Sunday visitors. Generally, these provisions required that proprietors who wished to visit the cemetery on the Sabbath could only do so, with their tickets, on foot (only Mount Auburn continued to allow proprietors to use their carriages on Sundays out of respect for the aged and infirm). Green Mount Cemetery in Baltimore went even further and made a blanket requirement that *all* visitors, whether in a carriage or on foot, were required to present a ticket to the gatekeeper.[34]

Most visitors appear to have taken such restrictions in stride, and some tourists wrote with bemusement about the problems of entry without a pass. As one visitor to Philadelphia wrote, "There were four other passengers in the omnibus beside myself. . . . When we arrived at the gate of the [Laurel Hill] Cemetery, they . . . had no ticket and couldn't get in! However, as mine gave me permission to take 'three friends' with me, I took them under my *friendly* protection, and, with the assistance of the gate keeper, got all *four* in."[35] Indeed, far from discouraging tourists and visitors seeking an afternoon promenade, the cemeteries only increased in popularity, to the point that the avenues and paths experienced overcrowding. The *New York Commercial Advertiser* reported that in June 1845 alone, twenty-three hundred carriages had passed through Green-Wood. Landscape architect Andrew Jackson Downing remarked that Laurel Hill Cemetery had received thirty thousand visitors between April and December of 1848, with an equal number heading to Mount Auburn and double that to Green-Wood.[36]

Restrictions notwithstanding, rural cemeteries became irresistible attractions for locals and tourists alike, for as Harriet Martineau wrote of Mount Auburn, "It is indeed a place for the living to delight in."[37] While on his grand tour of the United States in 1852, Englishman Henry Arthur Bright provided more detail in his travel diary concerning the variety of activities that took place within the cemetery enclosures: "Cemeteries here are all the 'rage'; people lounge in them, and use them (as their tastes are inclined) for walking, making love, weeping, sentimentalizing, and everything in short."[38] Rural cemeteries appear to have become especially popular for young lovers, and the city of the dead as a site for courting was lampooned in the comic novel *The Clockmaker: The Sayings and Doings of Samuel Slick of Slickville*, written by Nova Scotia politician Thomas Chandler Haliburton. Written in the Yankee dialect of the titular character, the book compares Mount Auburn with "Pair o' Shaise" in Paris. As the Clockmaker says,

> It's actilly like pleasure ground, it's laid out so pretty, and is the grandest place for courtin' in I know on, it's so romantic. Many a woman that's lost one husband there has found another in the same place. A widower has a fine chance of seein' widders there, and then nobody ever suspects them of courtin', bein' that they are both in black, but takes 'em for mourners, and don't intrude on 'em out of pity.

The character goes on to claim women must have invented Mount Auburn, "for they beat all natur' for contrivances, so they do." Any young man with a mind to find himself a rich young widow must go to the cemetery, he declares, where the shady walks "will put all the dead in creation out of your head a'most."[39] In stark contrast, writing with a sense of disappointment in his fellow Americans, Wilson Flagg complained, "People are attracted, in multitudes . . . to gratify their curiosity, not to yield up their hearts to pensive reflection." Whatever their purpose, with so many visitors on a monthly and seasonal basis—and in all likelihood the majority of them venturing out on the weekends—it is no wonder cemetery trustees felt the need to control visitors' behaviors and activities with firm regulations.[40]

Despite the publication of detailed rules and harsh penalties for offenders, however, cemetery trustees struggled regularly with breaches of conduct and vandalism of the landscaping. Mount Auburn established the principle that cemetery lots were the private real estate of those who purchased them and, as such, lot holders were "at liberty to manage [their] lot at will, to erect costly mausoleums, or record the death of a relative on a simple marble slab, to plant shrubs and flowers and enclose the hallowed spot, or let it remain in all its native wildness."[41] Harriet Martineau described the visual effect of such a liberal decoration policy: "I saw many lots of ground well tended, and wearing the air of luxuriant gardens; some surrounded with palings; some with posts and chains; and others with hedges of cypress or belts of acacia. Many separate graves were studded with flowers; the narrowest and gayest of gardens."[42] The decoration of a burial plot with flowers or shrubs could be a costly venture, never mind the expenses incurred with the erection of a monument, and the ongoing propensity of visitors to pilfer such plantings led lot holders to erect expensive cast-iron fences around their plots. In light of visitor complains that the "cast-iron exclusions" smacked of "aristocratic" tendencies in Boston, the *Saturday Morning Transcript* offered the defense that such an interpretation was "miserable reasoning, and a great mistake. It might as well be said that any fence round any farm in New England is a proof of the owner's being an aristocrat. He makes the fence to keep cattle and pigs off; and the 'cast-iron exclusions' are meant to answer *exactly the same purpose*." Emphasizing not only the protective role of the fences but also the destructive tendencies of visitors, the *Transcript* bemoaned, "Everybody knows that the monuments, the shrubbery, the flowers on the very graves in the Cemetery, would not be safe one day if the protection of the 'cast-iron exclusions' were relinquished."[43]

Mount Auburn's trustees were by no means alone in dealing with instances of vandalism despite all efforts to prevent such actions. The *New*

Cast-iron fence, Ralph Huntington Lot, Mount Auburn Cemetery.
(Photograph by the author)

Bedford (MA) Register reported with dismay that "wanton hands had also commenced their depredations on those simple efforts of taste, or pious offerings of friendship and affection, which have been planted" in the local rural cemetery, noting that anyone caught for such an offence would be liable to a fine "of not less than 5 or more than 50 dollars."[44] Despite reminders of the pecuniary consequences of such offenses, some visitors remained either thoughtless or defiant of the prohibitions. In 1843, the *National Aegis* (Worcester, MA) reported that the chairman of the local municipal board had entered a complaint "against one of our respectable citizens . . . for pulling a branch from one of the beautiful trees which decorate the common." The gentleman in question "submitted to his fine," with the *National Aegis* reminding readers, "It is vandalism to tear off one of the twigs." While the offense took place in the city common, the newspaper went on to relate that "we have heard frequent complaints from the owners of lots in the [Worcester Rural] Cemetery, of the almost total destruction, in some instances, of the plants and trees which affection and a due regard for the resting places of the loved and lost, have planted by the side of the monumental inscription" and expressed hope that the state laws would be used to bring the offenders to justice.[45] While rural cemeteries where theft and vandalism occurred received much press, burial grounds of all types suffered instances of unlawful behavior, many of which, while not new, were still actively in use, the graves still decorated with flowers. For instance, the *New York Commercial Advertiser* reprinted an advertisement from a Hartford newspaper that offered a reward for information regarding the theft of "a small oak-leaf geranium, in a pot" from the North Burying Ground, located adjacent to the city's rural Spring Grove Cemetery. The same person whose geranium was stolen wrote a few days later, "I found that another little plant had been taken away, a bridal rose. . . . These little flowers were once *her own*, and I had too good an opinion of human nature to suppose that anyone would be so heartless as to disturb them *there*. . . . This is a matter not only of private grievance, but one in which every member of our community has, or may have, a personal interest."[46] In addition to theft, older burying grounds, potter's fields, and Native American and African American burying grounds—those with the least amount of oversight, containing the bodies of the poor and the marginalized—were especially vulnerable to even worse offenses, most especially grave robbing.[47]

Rural cemetery lots were private property, but communities exhibited a sense of collective ownership over their rural cemeteries as institutions that reflected the community's identity, especially as it related to taste, refinement, and how "civilized" their residents purported to be. Desecration of any parts of their landscapes, either naturally occurring or designed, constituted a major breach of propriety, and the local newspapers took the lead as outlets for public shaming of such behavior. Despite their reputation as pleasure grounds, the rural cemeteries were nevertheless still considered holy ground for the burial of the dead. In some instances, misbehavior and vandalism were such common problems that the press could not suppress the feeling of exasperation that came with trying to shame the general public into better behavior. The disgust felt by one writer for the New York *Evening Post* in 1847 was especially palpable:

> Frequent instances have been known, even on ordinary occasions, when the vandalism of visitors has prompted them to scale the little enclosures, plunder the flowers which affection has planted upon the graves of the departed, and bear them away in the shape of bouquets, as gifts to those who are equally indifferent as to the source whence they were

procured. Some of the monuments, we are told, have had their corners knocked off in a spirit of mere wantonness, and the knife of the whittler may be traced in almost every portion of this sacred spot, where some Smith, Jones, or Jenkins, has been envious of recording his beautiful name in enduring letters.

Such acts of destruction within the cemetery landscape were clearly beyond the pale, as the author concluded, "The man that could be guilty of such conduct, is too mean to live, and certainly is in no fit condition to die. Withered be the hand, say we, that could pluck one flower that had been planted on a grave and nursed by the affection of one who mourned the departure of a loved friend or kinsman."[48]

Despite such excoriations, it was an uphill battle to induce the general public—men and women, young and old, working class and middle class—to be on their best behavior and to think about the rural cemetery landscape as a space where certain behaviors, such as wanton flower picking, were just not acceptable. One newspaper groused in 1854 that while Yankee boys could not suppress the urge to whittle on every wooden surface throughout New England, Yankee girls could not suppress the propensity "of pulling-up flowers [in a cemetery]; breaking the affectionate testimonials of respect planted by the sorrowful living, on the graves of the dead; and carrying off whole loads of branches of evergreens, for no other purpose but to gratify that propensity of destruction which is a characteristic of the race."[49] Young girls were by no means the only culprits. Nor were all perpetrators malicious in intent. While on a visit to Richmond's Hollywood Cemetery, Henry Arthur Bright reflected with humor in his travel diary how, with his host, "we found a wild yellow cactus (?a prickly pear) growing. Poor Burder [Bright's host] grasped at it energetically, but too late found that 'if every rose has a thorn,' every cactus has one no less. His hands were covered with subtle and venomous little darts. I escaped better, but not altogether, and the rest of the drive was spent in sucking our fingers!"[50] Bright's run-in with a prickly pear appears to have gone unnoticed by authorities, but a "respectable married lady" at Brooklyn's Green-Wood Cemetery was not so lucky. In what doubtlessly caused mortification for everyone involved, she "was arrested . . . for the offence of gathering a rose from one of the trees on the grounds. She was fined $5." Due to the status and respectability of the woman, "efforts were made to induce the wardens not to bring the suit, but as they are bound to protect the grounds from desecration, it was of no avail."[51] In these instances, the crime was more the result of thoughtlessness and overenthusiasm rather than the intention to do harm to the landscape.

Out of a desire to curb vandalism and other forms of misbehavior, whether committed intentionally or not, cemetery trustees often found themselves in the awkward position of sparring—both figuratively and even literally on occasion—with the public over access and admission regulations. Baltimore's Green Mount Cemetery offers an illustrative example of these struggles. Baltimore was the first southern city to participate in the rural cemetery movement, and Green Mount's proprietors proved to be torn between their sense of social conservativism and southern chivalry as they sought to establish Green Mount as a rival to its northeastern counterparts in both its landscaping and popularity as a tourist destination. To encourage greater numbers of visitors, the site purchased for the establishment of the cemetery was strategically located a little over a mile outside downtown Baltimore, making it a much more walkable distance for city residents than Mount Auburn or Laurel Hill. While desirous of public attraction, however, before its dedication in 1839, the cemetery's founders outlined in their prospectus a few preliminary admissions restrictions—"No boys, unless in company with their parents, *nor females unless accompanied by gentlemen* [emphasis added], will be admitted within the gates."[52] Every other rural cemetery established prohibitions against unattended children, but Green Mount was unique in its language specifying unaccompanied boys and the total exclusion of unescorted females. In the formal rules and regulations issued by the board of managers in 1840, the former restriction was expanded to include all children (not just the boys), while no mention as to female visitors was made.[53] However, the cemetery continued to adhere to the early regulation regarding women, and this proved to be a source of ongoing conflict in subsequent years.

A year following Green Mount's dedication, *The Sun* (Baltimore) began publishing reports to protest the institution's discriminatory admission policy for unescorted ladies. Based upon the testimony of a female correspondent, the newspaper relayed to readers accounts of two altercations that occurred within a few days of each other in 1840, in which groups of women, lacking tickets and a male escort, sought entry to the cemetery. In the first instance, after "a struggle on the porter's part, between duty and gallantry, respect for the sex and standing of the party," the porter relented and admitted the party "on his mere sufferance." The same situation occurred a few days later, but this time, the porter refused the women entry. In reflecting

Green Mount Cemetery, Baltimore, drawn from nature by Augustus Köllner. (Lithograph by Laurent Deroy; Goupil, Vibert & Co., publisher, ca. 1848, courtesy Library of Congress Prints and Photographs Division)

upon whether such restrictions were necessary, especially since they did not exist at any of the northern rural cemeteries, *The Sun* expressed the concern that should "the gates be thrown open to all, such ladies as our correspondent, might sometimes find themselves brought into the neighborhood of undesirable company" but that "regulations that will give greater freedom of admission, and avoid *this* unpleasant circumstance, would no doubt give great satisfaction to all respectable people." As *The Sun* aptly observed, any change in the regulations as they stood would be "a great convenience" to female visitors, since not only did "the requirements of business render it impossible to procure a male escort" during the week, but "it might often be the wish of female parties to dispense with male company."[54]

The idea that women might want to venture out of doors to a public space without a man to protect them or reaffirm their respectability was an especially complicated matter during the antebellum period, particularly in the South. American women were claiming the processes of death, mourning, and commemoration as existing within a feminized private sphere.[55] However, the rural cemetery existed within a liminal space between public and private wherein private activities—decorating a burial or mourning a loved one, for example—could be observed by strangers. In this way, the "social geography" of the cemetery became contested terrain—was it a public, masculine, and therefore possibly dangerous environment populated by sexual predators or was it private and feminine/feminized?[56] Urban middle-class women in the North were able to venture out into public alone without violating their claims to respectability, but as historian John F. Kasson has argued, women who did so "entered a realm in which they felt—or were expected to feel—particularly vulnerable. Possibilities for intrusion and symbolic violation abounded. From an impertinent glance, an unwelcome compliment, the scale of improprieties rose through a series of gradations to the ultimate violation in rape."[57] As The Sun had observed, throwing open the gates to unescorted female visitors might expose them to "undesirable company." That said, while the "ideal southern lady" was contained to the home, as Marise Bachand has shown, "elite women proved remarkably active in creating respectable public spaces within the southern city, thus expanding their own freedom of movement."[58] Baltimore's women proved equal to the task and appealed for changes in the cemetery's policy by writing open letters to The Sun and using the paper's editor as an ally to advocate on their behalf.

What complicated matters for the ladies of Baltimore, however, was a series of violent exchanges between men of various social classes within the cemetery's enclosure, which further highlighted the experimental nature and at times social instability of these new institutions. In May 1841, The Sun reported with dismay on two "violent and rather riotous occurrences" that were "deeply disgraceful and highly reprehensible." The first "fracas" occurred between two Irish gravediggers and a group of several "rowdies," in which "the shovels of the grave-diggers were freely exercised." The second "affray" actually involved Thomas P. Grant, director of the cemetery company, who objected to the admission of Henry Pollock, a local grocer, who had procured a ticket that would grant access to his family of nine and their carriage to the cemetery for the funeral of the Reverend S. G. Roszell. According to The Sun, Grant refused Pollock entry on the grounds that "persons were accustomed to obtain such tickets, and pick up thirty or forty people at the gate." Of a scene that smacks of Shakespearean drama, The Sun reported that Pollock accused Grant of not being a gentleman, to which Grant replied, "You are a blackguard." The verbal insults escalated until the two men came to blows, first with fists and then with sticks and stones, and only ended when Pollock nearly knocked out Grant with a rock to the head. In concluding its report of the "disgraceful" affairs in question, *The Sun* noted that such scenes may have been the result of the "alleged intoxication of some of the parties" and observed that liquor was available for sale near the cemetery.[59]

Within two weeks of these events, the cemetery trustees declared the gates closed to all but lot holders on Sundays, to which a correspondent for *The Sun* complained that "this indiscriminate exclusion . . . places the well-behaved and gentlemanly man under the same ban with the rowdy, and operates necessarily with equal injustice on the ladies."[60] Yet despite protests against the new provisions, the rule remained in place, to the consternation of "respectable" non–lot holders, who distinguished themselves from "rowdies." A young woman who identified herself as Alice wrote to the *Baltimore Saturday Visiter* in 1842 to express her frustration in this regard, "knowing that you are always ready to step forth and raise your voice in defense of the ladies." Having ventured to the cemetery on the Sabbath with a male companion who had a ticket of admission, the two were mortified when they were turned away since they were not lot holders. Disappointed at being thus rejected, the woman pointed out that one might suggest, "Why not go on a week day? You can have free access," to which she disdained, "for where is the true gentleman that can spend his time on a week day, to walk out with a lady. I say *true* gentlemen, because I am aware that there is a class, occasionally called gentlemen,—though better denominated exquisites, or walking-sticks—who are ready at any time, but they are not gentlemen, nor will any true lady be seen with them."[61] Class, respectability, and adherence to gender norms were necessarily intertwined—ladies could not gain entry to the cemetery without a male escort, but a "respectable" lady could not possibly bear to be accompanied by any other than a true "gentleman," none of whom were available except on the Sabbath. To take the arm of an "exquisite"—an alternative term in reference to a dandy—could tarnish a woman's reputation as respectable, and so, in short, Baltimore's women were stuck. What made matters worse in Alice's eyes was that the Sabbath prohibitions against non–lot holders were not working with regard to "the purpose of preventing the admission of ill-disposed young men," since she "observed several parties of young men—among which were those who were pointed out, as belonging to that class of rowdies, who create so much disturbance—entering at pleasure merely because one of their number, had been able to procure a lot-holder's ticket."[62]

Alice's concluding observation about the "rowdies" reflects the truism "necessity is the mother of invention," for disruptive young men were not the only ones who figured out how to get into Green Mount on Sundays. In the cemetery's "Second Report of the Board of Managers to the Lot Holders," published in *The Sun* in 1843, the board acknowledged "the decorum observed by the thousands on thousands of visitors since the gates were first thrown open" as "most praiseworthy and honorable." That being said, the report contained a final addendum, which was also sent out as a circular to each of the individual lot holders, that scolded the lot holders themselves for exacerbating the problems faced by the cemetery's managers; that is, the lot holders kept loaning their tickets to friends and visitors, which was against the rules. The result, as the board chastised, was that "on Sundays, especially, . . . Green Mount often presents more the appearance of a public garden than a place of interment for the dead." The lot holders were therefore "very earnestly requested to confine the use of their tickets to the limits prescribed by the rules printed on them." The report concluded with the final admonishment, "A person who does not pay for a lot, cannot complain if the right [to visit on Sundays] is denied to him."[63]

Despite ongoing efforts of cemetery boards to curb instances of public misbehavior and establish regulations to enforce the rules of respectability, it became increasingly clear to observers in the 1840s that the general public, which included the genteel middle class, viewed the rural cemeteries as genuinely public institutions wherein many considered the cemetery regulations more as guidelines and the acts of misbehavior as accidents rather than prosecutable offenses. To actually be charged for violating such regulations evoked surprise from offenders and a sense of responsibility on the part of newspaper editors to remind the public of the consequences of breaking the rules. As the *Sun* reported in September 1844, "A young man was arrested on Sunday" in Green Mount for some undescribed offense in the cemetery, "but it appeared to have been done more from thoughtlessness than otherwise; he was therefore released on payment of costs, and a promise of better behavior in future. Persons offending," the paper reminded its readers, "are subject to a fine of from $5 to $50."[64]

The ongoing struggles of cemetery trustees and the local press to regulate and shame the public into behaving themselves necessarily led to an increased awareness of the need to separate the park function from the cemetery. Among the early champions for such an idea was Andrew Jackson Downing, who praised the beauty and popularity of the nation's rural cemeteries but complained that "the only drawback to these beautiful and highly kept cemeteries, to my taste, is the gala-day air of *recreation* they present. People seem to go there to enjoy themselves, and not to indulge in any serious recollections or regrets."[65] Frederick Law Olmsted was in accord with Downing's view as he later criticized the "pleasure ground" aspect of the rural cemetery as out of keeping with what should have been the silent and peaceful nature of the burying ground and promoted the separation of the two functions into parks and cemeteries so that cities might have both without desecrating the one.[66] In short, the ability of the cemeteries to have a profound moralistic effect upon visitors was directly impeded by the greater desire and need within the population for green spaces where the general public could escape the confines of the city and let loose for an afternoon.

To rectify the incongruous double function of the rural cemeteries as places of both death and recreation, and thus encourage better behavior all around, Downing encouraged cities to build upon the success of the cemeteries by establishing public parks that would "civilize and refine the national character": "The finest band of music, the most rigid police, the certainty of an agreeable promenade and excellent refreshments, would, we think, as surely tempt a large part of the better class of the inhabitants of the cities."[67] Thus the parks, by providing an arena specifically designated for recreation, entertainment, and exercise, would remove those functions from the rural cemeteries. What is especially revealing about Downing's remarks is that he considered public parks as tempting to "the better class," which signifies his recognition that the genteel needed leisure space so that they would not continue to be tempted—whether consciously or not—to violate the rules of the cemetery and face public shame if caught. Rather, it would become the responsibility of the parks to shape public conduct within the secular landscape, and the cemeteries would continue to encourage behavior appropriate to the landscapes of the dead.[68]

Proving to be just as onerous as regulating the public's behavior, regulating matters of taste and choice regarding the kinds of monuments and tombs that lot holders erected on their plots dogged cemetery trustees, travelers, and art and architectural critics throughout the period of the rural cemetery movement and beyond. Embedded within the bylaws of the nation's rural cemeteries were notes concerning lot holders' choice of monuments—they were generally free to erect anything they chose, so long as the trustees did not deem it inappropriate or offensive. For example, at Laurel Hill Cemetery, while they denounced the erection of head and footstones over burials as illustrative of "bad taste," the "managers have no wish to interfere with individual taste in the construction of monuments" but reserved the right "to prevent the erection of large improvements which might interfere with the general effect, or obstruct any principal view."[69] Virtually all rural cemetery bylaws contained language stipulating the rights of lot holders to plant shrubs and flowers, to place boundary markers or short fences, and to erect whatever types of monuments they saw fit, all to be maintained at the lot holder's expense. As such, since the responsibility to adorn and maintain lots fell upon the lot holders—since rural cemetery burial lots effectively became the private property of the lot holders—the trustees' only real power lay within their ability to remove anything that clearly violated accepted codes of decency. The problem with having such an open-ended policy, however, was that matters of taste and what constituted an "appropriate" monument were entirely subjective, and policing peoples' preferences for adorning their plots proved to be nearly impossible. Further, new methods in stonecutting and quarrying, as well as an increasing number of trained sculptors in the United States by midcentury, allowed for an explosion in eclecticism on the cemetery landscape that mirrored the variety of new architectural styles that likewise dominated the cityscape.

The movement toward greater variety in sepulchral monuments began following Mount Auburn's consecration in 1831, first with the appearance of neoclassical forms such as shafts and obelisks, sarcophagi, and sidehill tombs with various temple facades. These were typically cut from Connecticut freestone or brownstone, but the material that quickly became most popular was marble.[70] Increasingly, as large stone quarries opened in various parts of the country, greater variety was available in material that lent itself to larger, more monumental forms of sepulchral art and architecture. The first commercial limestone quarries opened in Bloomington, Indiana, in 1827, for which a national market developed rapidly.[71] The Westerly Granite Quarry in Rhode Island, which opened in the 1840s, provided expanded options for both small and largescale monuments, sculptures, tombs, and mausoleums made out of this durable material by the 1850s.[72] Added to technological developments in stonecutting and quarrying, romanticism in art and the sentimentalizing trends in religious attitudes toward death resulted in a profusion of new types of sculptural and iconographic forms entering into the memorial lexicon—it was at this time that Americans began to embrace what June Hobbs has called "the clichés of death—clasped hands, fingers pointing up, ladies clinging to crosses, angels, gates ajar . . . those symbols least likely to arouse the interest of tombstone scholars simply because they are everywhere."[73] Historian David Charles Sloane conveys a similar sentiment as he describes the "seemingly endless combinations of these natural, mythological and religious symbols" that came to dominate the nineteenth-century cemetery landscape.[74] This cavalcade of new images and forms appeared at the same time that Americans began to experiment more enthusiastically with architectural revivalism. The rural cemetery thus became home to carriage gateways, tombs, and monuments in the neo-classical, Gothic, Egyptian, Tuscan, Romanesque, and Islamic styles.[75] Such structures were then adorned with all manner of iconography—upturned torches, hands, plants and flowers of every kind, angels, portraiture of the deceased, lambs, and doves—in short, anything that could be carved that suited the whim of the buyer. Reflective of the denunciations leveled by architectural critics of the late nineteenth century who hated the popular trends of their era, modern historians have looked upon eclecticism in the visual arts and architecture during this period with an equally critical eye, describing the great variety of buildings and monuments on the landscapes of both the living and the dead as a "riot" or "jumble of pseudohistorical styles" that embodied "the cultural confusion of men who no longer possessed a coherent vocabulary of symbols."[76]

On the contrary, the tendency toward variety and eclecticism was not born out of confusion. An enormous amount of change was then underway in the still young republic—industrialization was transforming the nature of labor as well as increasing economic stratification; the emerging middle class sought to define itself and establish its cultural authority; and immigration from western Europe was making the nation increasingly heterogeneous, both ethnically and religiously. Industrial manufacturing and extractive processes dramatically expanded the range of goods available to consumers, while the egalitarian trends of the Jacksonian era influenced Euro-American notions of individuality and personal freedom. It is not surprising, then, that as the economy and demographics of the nation expanded, and as new technologies spurred greater options for consumers, the memorials on the cemetery landscape subsequently became more diverse. Prior to these developments and the subsequent clash of opinions over monument styles, traditional eighteenth- and early nineteenth-century grave marker styles were relatively simple and uniform in style—upright headstones with accompanying footstones, made from locally quarried materials like slate, sandstone, or freestone and decorated according to the ideological principles of the period. By the eve of Mount Auburn's consecration, the American memorial landscape was therefore covered with headstones in the Anglo-Protestant tradition bearing winged skulls, cherubs (also referred to by some scholars as "soul effigies"), simple portraiture of the deceased, and, as had been in vogue since the 1790s, neoclassical urn and willow motifs.[77] While some headstones, such as those for ministers or prosperous merchants, were taller or more elaborately executed than others, and humble wooden posts or rough-cut fieldstones marked the graves of the poor or enslaved, the relative uniformity in design for so many eighteenth-century grave markers connoted the idea of Death as the great equalizer and established a visual rhetoric of homogeneity among both the living and the dead.

Immediately following Mount Auburn's consecration, periodicals like the North American Review and the cemetery trustees themselves urged the public to use the establishment of this new burying ground as an opportunity to cultivate a more refined aesthetic as they contemplated what kinds of markers to erect over the burials of their loved ones. In October 1831, the North American Review urged future lot holders to "not suffer the ground to be disfigured with dungeon-like tombs, which are only suited to the cellars of churches and burying-places in cities, where the dead cannot find room to lie dust to dust." The journal further admonished that the "stiff and ungainly head-stone should be banished" and replaced by "some simple form suited to resist the elements, and receive inscriptions."[78] Mirroring the North American Review's perspective, Mount Auburn's trustees issued a circular letter to lot holders in 1833 "prohibiting thin, perpendicular slab markers, and slate in particular." The trustees feared the traditional headstone material would "give a gloomy aspect to the scenery" and "would not harmonize with the natural and artificial beauties of a rural cemetery."[79] To further encourage the desired monumental aesthetic, cemetery trustees Joseph Story and Jacob Bigelow each erected their own family memorials, and theirs were among the first nine that visitors could see by the spring of 1833—a simple obelisk with Egyptian Revival base for Story and a broken column bearing a low-relief festoon of olive leaves set atop a neoclassical plinth and pediment for Bigelow.[80]

Even as the number of monuments at Mount Auburn remained few in number, the first major critique against the lot holders' sense of style appeared in the Saturday Morning Transcript (Boston) in September 1833. After having visited the cemetery, the newspaper's editor wrote evocatively of the melancholy feelings that the landscape evoked but concluded with his "regret at the execrable taste already exhibited by some of the proprietors in ornamenting of their lots, and in the ill-shaped and unclassical monuments they have placed on them." Fearing further reproach upon American taste "so liberally lavished upon us by the Trollopes, Fiddlers, and Hamiltons," the editor went on to suggest the publication of a book containing "five or six hundred designs of tombs, monuments and cenotaphs" that might then be distributed to all the stonecutters and their patrons.[81] One reader of the *Transcript* responded to the article to refute the charge against "bad taste," offering as a defense for the relatively rough execution of the monuments the absence of European "artists as [Antonio] Canova or [Bertel] Thorwaldsen [*sic*]." The editor followed this rebuttal with the clarification that "there are undoubtedly many of the monuments at [Mount] Auburn in excellent taste. We intended to cast no reproach upon the sculptor—we meant only to indicate the bad taste *of the proprietor* [emphasis added]."[82] In short, the sculptors could not be blamed for the poor choices of the purchasers.

The 1830s proved to be a period of great experimentation in sepulchral monuments and architecture, as new forms began to appear in both rural cemeteries and older reform cemeteries as well. Responding to the burgeoning criticisms of lot holders' aesthetic preferences and the variable quality evident in newly erected monuments, George Ticknor Curtis expressed in 1834 what would become a common refrain in subsequent decades—"Variety there must be, in these things, and ought to be; for the ornaments set up here, are but types and expressions of the variety in human feeling and affliction." Noting that all manner of emotions, including passion, grief, and sorrow, were expressed in the monument choices of individuals, Curtis admonished his readers that while there were "certain principles of taste to be violated or to be followed, yet we have need, before we condemn, to cultivate a catholic and tolerant spirit." The variety of human emotions and ways of mourning meant there would necessarily be an equal amount of variety in the monumental expressions of such feelings—some proprietors undoubtedly revealed a sense of refined artistic taste in the design and execution of their monuments or markers, while others erected what they personally liked or simply what they could afford (or what they chose to pay for). As Curtis suggested, then, visitors should therefore be cautioned to consider the diversity of potential styles—and of quality and execution—as a reflection of the diversity of humankind. Cemeteries like Mount Auburn would, indeed, become central locations for the display of an emerging sculptural tradition, but as Curtis warned, travelers should not visit the cemetery with the eye of an art critic. Not wishing "to deny the cultivation of the public taste," which would come in due time, he concluded that "whatever is done from feeling, will be, in this high and universal sense, natural and tasteful."[83] In short, visitors should regard whatever monuments people erected as expressions of personal grief or sentiment and not visit the rural cemeteries believing them to be outdoor art galleries.

By contrast, architect James Gallier saw American architecture in general, and sepulchral architecture in particular, as in a state of crisis that needed to be addressed by cemetery proprietors as quickly as possible to avoid cluttering the burial landscape with inappropriate and unseemly memorials to the dead. Writing for the *North American Review* in 1836, Gallier's language was remarkably prescient to those critics from half a century later who bemoaned Americans' abuse of architectural styles in fashioning an "artistically discordant" landscape.[84] Writing that "in no civilized country" were the rules of architecture "less regarded, than in the United States," Gallier complained, "Thus far the art, with us, is in a very chaotic state."[85] Regarding cemetery architecture, Gallier expressed concern that "the few models for monuments, which were at first displayed, have been very eagerly copied, and with no great variety," and further noted that the "public taste . . . should be well directed, before the cemetery becomes filled with uncouth structures and monuments."[86] Gallier's greatest concern was reserved for the influence that Mount Auburn's Egyptian Revival gateway evidently had upon the tastes of the cemetery proprietors. To the architect's dismay, despite his own low opinion of the Egyptian Revival, Gallier noted that "in imitation, the principal portion of the monuments [in the cemetery] are in the same style. We have, accordingly, a great number of pyramids, and obelisks, and tombs supported by Egyptian columns, and fashioned in the heavy proportions of that style." As a more overtly Christian alternative to Egyptian architecture, especially for the gateway, which was to be replaced with a more permanent stone structure, Gallier suggested "the sublime, the glorious Gothic."[87] Such a suggestion went unheeded at Mount Auburn, where the carriage gateway was reconstructed in 1842 according to the original design, but by the 1850s, the Gothic easily rivaled the Egyptian as the most popular of the revival styles for cemetery entrances and monuments.[88]

The late 1830s into the 1840s witnessed the elaboration of neoclassical and Egyptian forms as well as the introduction of freestanding sculptural works of art into the rural cemetery landscape. Travelers' accounts reflected an overwhelming approval of these developments. One correspondent for the *Columbus Democrat* in Ohio remarked in 1837 on the "correct clas-

Samuel Appleton monument, Mount Auburn Cemetery. (Photograph by the author)

sical taste . . . frequently displayed in the erection of the monuments" at Mount Auburn.[89] Another visitor in 1838 breathlessly described his rambles through the cemetery and how at various turns he witnessed "some new glory of art in the shape of an obelisk, a column, a sarcophagus, or some other sepulchral monument, of marble, or of granite, each vying with the others in the purity of the taste with which it was designed, and in the perfect elegance and finish of its workmanship." Noting that "scarcely two monuments are exactly alike," the writer declared that "the charm of variety was yet perfect." His most enthusiastic description was for the monument to Samuel Appleton, which remains today one of the most well-known at Mount Auburn. Sculpted in Italy and "imported at an enormous expense," the Appleton monument is a solid, miniature Grecian temple, ornamented with the Ouroboros (self-devouring snake) inside of which is the winged hourglass. Sculpted bas-relief lions' heads appear on the false doors, with evergreen leaves overhead; the roof at each end is surmounted by a "sepulchral lamp," described by the writer as "purely classical, and of inimitable workmanship. The entire structure forms a *tout ensemble*, which satisfies the eye, the imagination, and the taste."[90]

Writers continued to comment on the novelty of new designs and poignant symbolism as monumental and architectural forms proliferated in the new rural cemeteries. The broken column, for instance, had appeared as a device on slate headstones since the early nineteenth century, but its execution as a freestanding memorial only began in the 1830s. On the erection at Laurel Hill Cemetery of a broken column monument for the James N. Barker family in 1838, *The Pennsylvanian's* description was especially evocative of the emerging predilection for romantic symbolism—"The capital, alas, is wanting; and the broken fragment with its chaste and touching eloquence, tells the story of the husband's and the parent's loss. How like the story of human life and human hopes! The column of hopes and wishes erect on earth, is always broken before the capital can be placed on its appropriate summit."[91] Portraiture also began to manifest in new ways during this period. Since the mid-eighteenth century, portraits of the deceased had appeared on American gravestones. The installation in 1840 at Mount Auburn of the Binney monument—a full-length sculpture of four-year-old Emily Binney lying in bed, protected by a canopy supported by Doric columns—marked the introduction of fully three-dimensional sculptural works to the cemetery landscape, and as Elise Ciregna has noted, "*The Binney Child* soon became a great attraction."[92] As Cornelia Walter would reflect in the 1847 cemetery guidebook *Mount Auburn Illustrated*, "Monumental tributes of this class are as yet rare in our country, though no style can be more appropriate in memory of buried friends."[93]

By the 1840s, eclecticism had become the order of the day in the cemetery landscape. Some authors, like Nathaniel Dearborn, who wrote one of the many guidebooks for Mount Auburn, gloried in the new diversity of monuments. Writing in 1843, he enthused, "Hill and glen salute the eye at almost every stopping point, and the ever varying forms of mausoleums, temples, and obelisks, from the most splendid production of the sculpturing art, to the neat and simple pyramid, claim attention in every direction."[94] The elaboration of new designs further meant an increased variety in the size and cost of funerary monuments, especially as a greater number of local stonecutters and carvers were able to meet the consumer demand. The size and cost of monuments began to reach such proportions that other writers began to express concern that while variety in sepulchral art was a good thing, proprietors might disregard proper taste in favor of expensive ostentation. The *North American Review* was ever the champion of Mount Auburn as reflective of good taste, its monuments "singularly free from conceit, prettiness, and affectation."[95] Nevertheless, one observer could not help but note the contrast between the newly erected memorials at Mount Auburn and the headstones at one of Boston's ancient burying grounds, Copp's Hill:

> In the latter [Mount Auburn] the hand of wealth and art and taste has reared columns—has sculptured in all the beauty of exquisite chiseling, busts and devices and statues, and the impression cannot be shaken off that you are in the burial place of the wealthy. I can readily imagine that in the midst of so much luxury and ornament the poor man shrinks back, and doubts for the moment the loudly published equality of the grave. At Copp's Hill there is no such triumph of riches. Many a man of character and some of fame lie here beneath a plain free-stone tablet. Even the monuments which display, as many of them do, heraldic bearings, and armorial devices, are but rudely sculptured, and would be sadly out of place at Mount Auburn.[96]

Other rural cemeteries likewise received their fair share of praise or censure for the degree to which their monuments reflected wealth or pride. As one visitor to Laurel Hill Cemetery noted, while some of the monuments were "chaste, simple, and pleasing,—others strik[e] the beholder unpleasantly from their ostentatious display of the efforts of the sculptor, or, of the praises of the deceased."[97] By contrast, *The Sun* (Baltimore) dismissed the folly of pride in any monuments at Green Mount Cemetery with "ah! How pardonable!" for, as the newspaper concluded, "each monument is a monument of humanity—each epitaph is our own."[98]

Many commentators wrote generally about the importance of finding a happy balance between taste, monetary expenditure, and skillful execution. Cornelia Walter exhorted the readers of *Mount Auburn Illustrated* to recognize that good taste and wealth did not necessarily go hand in hand. "But *good taste*," she wrote, "is not subservient to the power of gold, and should ever be consulted even in the simplest memorial. The wealth which justifies large expenditures is not always successfully applied, and we have seen sepulchral structures of high cost, which, to the beholder, admitted of no other feeling than that they were monuments of the bad taste of the designer." Walter concluded that if a proprietor was incapable of purchasing and erecting a properly executed, tasteful memorial, they would do well to simply plant flowers upon the elevated mound of their plot; they would be "a far better and more pleasing monument than an unsuccessful effort of the other kind, and infinitely more grateful to the traveler's eye."[99]

Nehemiah Cleaveland pressed the issue in even more forceful terms in the guidebook *Green-Wood Illustrated* in 1847. Noting that the subject of monumental erections presented "a question both of taste and durability," Cleaveland acknowledged that it was necessary to approach the matter with "some delicacy" given that each individual possessed the right "to have his own way in such matters." Encouraging variety as "essential to pleasing effect," Cleaveland remarked upon the most commonly employed forms, including the headstone, the "pyramidic forms" (obelisks and pyramids), the sarcophagus, and the column. The problem, as he saw it, was that the popular taste was "ever prone to servile imitation," so even as the sepulchral aesthetic had become more eclectic, the American enthusiasm for these newer forms resulted in "the multiplication of one thing, producing, as it must, a wearisome sameness." Reminiscent of Gallier's critique, Cleaveland further expressed disappointment that Americans relied so much upon "superstitious Athens" and "calf-adoring Egypt" for architectural inspiration and hoped that, at the very least, proprietors would include "the cheering emblems of the living faith," such as the allegorical figures of Hope or Immortality, to decorate their memorial structures.[100]

Nehemiah Cleaveland's frustration with the direction of American memorial taste was palpable, and his warnings in *Green-Wood Illustrated* were a harbinger for what was to come in subsequent years. In 1848, the *Christian Review* noted with approval the widespread establishment of rural cemeteries but denounced the "desire for singularity, and for a display of expense, in monuments and monumental inscriptions." Cognizant of the "great diversity of taste" evident on the cemetery landscape, the periodical applauded the idea of variety—"We are made to love variety; all nature is full of it; and in its endless beauty true taste finds much of its gratification." It was the idea of singularity, "a desire for something unlike everything of the kind . . . , an attempt to be original," rather, that the *Review* found so offensive. Even worse was "the great and growing love of expense" throughout the nation, which had carried into memorialization to "the utter violation of that simplicity which should characterize all such memorials."[101] The following year the *New Englander* echoed Cornelia Walter's concerns when it denounced ostentatious monuments as "no longer a memorial of the dead but of the folly of the living." Encouraging proprietors to think upon the propriety of context, the journal urged, "Good taste must condemn costly and magnificent structures over the remains of an infant however dear, while a public benefactor, a father of his country, may be properly honored with a monument equaling in splendor anything which his country can boast." *The New Englander* complained in its concluding remarks, "We copy the great, but its grandeur vanishes; for we cannot succeed in retaining grandeur on a reduced scale."[102]

Wilson Flagg offered a particularly colorful denunciation of what he considered to be ostentatious displays of wealth and bad taste in an 1853 essay for the *Magazine of Horticulture*. Whereas cemeteries like Mount Auburn, Laurel Hill, Green-Wood, and others were established in the hope, at least in part, of elevating the spirit and improving the morals of the public, many had become covered with "gewgaws and expensive follies," which had transformed the landscape into "a mere magnificent toy-shop." Proprietors had exhibited, in their choice of monuments, "too many sad attempts to carry the arbitrary distinctions of social life down to the grave," which had struck Flagg "with a sensation of the ludicrous, which expels every feeling of sympathy or solemnity." The worst offense, in his view, was that after "one's thousands have been lavished upon a monument, which can serve only as evidence of the folly and pride of the owner, the iron fence is set up around it, like the palisades around one's front yard in the city, that the vulgar may be obliged to stand at a distance and admire it."[103] Andrew Jackson Downing had denounced what he regarded as "hideous *ironmongery*" prevalent in the rural cemeteries several years earlier, but to Flagg's abhorrence, the fashion for decorative iron fences around private lots had not diminished.[104] Flagg concluded his essay with the firm belief that future generations would condemn "the absurdity of the taste that has frequently guided the artist and proprietors" and that "disgusted with their ostentation . . . it will become the fashion to labor for simplicity combined with grandeur and cheerful solemnity."[105] Unbeknownst to Flagg, the rise of the memorial park in the twentieth century with its emphasis on sepulchral minimalism would ultimately prove him right.

What had begun as an expansion of the burial reform movement, with cemetery trustees' and landscaper designers' efforts to afford the public an opportunity to enjoy expansive naturalistic spaces outside of the city, very quickly transformed into a massive experiment in how Americans would engage with parklike burying grounds and memorialize the dead. The result was a perpetual tension between how the general public sought to engage with these landscapes, how lot holders saw fit to adorn their burial plots, and the desire on the parts of cemetery trustees and critics to effectively engineer what constituted proper behavior and aesthetic taste. Part of the reason why rural cemeteries became a hotbed for such tensions was that not only were they sacred spaces for the burial of the dead, but they were also arguably one of the most important emerging cultural institutions that reflected the progress of the nation and its people. As one writer in 1855 declared, "Rural cemeteries . . . exert an important influence on the public taste. When properly laid out, they present to the eye a pleasing landscape adorned with trees and shrubs and vines, with well-kept roads and walks, and tasteful monuments. All classes in society can obtain easy access to them, and can learn by their own inspection how beautiful is nature—how beautiful in her own simplicity, and also when her charms are heightened by the hand of art."[106] For as much as trustees and writers wanted rural cemeteries to shape public morals, behaviors, and tastes and to generally provide a civilizing function, the public themselves ultimately engaged with the cemeteries and erected monuments according to their own whims. And despite efforts to outsource most forms of outdoor pleasure to public parks, beginning with the establishment of New York's Central Park in 1853, and the increasingly vehement language of architectural critics during the second half of the century against the American predilection for eclecticism, clashes over public misbehavior within the cities of the dead and cemetery proprietors' desire to erect increasingly lavish and expensive monuments persisted well beyond the principal years of the rural cemetery movement. Yet, even as these clashes unfolded, the establishment of rural cemeteries expanded beyond the confines of the Northeast into the urban South and the Midwest during the 1840s and 1850s, transforming a regional cultural phenomenon into a genuinely national movement with major implications for how communities fashioned their own local, regional, and national identities.

4

"A Tabernacle for the Dead"

National Expansion of the Rural Cemetery

By the 1840s, the rural cemetery model had begun a dramatic expansion beyond the confines of the Northeast, with cities in virtually all of the states east of the Mississippi River establishing their own contributions to the rural cemetery movement by the eve of the Civil War. As early as 1849, Andrew Jackson Downing declared, "There is scarcely a city of note in the whole country that has not its rural cemetery." Referring to Mount Auburn, Downing observed, "No sooner was attention generally roused to the charms of this first American cemetery, than the idea took the public mind by storm. Travellers made pilgrimages to the Athens of New England, solely to see the realization of their long-cherished dream of a resting-place for the dead, at once sacred from profanation, dear to the memory, and captivating to the imagination."[1] At the dedication of Magnolia Cemetery in Charleston, South Carolina, the following year, artist and orator Charles Fraser reinforced Downing's sentiments to the crowd in attendance: "The establishment of Mount Auburn was an era of taste in our country. . . . Since then, almost all our chief cities have introduced rural cemeteries into their neighborhood, recommended, as it is said, by similar advantages of situation and embellishment."[2] It was thus during the two decades before the Civil War that the rural cemetery movement became a genuinely national cultural phenomenon, as Americans north, south, and west embraced the common principle of creating expansive and beautiful resting places for the dead outside the immediate boundaries of the city. For many of the new cemeteries founded during these years, it was specifically because of tourism in the northeastern cemeteries, and especially at Mount Auburn, that civic-minded urban elites returned to their home cities in the expanding Midwest and urban South to propose the establishment of their own such burying grounds.

Notable among the new cemeteries of the 1840s were Cypress Grove Cemetery (1840) in New Orleans; Rose Hill Cemetery (1840) in Macon, Georgia; the Cincinnati and Covington Cemetery (1843) in Covington, Kentucky; Mount Holly Cemetery (1843) in Little Rock, Arkansas; Frankfort Cemetery (1844) in Kentucky; Allegheny Cemetery (1844) in Pittsburgh; Albany Rural Cemetery (1844) in New York; Spring Grove Cemetery (1845) in Cincinnati; Swan Point Cemetery (1846) in Providence, Rhode Island; Elmwood Cemetery (1846) in Detroit; Bonaventure Cemetery (1847) in Savannah; Cave Hill Cemetery (1848) in Louisville and Lexington Cemetery (1849) in Kentucky; Prospect Hill Cemetery (1849) in York, Pennsylvania; and Hollywood Cemetery (1849) in Richmond, Virginia. Added to these in the following decade were Magnolia Cemetery (1850) in Charleston; Greenwood Cemetery (1852) in New Orleans; Elmwood Cemetery (1852) in Memphis, Tennessee; Mount Moriah Cemetery (1854) and Mount Vernon Cemetery (1856) in Philadelphia; Odd Fellows Rural Cemetery (1854) in Salem, Oregon; Oakwood Cemetery (1854) in Richmond, Virginia; Evergreen Cemetery (1855) in Portland, Maine; and Rosehill Cemetery (1859) and Graceland Cemetery (1860) in Chicago. In some places, preexisting burying grounds that did not possess the rural cemetery aesthetic were developed over time so that they fit within the movement. For example, Atlanta, Georgia, was still a relatively new city when, in 1850, it established its first municipal cemetery. This burying ground was originally designed according to the reform cemetery model and was thus similar to the Grove Street Cemetery (formerly known as the New Burying Ground until 1845) in New Haven, Connecticut. As it expanded, however, planners incorporated more "rural" elements, and the public cemetery was renamed Oakland Cemetery in 1872.[3]

Significantly, the nationalization of the movement during the 1840s and 1850s highlighted the great heterogeneity of both the American landscape and its people. Northeastern rural cemeteries served as models of inspiration, but out of necessity landscape architects worked with the natural topography and flora available to them and sought to magnify the best features of local landscapes rather than attempt to just copy what already existed. Further, as the rural cemetery movement expanded into the urban South and the Midwest, the new cemeteries took on the important role of reflecting and reinforcing local and regional, as well as national, identities. While acknowledging the Northeast as the place of origin for the first rural cemeteries, urban white southerners and midwesterners embraced the idea of the rural cemetery as an inherently American—not a uniquely New England—cultural institution and then used the landscape in ways that affirmed the role of their particular state or region in the national historical narrative and collective identity. In the Midwest, the adoption of the rural cemetery was part of community leaders' efforts to shed their towns and cities of their unrefined frontier status. For residents of the urban South, the introduction of burial reform with rural cemeteries was often fraught with tensions over tradition and politics even as proponents saw rural cemeteries as a mark of modern progress. Further, as increasing numbers of cities embraced the rural cemetery model, there emerged a broadly shared sense of competition between communities over whose rural cemetery might be considered the most beautiful or impressive. Such competitive spirit and pride of place increased during the antebellum period and fed into a burgeoning regional exceptionalism that came to full fruition in the aftermath of the Civil War, particularly in the South, with the apotheosis of the Confederate dead and the emergence of the Lost Cause mythology. Finally, while cemetery proprietors in the Northeast had promoted their rural cemeteries to the public as beautiful and wholesome tourist destinations and places where locals could promenade or engage in moral introspection, those beyond the region sought to transform their cemeteries into meccas of the illustrious dead—hallowed grounds where not just the community's but also the nation's "special dead" rested—and, by their presence, to convert the cemetery landscape into a shrine of national significance.[4] The national growth of the rural cemetery movement thus highlighted the challenges, tensions, and opportunities involved in cultivating a shared national identity with common institutions while maintaining distinct community or regional identities.

The problems of burial overcrowding and fears of infectious epidemic disease, linked directly to population increase and urban development, had spurred the development of the nation's first rural cemeteries, and by the late 1830s, an increasing number of cities beyond the confines of the Northeast began experiencing the same issues as Boston, New York, and Philadelphia in the preceding generation. Unsurprisingly, urban elites from the South and the expanding Midwest looked to that region and its wildly successful and popular cemeteries for inspiration. The turnpike era had given way to canal development, and with the completion of the Erie Canal in 1825, westward travel became much easier, and populations in what were previously frontier towns—places such as Pittsburgh, Akron, Cincinnati, Louisville, St. Louis, and Detroit—began to boom, and those communities' original burying grounds quickly reached and exceeded their maximum capacity. In the urban South, the major cities dated much earlier, to the seventeenth and early eighteenth centuries, and in places like Baltimore, Richmond, Charleston, Savannah, and New Orleans, burial practices had long been undertaken by individual churches, each of which had their own accompanying churchyard. With the exception of potter's fields—many of which doubled as the only burying grounds available for the burial of both free and enslaved people of color—public burying grounds fashioned on the reform model of New Haven's burying ground were few in number. But even these cities, with long-established burial systems, experienced significant population increases that put major strains on their older burying grounds. Reflecting this particular concern in his dedicatory oration at Green Mount Cemetery, Maryland novelist and politician John Pendleton Kennedy declared, "I do not wish to lie down in the crowded city. I would not be jostled in my narrow house,—much less have my dust give place to the intrusion of late comers: I would not have the stone memorial that marks my resting place to be gazed upon by the business-perplexed crowd in their every day pursuit of gain, and where they ply their tricks of custom. Amidst this din and traffic of the living is no fit place for the dead."[5] Echoing this sentiment at the dedication of Cave Hill Cemetery in Louisville, Connecticut native and Presbyterian minister Edward P. Humphrey complained, "Is there a city in the country, which has attained the antiquity of half a century, that is not obnoxious to the reproach of a neglected or desecrated graveyard?"[6] In his estimation, even relatively new cities could not escape the problems of burial overcrowding and dilapidated conditions in the face of urban expansion and development.

Indeed, despite the imbalance in population densities between the North and the South generally, several southern cities ranked in the top twenty by population in the nation according to the 1840 census: Baltimore (2nd), New Orleans (3rd), Charleston, South Carolina (10th), Louisville, Kentucky (16th), and Richmond, Virginia (20th). By 1850, with the exception of Richmond, which had dropped to 26th most populous, these cities still ranked in the top twenty, with the addition of St. Louis, Missouri (8th). Added to these were two of the newer midwestern cities among the nation's most populous in 1840—Cincinnati (6th) and Pittsburgh (17th).[7] For young cities like Cincinnati, which styled itself as the "Queen City" or "Metropolis of the West," establishing a rural cemetery was an integral part of urban development and of efforts by locals to cultivate the image of their community as a modern city rather than as a frontier town.[8] For their part, white southerners who supported rural cemetery development regarded it as critical to both their cultural development and their public health. "A rural Cemetery is to be found in the neighborhood of nearly all the considerable cities of the North," opined the Magnolia Cemetery Company; "how much more necessary is such a facility in the warmer climate of the South?"[9] For many in the urban South who sought to acquire the features of metropolitanism as well as stave off the ravages of epidemic disease, they would not be charged with backwardness.

Given the relationship between population expansion, urban development, and embrace of the rural cemetery model, it was unsurprisingly the nation's two most populous cities after New York City that brought the rural cemetery movement out of the Northeast—Baltimore and New Orleans. In Baltimore, tobacco merchant Samuel D. Walker first proposed the creation of a new burying ground in 1834 after a visit to Mount Auburn. When an official cemetery company formed in 1838 with the aim of establishing Green Mount Cemetery, Samuel Moore, who served as president, explained in the cemetery's prospectus that the company's "object is the establishment of a public cemetery, upon the plan of 'Père-la-Chaise,' in France, and 'Mount Auburn' and 'Laurel Hill,' in this country."[10] The Sun (Baltimore) became an early champion of the cemetery, predicting that should Green Mount "meet with the favor that is anticipated, it will not be many years before . . . it [is] an object of pride, not only to the city more immediately connected with it, but to the State of Maryland."[11] The Sun published news on the rate of subscriptions for burial lots and printed in full the prospectus for the cemetery and the terms of subscription. After much promotion, Green Mount Cemetery was formally dedicated on July 13, 1839, before a crowd of "hundreds," who had arrived "on horseback, in carriages, and on foot, eager to witness the consecration of the spot which perchance would be their last resting place."[12]

Despite the geographical distance that separated Louisiana from New England, word of the attractions embodied by rural cemeteries spread swiftly via print media, and New Orleans, having a sizable population already in need of expanded burial space, followed suit shortly thereafter with the establishment of Cypress Grove Cemetery in 1840. Situated below sea level, New Orleans had presented unique challenges for the burial of the dead since it was first colonized by the French in 1718. Burial belowground proved unreasonable, as the graves quickly flooded, and so residents eventually adopted aboveground burial systems derived from the French and Spanish, including family and society mausoleums, oven tombs (so named because of their oven shape) called *fours*, and loculi, "niches large enough to hold a single coffin end on, [that] were customarily built in blocks or walls four to six tiers high." As noted by Dell Upton, it was because of the preponderance of aboveground burials that dominated the city's landscape that "the complex relationship between the living and the dead was particularly poignant" since "the abodes of the two were visually so similar to one another."[13] Although New Orleans lacked the kind of undulating topography so intimately associated with the rural cemeteries of the Northeast, the Firemen's Charitable Association, which established Cypress Grove, nevertheless referred to the city's first nonsectarian cemetery (which also came to be known as Firemen's Cemetery) as a "rural cemetery." Moreover, given the difficulties for burial presented by the city's situation below sea level, the cemetery's organizers highlighted its location as its greatest attribute, "the ground being the highest in the vicinity of New Orleans."[14] Once opened to the public for interments, the *Daily Picayune* (New Orleans) wrote favorably of the city's new cemetery as a local expression of the broader movement: "It is pleasant to observe in various sections of the country, a growing disposition to deprive grave yards of their gloom and to render them what they ought to be, beautiful and pleasant retreats from the turmoil and cares of our daily existence. Mount Auburn, near Boston, sweet and lovely spot! the cemetery near Philadelphia, our own Cypress Grove Cemetery, are noble evidences of the existence of this feeling."[15] Even so, the ongoing commitment to using densely packed, French- and Spanish-influenced "reusable family and society tombs that emphasized family and community over individualism . . . perplexed many American and English travelers and added to their sense of the exotic otherness of Creole New Orleans, its climate, culture, and architecture."[16] Further, while Cypress Grove as a non-sectarian cemetery reflected the increasing presence of Anglo-Protestants in the region following the Louisiana Purchase in 1803, the "Crescent City" remained dominated by Roman Catholics, who continued to be buried in cemeteries owned and operated by the Archdiocese of New Orleans.[17]

Concerns about overcrowding, neglect, and vandalism were not the only major factors behind the establishment of rural cemeteries outside the Northeast. Epidemic disease was a significant reason why some communities, especially in the South, looked to establish extramural burying grounds. Yellow fever had abated in the North in the aftermath of the 1822 epidemic that caused New Yorkers to ban intramural burial, but the disease continued to wreak havoc with intermittent epidemics throughout most of the rest of the century in a number of southern port cities. In Charleston, where residents had argued since the late 1830s about the potentially negative health ramifications of perpetuating churchyard burials, the announcement of the formation of the Magnolia Cemetery Company was met with general favor. As the *Charleston Courier* noted, "An extra-mural place of sepulture has long been a great public want with us, and we rejoice to see it in the act of being supplied."[18] In New Orleans, when the city's first rural cemetery, Cypress Grove Cemetery, became overcrowded by yellow fever victims from the 1852 epidemic, a second cemetery established on the rural cemetery model, Greenwood Cemetery, opened that same year.[19] Writing about the trend for rural cemeteries during the 1850s, authors continued to reinforce the argument that had been made since Jacob Bigelow first developed the idea for Mount Auburn Cemetery. As one writer noted, "The connection of such burial-places with the public health, is a consideration not to be overlooked. When a multitude of bodies are interred side by side, and, as is sometimes the case, one above another, it is impossible but that the surrounding air should be tainted with a noxious effluvia. The atmosphere of a church can hardly be wholesome, when the soil about it and beneath its floors is crowded with the decaying relics of the dead." Reflective of the continued adherence among the medical profession and even the general population to the miasmatic theory of disease and to the notion that the dead specifically posed a health risk to the living, they concluded, "It can not be healthful to visit such places often, nor to live in their immediate neighborhood. Much better is it to commit the remains of our dead to the fresh earth, where the pure winds blow, and amid flowers and verdure."[20]

The 1830s had been an era of experimentation with the new rural cemeteries, a period of trial and error in terms of landscape design and, more importantly, ways to manage and police the cemetery and those who traversed its paths. By the beginning of the next decade, virtually every rural cemetery had its list of policies and procedures, rules for lot holders, regulations concerning visitors, and regularly published pamphlets or booklets with reports from trustees that included matters concerning the history and development of each cemetery, challenges faced by managers and subscribers, and significant burials and monuments, as well as exhaustive lists of lot holders and burials. In short, the foundation had been laid so that during the 1840s, the rural cemetery as a firmly established model could easily be replicated with modifications dictated by local priorities, tastes, and, of course, topography. The cemeteries regarded as the principal models were considered so different from each other while still embodying the ideal of what a rural cemetery was meant to accomplish for its community—observers felt that Mount Auburn best reflected the wild sublimity of seemingly untouched nature, while Laurel Hill, a much smaller rural cemetery, embodied the picturesque, and Green-Wood, the largest of the nation's rural cemeteries, was impressive for the sheer vastness of its landscape—that the very term "rural cemetery" was ultimately a fluid concept. The result was the establishment across the nation of burying grounds labeled by their proprietors as "rural cemeteries" that were vastly different in size, terrain, landscaping, and flora, but unified by the desire to have an expansive and picturesque burying ground where lot holders owned and controlled their burial real estate, and that represented the neighboring citizens' cultural progress.

Since rural cemeteries were nonsectarian, no one was barred from interment on account of religious denomination.[21] Race, of course, was another matter altogether, and there was no consistent pattern regarding policies of racial inclusion or exclusion—such issues were entirely local in nature and even varied according to whether the rural cemeteries were established by privately held corporations or were municipal ventures. Further, there was no simple North/South dichotomy in terms of racist or antiracist burial policies. Mount Auburn, Allegheny, and Albany Rural Cemeteries neither barred non-white burials nor had segregated sections within those cemeteries, while Green-Wood Cemetery in Brooklyn maintained a segregated "colored" section, and Philadelphia's Laurel Hill Cemetery barred Black burials altogether (see chapter 3). Because Black Philadelphians were barred from Laurel Hill, in 1849 they established and buried their dead in the privately owned Lebanon Cemetery in South Philadelphia and Olive Cemetery in West Philadelphia. At the time of its operation, Olive Cemetery was one of the largest African American–owned enterprises, and the donor of the land for the cemetery, Black businessman Stephen Smith, also established the Home for Aged and Infirm Colored Persons adjacent to the burying ground.[22]

Even in the slave South, there were no universal patterns for burial according to race. At Frankfort Cemetery in Kentucky and Elmwood Cemetery in Memphis, cemetery trustees had established policies to allow for the burial of free persons of color and enslaved African Americans. Of course, as Angelika Krüger-Kahloula has observed in her analysis of racial segregation in American cemeteries, "The categories of caste and class that affect the residential patterns of the living also touch the homes of the dead."[23] According to the original deed for Frankfort Cemetery, Lot no. 1 in the rear of the cemetery, in what became known as the Glenns Creek section, was established as "a burial place for Slaves and persons of Colour and none are to be buried therein but such as actually die within the town limits or are the slaves of lot owners or of citizens of the town." Despite Frankfort Cemetery's eventual desegregation, the Glenns Creek section remains a central location even today for the burial of people of color in Frankfort.[24] In a history of Elmwood Cemetery published in 1874 for lot holders, the cemetery trustees noted with pride the liberal attitude of the institution with regard to Black burials: "Prior to the enactment of social equality laws by the Federal Congress, even in 1857, the managers and stockholders of Elmwood assented to the interment of colored people within the Cemetery. A 'section' was set apart for use and occupation by colored people exclusively; and it was further declared, by a special resolution of the managers, that colored people should not be buried in any other portion, or private lot, of the Cemetery."[25] At Bellefontaine Cemetery in St. Louis, no separate section was created for the burials of people of color, free or enslaved, but a number of white lot holders maintained the enslaver-enslaved relationship even in death as they opted to bury certain "beloved" servants within their family plots.[26]

With the exception of Cave Hill Cemetery in Louisville, whose governing documents specified that burial was strictly reserved "for the white race," most southern rural cemetery regulations contained no specific language that either barred or included African Americans for either burial or visitation.[27] This was likely because no such language was considered necessary in the first place—prevailing laws and custom already dictated what African Americans could and could not do and where they could and could not go within their local communities. In Richmond, for instance, local ordinances passed during the 1830s and 1850s regulated Black funerals held within the city. Richmond already contained several burial places established for free and enslaved African Americans by the time Hollywood Cemetery was dedicated as an exclusively elite white institution—the Burial Ground for Negroes (aka the African Burial Ground), established in the mid-eighteenth century; the potter's field, established in 1814 alongside the Hebrew Cemetery; Phoenix Cemetery, a reform-style cemetery established in 1815 by the Burying Ground Society of the Free People of Color of Richmond; the Second African Burial Ground, set aside by the city on Shockoe Hill in 1816; a private cemetery established in 1832 by Robert Smith, a free Black merchant, informally known as Smith Cemetery; and Union Burial Ground, established in 1848 by the Union Burial Ground Society. Building upon the success of Hollywood Cemetery, the city of Richmond established a second rural cemetery, Oakwood Cemetery, as a municipal burying ground in 1854 that *did* include a section for African Americans. Indeed, at Oakwood, African Americans were the first to be interred there beginning in 1855, while middle-class and elite whites shortly thereafter began to purchase lots once the landscaping for the white sections was finished. And although it was not created until 1891, Evergreen Cemetery represented Black Richmond's counterpart to Hollywood, intended to be a beautiful burial ground for the city's emerging Black middle-class designed on the rural cemetery model.[28]

The situation for free people of color was similar elsewhere, with burial in parish churchyards and the formation of Black burial societies being the most common trends. In Baltimore until the 1840s, for example, most of the free Black population was buried in their church burial grounds. In 1851 a group of men purchased part of the land owned by Thomas Burgan Jr. and established Laurel Cemetery, which functioned as the rural cemetery for Baltimore's free Black population.[29] Following the cemetery's consecration, *The Sun* (Baltimore) reported on the universal approval of the new cemetery by "the authorities of the State, who have incorporated the company," and declared that Laurel Cemetery would "not fail to exercise a moral influence, affording as it does a pleasant and safe place of resort for the colored population."[30] The language here is telling, for not only would Laurel Cemetery be, like other rural cemeteries, a place of retreat for visitors, but it would also be a safe outdoor space owned and controlled by African Americans for their own use. For the most part, throughout the antebellum period, the number of rural cemeteries established specifically by and for African Americans remained comparatively few in number, largely due to prevailing social and legal restrictions, even for free people of color, and many of the urban burying grounds designated explicitly for the burial of free and enslaved African Americans—including Lebanon and Olive Cemeteries in Philadelphia and Laurel Cemetery in Baltimore—would eventually fall prey to eradication from overcrowding and urban development in the twentieth century.

For elite white populations, however, there were virtually no social or legal restrictions that stood in the way of establishing expansive cities of the dead. In some instances, the land purchased for the development of a rural cemetery was truly vast when compared to the postage stamp–sized plots of land designated for churchyards and older public burying grounds. Among the largest of the new crop of rural cemeteries, which was touted by its promoters and visitors as reflective of the city's rapid development, was Spring Grove in Cincinnati. The original cemetery committee purchased the Garrard Farm in 1844, constituting about 166 acres and located roughly four miles from the city. As noted in an account of the cemetery published in 1849, "This ground presents every variety of landscape, very beautifully diversified with hill and dale, forest, lake, and lawn, and running brook, while the soil is admirably adapted to the purposes of sepulture. It is sufficient in extent to accommodate a great population for many generations, and remote enough from the city not to be disturbed by its extension."[31] Like many of its counterparts elsewhere, Spring Grove quickly superseded the city's older churchyards and burying grounds as the principal burial location for Cincinnatians, and with the cemetery company's success with selling lots and the general popularity of the site, further land was purchased that increased the cemetery's size such that by the early 1850s, it encompassed 217 acres, making it one of the largest rural cemeteries in the nation.[32] Lot holders quickly erected costly monuments and tombs, which added to the cosmopolitanism of the city and reflected the wealth of its inhabitants. By 1852, there were "220 monuments; 300 head stones; 245 inclosed lots; [and] 12 private vaults." Some of the monuments erected by then were incredibly costly by midcentury standards, with one costing an estimated $9,000 and others in the $2,000–3,000 range (in today's dollars, the $9,000 monument would be the equivalent of $332,309, a truly extraordinary expenditure).[33] In addition to the cemetery's display of the wealth of the city's inhabitants, Spring Grove's promoters saw in their institution "a testimony of the moral and mental progress" of their city in the modern age, as "impressive as is the enslavement of steam and electricity to our physical progress."[34] This

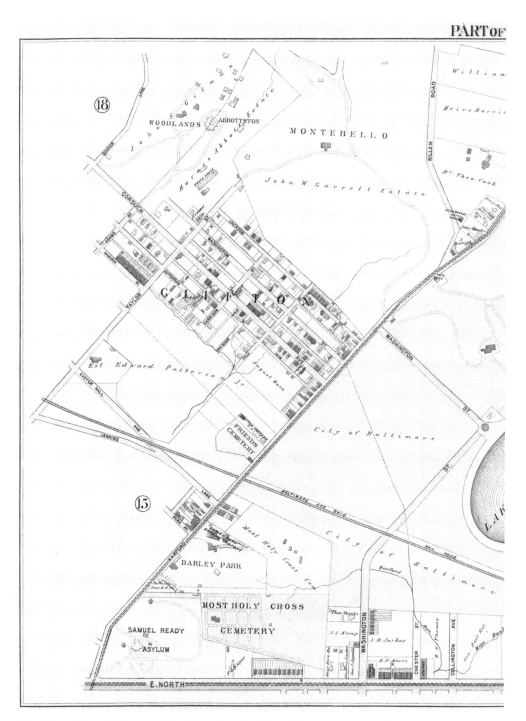

"1896 Map of Laurel Cemetery from Bromley Atlas," *Laurel Cemetery Memorial Project.*
(Philadelphia: G. W. Bromley and Co., 1896; accessed February 14, 2023,
https://laurelcemetery.omeka.net/items/show/19)

20

Scale 300 feet to the Inch

Daniels

Adam G. Erdman

Idreon

ERDMAN ROAD

John K. Garrett Estate

MAYFIELD

Clark

ROAD

Samuel Richmond

A. G. Erdman

CITY LINE

James Simpson

John Dunn

A. G. Erdman

A. G. Erdman

George M. Lawler

AVE.

CLIFTON PARK

City of Baltimore

George Brehm Ave.

ICE POND

George Brehm

JEWISH CEMETERY

ST. VINCENT CEM.

Francis White

LAKE CLIFTON

ROAD

BOUNDARY

EASTERN LANE

H. Gray
J & R Buchwald
Chas. Sergyel

LAUREL CEMETERY

HEBREW CEMETERY

H. C. Logemann

Francis White

George Ramming

BELT LINE

BELAIR

SINCLAIR

Ren

LANE

LONEYS

SINCLAIR

BALTIMORE CEMETERY

AVE.

8

observation is noteworthy, for while the rural cemetery reflected midcentury Americans' desire for natural spaces from which they could escape the noises and smells of the urbanizing and industrializing environment for an afternoon, it was by no means considered by contemporaries to be an anti-modernist institution. Rather, it was quite the contrary. The development of the rural cemetery as a progressive institution where Americans could model the best approaches to the care for and memorialization of the dead and the adoption of new technologies with which to conquer the natural world were ultimately two sides of the same coin.

Despite the enthusiasm by cemetery companies for the adoption of the rural cemetery as a mark of urban progress, there were, in some cities, substantial hurdles to overcome to gain public acceptance of the new burial landscapes, including resistance to abandoning traditional modes of sepulture. In Charleston, for instance, the movement to establish a rural cemetery dated to 1839, when Mayor Henry Pinckney, observing that the city's burying grounds had become overfilled to the point that they threatened the health of residents, called for the creation of a new extramural burial space. It took until the late 1840s for the Magnolia Cemetery Company to form and until 1850 to dedicate the new cemetery.[35] While Magnolia was created in the interest of public health and in the hope that it would become the city's preeminent burying ground, its promoters faced stiff resistance from the local churches, each of which buried the dead from their congregations. Even after Magnolia's dedication, local churches continued to fight against city officials' efforts to ban churchyard burials in favor of burying the city's dead strictly within the grounds of Magnolia Cemetery, and the issue came to a head in the aftermath of the 1858 yellow fever epidemic. In 1859, representatives from the city's First Baptist Church refuted the claim that churchyard burials exacerbated the epidemics and pointed to the increased number of burials in Magnolia as mitigating any problems of overcrowding. Reflecting the problematic class dynamics involved as well, these resolutions urged officials to consider "the convenience of the poor, to whom the proposed measure would greatly increase the expense of burials."[36] Magnolia Cemetery did include "two *public* or *general* burial lots," but the prices ranged from ten to fifteen dollars (depending on whether one wanted to erect a headstone), an impossible sum for the poor and indigent.[37] The petitioners prevailed over the city council proposal, and, as such, churchyards remained in direct competition with Magnolia Cemetery for interments. Given the devotion of most parishioners to their church-affiliated burying grounds,

Magnolia's promoters were challenged in their efforts to make their institution the foremost location for the city's dead. As noted by Thomas J. Brown, "Under these circumstances, Magnolia made limited early progress toward matching the churchyards as a repository of community memory."[38] It would ultimately take a variety of factors, including positive press and travelers' accounts, as well as securing burials of notable figures, to turn the tide of public opinion and make Magnolia the most attractive and in-demand location for the interment of elite Charlestonians.

In Richmond, resistance to the proposed location for Hollywood Cemetery became so fierce that it nearly killed the venture altogether. Elsewhere across the country, cemetery companies sought to find the perfect balance in the distance of their cemeteries from the urban centers—usually three to four miles in the Northeast and the Midwest, closer in the case of cities in the South, where the rural cemetery was regarded as an integrated part of the process of urban expansion in which ease of access was a priority. Cemetery companies would scout sites that might be ideal for burial as well as for planting, landscaping, and, of course, offering optimal views of the surrounding countryside or urban landscape for visitors. Choosing as their location a portion of land overlooking the James River, the Hollywood Cemetery Company purchased the property for their burial ground in 1847, but the Virginia state legislature refused to pass an act of incorporation until 1856.[39] Influential Norfolk lawyer Peter Porthress Mayo, who owned a tract of land adjoining the western edge of the proposed cemetery, claimed the new burying ground would ruin his investment. As Mary Mitchell has illustrated, Mayo's opposition to Hollywood was largely out of self-interest, but "political considerations also played a part," as he belonged to the Whig Party, whereas many of Hollywood's subscribers were Democrats.[40]

To persuade the legislature to permit the incorporation of Hollywood Cemetery in the face of opposition driven by Mayo, company president Thomas H. Ellis issued a statement in January 1849—six months before the cemetery's formal dedication—in which he explained, "A number of citizens of Richmond, having visited the beautiful cemeteries of the northern cities, and perceived how much they contributed to adorn the environs of those cities, while they afforded a secluded and safe depository for the dead, conceived the idea of providing a similar cemetery here." Acknowledging sources of opposition to the project, Ellis admitted, "It is objected that the location of the cemetery is such as to retard the growth of the city in that direction; that it will injuriously affect the health of the citizens; that it will prejudice the city water works; and that it is a 'Yankee' speculation in graves." This last point is telling, especially given the fact that several of the initial backers of the cemetery were New England transplants. To mitigate these concerns, Ellis furnished letters from Henry Hardesty Jr., president of Green Mount Cemetery in Baltimore, B. W. Richards, president of Laurel Hill Cemetery in Philadelphia, and J. A. Perry, comptroller of Green-Wood Cemetery in Brooklyn. Hardesty attested to the quick public acceptance of Green Mount, while Perry explained the positive effects of his cemetery on the surrounding community. For his part, Richards at Laurel Hill pointed out that "rural Cemeteries are now so numerous" throughout the Northeast "that one hears with surprise of any objection to them."[41]

Despite Ellis's appeals, the legislature persisted in its refusal to incorporate Hollywood Cemetery. The negative vote by the legislature, however, was not due to any significant opposition to the idea of rural cemeteries. Two weeks later, "the same assembly incorporated the Mount Wood Cemetery, a private joint-stock company in Wheeling, Virginia (now in West Virginia)." On top of this, back in 1844, rural cemeteries in Fredericksburg, Winchester, and Fairmont (now in West Virginia) had also received charters.[42] It was thus eminently clear that the problem lay in Richmond itself, where Hollywood Cemetery revealed the city's political sectionalism.

Opposition notwithstanding, this did not halt the dedication of the cemetery or impede the company's efforts to spark public interest in purchasing lots. Rather, the greatest threat to the cemetery's survival was the extensive campaign undertaken by the *Richmond Whig* to denounce the cemetery's location and rally public outcry. In direct competition with the *Richmond Enquirer* and *Richmond Republican*, both of which supported Hollywood, the rivalry between the papers meant that Hollywood's "fate became trapped in the crossfire."[43] No sooner was Hollywood formally dedicated in June 1849 than the *Whig* began a smear campaign against the cemetery planners' choice of location, in the hopes that city residents would not purchase plots and thus force the cemetery to close. "We object to this Cemetery, on account of its location, and the numerous disadvantages which are certain to arise," the *Whig* wrote in July. "It is directly in the path of the advancing population of the city, and now but a short distance beyond the corporation line, in a very few years, it will be in the very centre of population. There is no hope for it. There it lies, an impassable obstacle in the path of progress, and improvement must either come to a dead halt or go around." Where other cities, like Cincinnati, regarded the rural cemetery as a mark of progress, here it was denounced as an impediment. "There is room for almost unlimited manufacturing establishments," the *Whig* declared, but with Hollywood situated where it was, the "advantages which it presents will be absolutely destroyed—the property itself rendered entirely unproductive—by the prosecution of this scheme."[44]

The *Whig* took great pains in expressing as genuinely (and dramatically) as possible its concerns about the city's expansion and industrial development, but, ironically, chief among the newspaper's stated objections was the potential negative health ramifications of the new cemetery. Where cities elsewhere regarded rural cemeteries as a solution to burial overcrowding and a prophylactic against epidemic disease arising from miasmas, the *Whig* took the position of strenuously arguing that Hollywood would *create* a public health crisis because of its location. "What will our worthy citizens think," its editors railed, "when they are told that this Cemetery lies on a hill, directly overhanging the Pump House, which supplies this reservoir?"[45] Persisting in this line of argument throughout 1849 and 1850, the paper's editors deployed increasingly maudlin language reminiscent of what one might find in a tale of terror by Edgar Allan Poe. In late March 1850 the paper concluded a front-page article by stating that "the bare idea of drinking water impregnated with drainings from dead bodies is too disgusting to be endured for a moment."[46] About a week later, in a lengthy front-page essay appealing for public outcry to close the cemetery, the *Whig* went even further and railed, "In 30 years the city of Richmond will, in all probability, be spread all around this burial-ground. Our citizens will then inhale the noxious vapours which will issue from the receptacles of the dead—and in the meantime we, of this generation, shall have the agreeable task of daily consuming in our water, tea and coffee and grog, the putrescent oozings of the illustrious defunct."[47]

Hollywood's proprietors ultimately caved to the pressure from the *Whig* articles and responded by "disposing of an extensive section of their grounds [near the waterworks], large enough to remove every shadow of cavil and prejudice on the part of the most bigoted opponent of the cemetery," as reported by the more supportive (and Democrat-owned) *Richmond Enquirer*.[48] The *Enquirer* also published the cemetery company's report of March 26, 1850, which included details about Hollywood's proprietors, all of whom were men of standing within the community.[49] The publishers of the *Whig*, perhaps hoping to avoid charges of libel and calling the named individuals "our personal friends," reaffirmed once more their opposition to the cemetery but noted they would no longer pursue this line of argument, thus leaving it in the hands of "the Common Council . . . to take measures to protect the health of the city by suppressing this nuisance."[50] Without the regular public criticisms generated by the *Whig*, opposition to the cemetery's existence dissipated. As the *Enquirer* reported in 1852, "We are glad to know that the unfounded prejudices, once entertained against Hollywood, have wasted away."[51]

Even as these scattered hurdles were overcome, southern rural cemetery promoters discovered the unanticipated challenge of attracting lot holders from beyond the city, especially those from plantation districts. Historically, southern burial grounds were often in far worse condition than even the most overcrowded northern sites due to "the decentralization of the population" and "a general replacement of community burial grounds by individual family plots on private land."[52] Isolated family plots located on farms were common in the Northeast as well, but on southern farms and plantations such plots tended not to survive changes in landownership. Edward P. Humphrey lamented this particular issue in his address at Cave Hill Cemetery: "The plantations, in this region, have been cultivated less than three quarters of a century; and yet in passing from the possession of one proprietor to that of another, the family burial place has, in some instances, gone into neglect and become covered with rank vegetation; or perhaps, the fences have been removed, and the place burned over and 'turned out,' as the expression is, into the common field. Soon even the fact, that the dead are buried there, will be forgotten forever, unless the spade shall accidentally reveal their crumbling relics."[53] The new rural cemeteries were intended to rectify this problem by offering rural inhabitants a large, centralized place for burial where multiple generations of families could bury their dead without fear of future accidental desecration. Champions of the new institutions felt confident that people from both near and far would be inclined to purchase burial lots. For example, in praising the newly established Elmwood Cemetery in 1854, the *Memphis Daily Eagle and Enquirer* contended, "There are, doubtless, many of our readers at a distance, as well in the Interior as on the River, who would become owners of lots in such a Cemetery here, if they knew that there was a guaranty of its affording them a secure place of repose for their dead. Knowing that the auspices, under which 'Elmwood Cemetery' is established, afford such a guaranty, we have designed to serve them by this notice of it."[54]

What rural cemetery proprietors did not anticipate, however, was that

Family Burying Ground, ca. 1840, oil on canvas. (Courtesy National Gallery of Art)

many rural inhabitants simply did not embrace the idea. Similar to Charlestonians' affinity for their church burying grounds, most white rural southerners preferred burial close to home rather than in distant, suburban cemeteries. The *Southern Literary Messenger* lamented the ongoing practice in Virginia as a grievous problem, the results of which could be observed, despite the establishment of Hollywood Cemetery in Richmond: "In wandering over the State of Virginia, we have been struck most painfully with the fact that . . . there is no abiding place for the living or the dead. The father plants and the stranger to his blood and family waters. His descendants flee the land of their birth, and are found in distant regions. Change is the order of the day with us, and the graves of our relatives are overgrown with briars and noxious weeds, and the ploughshare sooner or later destroys all vestige of the spot where they rest from their labors." Approving the establishment of Hollywood and the other "great and beautiful republics of the dead," the *Messenger* promoted legislative action for the establishment of permanent cemeteries in each county, but such measures were never undertaken—rural cemeteries remained, for the most part, ventures undertaken by private individuals who worked collaboratively and formed incorporated cemetery companies.[55] Generating interest from rural inhabitants in purchasing burial plots remained a struggle beyond the antebellum period as well. As late as 1875, Hollywood Cemetery's trustees were directing particular efforts at securing "country families" to purchase burial plots and to so avoid "using their own fields, which . . . are so liable to be ploughed over by subsequent proprietors." The trustees expressed surprise, however, that despite the improved accessibility of Richmond from the countryside "by rail and water," such purchases "have not been more numerous."[56] Northeastern rural cemetery promoters did not have to grapple with these problems, because smaller towns beyond the major metropolitan areas throughout the region simply established their own new cemeteries; by contrast, the failure of southern cemetery proprietors to entice rural inhabitants to purchase lots further entrenched the image of the rural cemetery in the South as an indelibly elite urban institution.

Even as some cemeteries faced challenges from various sectors of the community—whether from the local churches, from the press, or in their struggle to attract lot holders—once established and open to the public, they quickly became sources of immense pride for the cities with which they were associated as well as symbols of elite cosmopolitanism and urban progress. For each cemetery, its layout and design, the notability of the dead interred within, the genteel taste exhibited by the monuments that dotted the landscape, and the variety of trees and flowers (both native and introduced from foreign countries) all reflected back upon the community as a whole and their place within the national culture. Baltimore's Green Mount Cemetery, situated on the northern boundary of the city on land that had been part of the country estate of wealthy merchant Robert Oliver, was established by its proprietors in the hopes that it would "grow to be an object of value and interest to this community, and honourable to the state."[57] At that cemetery's dedication, John Pendleton Kennedy observed the positive impact of Mount Auburn and Laurel Hill on their communities and imagined what these effects would mean for Baltimore's residents now that they had their own sanctuary for the dead. There is, he asserted, "scarce an inhabitant of Boston or Philadelphia who does not testify to the pride with which he regards the public cemetery in his neighborhood." Illustrative of the competitive spirit that would become a hallmark feature of the rural cemetery movement, Kennedy stated that Green Mount would "advantageously compare" to its northeastern counterparts, being "more accessible than Mount Auburn" and "more spacious than that in the neighborhood of Philadelphia. . . . And in point of scenery, both as respects the improvement of the grounds, and the adjacent country," Green Mount "is, at least, equal to either." Kennedy concluded, "I know not where the eye may find more pleasing landscapes than those which surround us."[58]

The relationship between cemetery and city identity remained clear at the consecration of Chicago's Rosehill Cemetery two decades later. Chicago experienced "explosive growth" during the 1830s, when during that time its population increased twentyfold, "the value of its land grew by a factor of three thousand, and boosters began to speak of it as a future metropolis." As Chicago became the terminus for the eastern *and* western rail lines by midcentury, city leaders labored to promote their home as the fulcrum between East and West.[59] The Reverend Noah Hunt Schenck's address in 1859 reinforced this image of the city's position as gateway to the expanding West as he declared,

> At the east of us and so near at hand lies the lake [Michigan], that its waters become a very important feature in the landscape. At the west the prairie spreads away to the setting sun, now dotted with the signs of a dense population where but a few years ago the Buffalo was monarch of the grassy plain. . . . Thus the life of the city, the grandeur of the lake and the prairie, the association of the Indian and the Buffalo, the beauty of these native oaks, and the topography and composition of the ground all unite in the pledge which is this day made that Rosehill shall ere long be a wilderness of beauty.[60]

It was undoubtably because the northeastern cemeteries had served as the initial inspiration that so many writers and orators drew comparisons between the newer and older rural cemeteries when they made such declarations of superiority. The early history of Richmond's Hollywood Cemetery, before its directors faced the challenges to their venture posed by the *Whig*, is illustrative of this trend. While visiting Boston in the spring of 1847, Richmond businessmen Joshua J. Fry and William H. Haxall toured Mount Auburn. Inspired by their experience, Fry and Haxall returned to Richmond to garner support to establish their own rural cemetery. After making appeals to silversmith William Mitchell Jr. and Isaac Davenport, a senior partner in the firm of Davenport and Allen, the four men purchased Harvie's Woods, a plot of land that "bordered several sites already popular with those escaping the bustle of the city, including Clarke's Springs, the grounds of Major John Clarke's estate, and Belvidere, the former home of William Byrd III."[61] In August, the men organized a board of directors, whose members included Thomas H. Ellis, president of the James River and Kanawha Canal Company, and New England transplants James Henry Gardner, a shoe merchant, and Horace L. Kent, a wholesale dry goods merchant. In February 1848, Philadelphia architect John Notman furnished the design for the proposed cemetery as well as its name—Hollywood Cemetery, due to the abundance of holly trees on the grounds. At the cemetery's formal dedication on June 25, 1849, Oliver P. Baldwin declared that, in comparison to its counterparts in the Northeast, "a more beautiful place could not have been selected for a tabernacle for the dead."[62] Later, Hollywood Cemetery president Thomas H. Ellis concluded in his first annual report that the board of directors was "satisfied that in Holly-Wood the citizens of Richmond have the site of a Rural Cemetery of unsurpassed beauty; and they have set before them as their object the sentiment appropriately expressed by Washington Irving, that 'the grave should be surrounded by everything that can inspire tenderness and veneration for the dead, or that might win the living to virtue.'"[63] In the *Southern Literary Messenger*, the South's counterpart to the *North American Review*, a description of Hollywood in 1856 claimed that "this is, or will be, one of the most beautiful [cemeteries] to be found in any country."[64]

Writers, orators, and cemetery trustee reports all reflected similar sentiments about their respective rural cemeteries as sources of local pride and beautiful attractions that enhanced both the appeal to and the reputation of their cities. The *Baltimore Clipper* reported with approval in 1841 that Green Mount Cemetery would, "ere long, become one of the most charming resorts in our country" and that it was a place of which "our city may be proud."[65] *The Sun* (Baltimore) likewise exulted, "The improvements that are being daily made at Green Mount, will in time make it one of the most delightful resorts of the kind in the world."[66] Frankfort Cemetery, located on the southeastern edge of Kentucky's capital city and overlooking the Kentucky River immediately to the west, became regarded within a short time of its establishment as "The Westminster Abbey of this Commonwealth."[67] Linden Grove Cemetery (originally called the Cincinnati and Covington Cemetery), established by the Western Baptist Theological Institute in Covington, Kentucky, in 1843, was not a rural cemetery that garnered national attention, and yet the *Cincinnati Enquirer* declared that with the whole cemetery "laid out in the best modern style," it was "one of the most inviting burial places in the Western country."[68] Writers to the *Detroit Free Press*, having visited the city's Elmwood Cemetery in 1847, declared that it "bids fair to be equal in beauty and order to anything of the kind in the country" and that the "site possesses natural beauties equal to any of our rural Cemeteries" elsewhere in the nation.[69] Thomas M. Howe, president of Allegheny Cemetery's board of managers, concluded in his first report in 1848 that in the work that had already been accomplished by the cemetery's architect, John Chislett, "a foundation has been laid, on which a liberal and generous public will rear a mighty 'city of the dead.'"[70] When the editors of the *Pittsburgh Gazette* visited Allegheny Cemetery in 1850, they declared that the "grounds are the finest in America," having become "the wonder and delight of all visitors, especially of intelligent strangers, who have had an opportunity of examining the beautiful Cemeteries of the East, such as Mt. Auburn, Greenwood, and Laurel Hill."[71] In Charleston, the *Courier* boasted in 1853 that while Magnolia Cemetery was as "yet in its infancy," it would "ere long, vie, in every charm and beauty, natural and artificial, with its predecessors and models of the North."[72] And in Tennessee, the *Memphis Daily Eagle and Enquirer* published its approval of the city's Elmwood Cemetery in 1854, anticipating that "in ten years, it will vie with any of the older [rural] Cemeteries of the Union, in beauty of locality, and will be a credit and an honor to our city."[73]

The new rural cemeteries also played a symbolic role in their relationship to their respective cities. Oliver Baldwin, for instance, stressed the superior views of Richmond from the summit of Holly Wood Hill within Hollywood Cemetery. In his remarks, Baldwin painted a vision of a landscape unrivaled by any other in the nation—one that included "a wide expanse of country glowing with rich verdure" as well as "the stream [James River] . . . seized for manufacturing purposes." From the cemetery, one could see "that most beautiful city of the South, so happily called the 'City of Gardens,' in full view of this Garden of Graves."[74] At the dedication of Magnolia Cemetery in 1850, Charles Fraser observed, "Nor can we be indifferent to the prospects which attract the eye on every side—Cooper river pursuing its quiet course towards the ocean, and the ocean blending its dim line with the mists of the horizon; the harbor, with Sullivan's Island and Forts Moultrie and Sumpter [*sic*] in the distance; the approach and departure of vessels; and last, though not least, Charleston itself, with its lofty steeples and its forest of masts in beautiful perspective."[75] Each cemetery was itself a gem to be added to the diadem of any city, but many cemetery planners were likewise strategic in their endeavors to choose locations that would provide visitors with the best possible perspective of the city and environs. Not to be outdone by communities farther east, the proprietors of Bellefontaine Cemetery in St. Louis laid out their city of the dead "upon a more enlarged and liberal plan than any heretofore adopted for a similar purpose in this country." The *St. Louis Intelligencer* declared, "The location of the Cemetery grounds is beautiful, in the extreme. They afford scope for every variety and extent of improvement and decoration. They lie about five miles north of the Court House, and embrace about one hundred and thirty-eight acres. The drive to the Cemetery will ultimately be one of the most interesting leading from the city."[76] In Louisville, Edward Humphrey was more modest in his address at the dedication of Cave Hill Cemetery and offered humble praise for the diverse and unique qualities of the landscape encompassing the new burial place. "If it be wanting in the elements of grandeur, it is rich in those of rural beauty. The green meadow, the fields of waving grain, the cultivated garden, the homes of our friends half revealed amid the foliage, the sunny lawn, the deep old wood, the shadowy cave, the weary highway, and the gushing and redundant fountain, all are here."[77] All were established as rural cemeteries, and all were designed with the impulse to highlight the best and most attractive qualities of the surrounding landscape and cities with which they were affiliated. No two rural cemeteries were alike, and yet they were all unified in the desire of their promoters to exhibit the cultivated taste and "advancing civilization" of the era.[78]

In addition to the importance of the geographical relationship between the rural cemeteries and their cities, there was the further significance vested in their function as repositories for the notable dead, an element that proprietors believed would bind communities to these spaces in perpetuity. In his consecration address for Cincinnati's Spring Grove Cemetery in 1845, the Honorable John McLean declared, "Within a century to come, what diversity of character will meet within this field of death! Here may be interred the mighty dead, who, in life, made a deep and lasting impression on the age in which they lived—who lived more for the world and their country, than themselves. These being honored in life, will be honored in death, by the grateful sense of their country. And every one who passes by will pause to read the inscriptions on their tombs." As McLean noted, however, not all persons interred would be cherished because of their great achievements. "A

Entrance to Cave Hill Cemetery, Louisville, Kentucky. (Detroit Publishing Co., ca. 1906, courtesy Library of Congress Prints and Photographs Division)

great majority will not be thus known to fame. But they will not be the less dear to their kindred and friends, who will cherish a remembrance of their virtues."[79] The trustees of Detroit's Elmwood Cemetery echoed this sentiment in their *Second Report* of 1857: "Elmwood has already become to our citizens hallowed ground. Here lie the mortal remains of our best and noblest and truest of both sexes, and thither will be borne, ere long, all that is earthly of those who now address you."[80] The underlying message in this exhortation was that while the bones of the illustrious (and not so illustrious) dead of earlier generations lay moldering in churchyards and burying grounds that were overcrowded and soon would be overrun by the city's development, those interred in the local rural cemetery would remain untouched and protected forever. That was at least the intent by those who established and supported rural cemetery development, for like the civilizations of antiquity, they sought to build institutions that would stand the test of time. As Simon Perkins and J. D. Commins, president and secretary of the Akron Rural Cem-

etery (later renamed Glendale Cemetery) in Ohio, wrote, "We are not building for a year or century, but for all future time. And shall we not beautify and
embellish these hallowed precincts, where sleep the loved remains of those
whose persons were once so dear to us? Where we ourselves must also soon
find our own resting place, to wake no more forever."[81]

Of course, many of those who established and managed the new rural
cemeteries were not satisfied with creating institutions that would only be
cherished locally; they also sought to fashion hallowed cities of the dead
vested with national significance that would further elevate the reputation of
their city. For many, rural cemeteries were a national cultural phenomenon
that were likewise linked to the cultivation of a modern American national
identity. The most profound declaration of any community's uniqueness
and importance to the national historical narrative manifested through
the focused activities of several cities and states to use their rural cemeteries as repositories for the nation's "special dead," that is, their civic saints.[82]
In some instances, rural cemeteries garnered national repute because they
happened to be the burial place of choice upon the deaths of important contemporary figures—such was the case for Lexington Cemetery in Kentucky,
where statesman Henry Clay was laid to rest when he died in 1852. As noted
by Sarah Purcell, Clay's remains "functioned as civic relics as a fascinated
and reverent public looked upon and read about his body." Prior to burial,
the public had the opportunity to view Clay's body on a tour, his body
treated as a relic in such a way that it "anticipated the same kind of treatment that would be given to Abraham Lincoln after his assassination more
than a decade later." The corpse itself symbolized national unity through the
shared grief felt by Americans, as well as sectionalism and conflict, as it was
Clay who had been the principal architect of the Compromise of 1850. The
actual funeral, held on July 10, 1852, drew an estimated crowd of between
thirty thousand and one hundred thousand people and was "the largest cer-
emonial occasion ever witnessed in Lexington" to that point in time.[83] To
further honor the nation's great compromiser, the Clay Monument Association formed shortly thereafter and raised funds for the construction of an
enormous Egyptian Revival mausoleum surmounted by a shaft atop which
stood a larger-than-life statue of Clay. In a moment of historical irony, the
monument was completed and dedicated with great fanfare locally and in
the national press on the Fourth of July in 1861, and the cemetery became a
pilgrimage site for soldiers and civilians alike throughout the Civil War and
beyond.[84]

Elsewhere, reburial campaigns of important figures from American history became the principal method by which communities used their rural cemeteries to stake their claim to national importance. As one proponent of reburial in Baltimore exhorted in 1839 before Green Mount's dedication, "These relics are the moral property of the people, that no private claim can bar, and that no apathy should cause us to neglect; they would form a treasure if collected together, of inestimable value, upon which posterity might draw, without consuming; it would be a widow's cruse of holy impulses, forever flowing and forever full." Of the important "Fathers of Maryland" whom this advocate proposed for reburial, two such individuals, War of 1812 general William Henry Winder and poet Edward Coote Pinkney, "whose voices were so often heard in 'fierce extremes' of national vicissitude, and who in the matched conflict of eloquence, 'could raise a mortal to the skies or bring an angel down,'" were ultimately moved to Green Mount Cemetery.[85] In 1857 Charleston celebrated the reinterment in Magnolia Cemetery of the remains of U.S. attorney general Hugh Swinton Legaré, who had died in Boston in 1843 and been buried at Mount Auburn Cemetery without a monument. In this instance, not only did the acquisition of Legaré's remains elevate the reputation of Magnolia Cemetery, but it marked a turning point in the cemetery's fortunes in terms of attracting more Charlestonians to choose Magnolia for their final resting place.[86]

As cities and cemetery managers continued to accumulate the relics of the nation's special dead, the most high-profile reburial campaigns took place in Kentucky and Virginia. In 1845, Kentuckians successfully lobbied for the exhumation and reburial at the newly established Frankfort Cemetery of "those most famous 'Pioneers of the West,'" Daniel Boone and his wife, Rebecca.[87] The Frankfort Cemetery Company sent a committee consisting of Colonel William Boone, Daniel Boone's oldest surviving nephew; Thomas L. Crittenden, a lawyer and future Union Army general; and Philip Swigert, a banker who went on to become mayor of Frankfort in 1849, to retrieve the remains of the Boones from Warren County, Missouri, where "these noble and fearless pioneers" were originally buried.[88] As the *St. Louis New Erie* reported, the representatives from Frankfort met with Boone family descendants who still lived in Missouri, explained why they wanted the remains of Boone and his wife, and received permission to do so. Following the exhumation of what little remained of the Boones (if the bones they exhumed were even those of the Boones at all), Crittenden delivered an address in which he thanked the Boone relatives for allowing the committee to remove to Kentucky what the state considered "a prize of inestimable value."[89]

The reacquisition of the Boones' remains was a point of significant pride for both Frankfort Cemetery and the state of Kentucky, for as *The Commonwealth* (Frankfort, KY) explained, the Boones' "early adventures, indomitable perseverance, unswerving patriotism, and pure and spotless lives, are indissolubly interwoven in the early tradition of our State."[90] The reburial ceremony itself was a grand affair, with businesses closing for the day and all residents of Frankfort encouraged to attend. The elaborate procession featured Boone relatives, aging survivors of the early expeditions into Kentucky led by Boone, including "the first black man who ever trod the soil" of that state, officers and soldiers, members of the cemetery company, politicians from the state and federal governments, fraternal organizations, teachers and local schoolchildren, and the general public "from all the Western and Southern states." In all, it was estimated that about fifteen to twenty thousand people gathered in the cemetery for the event.[91] The presence of the Boones enhanced the national awareness of Frankfort Cemetery as both a tourist attraction and a pilgrimage destination, especially for high-status visitors. General Winfield Scott, for instance, included as part of his 1852 presidential campaign a stop at Frankfort Cemetery to view the graves of the Boones; and while Scott visited Henry Clay's widow at their Ashland estate, General Thomas Lawson of the campaign entourage went to see Clay's grave in Lexington.[92] Cemeteries today continue to draw visitors by advertising the presence of famous corpses, but for twenty-first-century tourists, the monuments above the graves tend to be the focus of attention. By contrast, as the case of the Boones in Frankfort Cemetery and the grave of Henry Clay in Lexington illustrate, the semisacred quality of the bones of the dead were what many considered most important for sanctifying the landscape and drawing crowds—the cornerstone for the Clay monument was not laid until 1857, and the Kentucky state legislature did not make appropriations for the erection of a monument over the bodies of the Boones until 1860, despite a steady stream of visitors to their place of reburial.[93]

The Boone reburial received national press coverage and was justly regarded as an important event expressive of Kentucky's heritage and role in the narrative of westward expansion; even so, the events in Kentucky paled in comparison to the exhumation and reburial of the remains of President James Monroe in 1858 at Richmond's Hollywood Cemetery.[94] This endeavor, which was a collaborative effort between the cemetery's proprietors, city and state leadership, and the state of New York, highlighted Virginians' desire to center their state as crucial in the history of America's development. In her history of Hollywood Cemetery, Mary H. Mitchell explains, "The initial idea to pay tribute to James Monroe on the hundredth anniversary of his birth in 1858 came from a Virginia-turned-New Yorker named Alexander Jones." After Jones made inquiries both to the city of New York and to Virginia's governor, Henry A. Wise, regarding what plans were in place to honor Monroe's centennial, the Virginia General Assembly passed a resolution to appropriate $2,000 for the exhumation and reburial of the former president, whose remains at that time rested in the New York City Marble Cemetery, a public burying ground designed on the reform cemetery model established in 1831 in Manhattan. The plans for the reburial proceeded as a joint effort between New York City and the state of Virginia as a way to honor Monroe's contributions to the nation's founding by returning him to his native soil. Governor Wise agreed "to purchase three triangular lots in the circle reserved for dignitaries" at Hollywood Cemetery for the reburial. This ceremony marked only the first of the governor's far more ambitious plans. He further intended to secure the remains of Thomas Jefferson and James Madison for removal to Hollywood's "Presidential Hill," so that "the three old friends could be reunited." However, the descendants of Jefferson and Madison refused Wise's request, and the additional reburials never transpired as the governor planned.[95]

At the behest of the Monroe family descendants, the exhumation in New York City on July 2 was a relatively quiet affair, undertaken in the early morning hours; by contrast, the president's reburial, which took place on July 5 at Hollywood Cemetery, was an enormous and widely publicized event. On an occasion marked by excessive ovations to American patriotism and national unity, despite the vituperative state of national politics, Governor Wise used the reburial ceremony as an opportunity to declare the solvency of the Union, painting the cooperation between New York and Virginia as symbolic of the state of the nation. Employing dramatic language, Wise declared:

> Thrice grateful are we for this one more binding link in the chain of affection and union. It makes this no funeral, it wails no dirge.—It is an anthem of praise and gladness and glorification. Thank God! that we have lived to this another day of liberty and National Independence, in the bonds only of State amity and union. . . . Who knows this day, this

hour, here around this grave, that New York is of the North and that Virginia is of the South? "The North has given up," and "the South shall not hold back," and they are *one*, even as all the now proud and pre-eminent *thirty-two are one*.[96]

Wise's flamboyant rhetoric aside, the reburial ceremony, which received national attention, effectively sanctified Hollywood Cemetery as a site of national significance and further reinforced Virginia's claim to have played a central part in the history of the Early Republic. With Monroe's physical remains returned to his native soil, the cemetery would then be marketed as a national shrine. Hollywood's proprietors fully understood and promoted the cemetery's role as a symbol of local and national identity by placing a sign over the entrance to the grounds for the Monroe plot that read: "'The Pantheon of departed worth, / The future Mecca of the Old Dominion.'"[97] The great irony was that Hollywood Cemetery indeed eventually became the Mecca of the Old Dominion—and, more broadly, of the South—for its status as a shrine not for the holy relics of the republic but rather for those of the Confederacy (see chapter 5).

In his description of President Monroe's new place of burial, the Richmond correspondent of the *New York Tribune* proclaimed, "Hollywood Cemetery is a very beautiful tract. . . . Like Greenwood and Mount Auburn, this cemetery is everywhere traversed by winding roads and shady footpaths . . . [and] already the area is dotted all over with gleaming monuments."[98] Such a description necessarily reflected the interconnectedness not only of Hollywood, Mount Auburn, and Green Wood but of all the nation's rural cemeteries, north, south, and west, as part of the national rural cemetery movement. As so many orators had already acknowledged in their cemetery dedication addresses, the cultural phenomenon may have been birthed in the Northeast, but it was embraced wherever urbanization occurred. Tied to midcentury impulses to cultivate institutions and practices that would illustrate the progressive development of American society and, more pointedly, the transformations underway in individual communities, rural cemeteries reflected what many Americans hoped were the best features of antebellum culture—taste, refinement, a proper respect for and care of the dead, and an appreciation for landscapes designed according to the principles of beauty as well as function. Simultaneously, the explosive popularity of the rural cemetery model across the nation illustrated the great variability of urban environments and populations beyond the Northeast. Simply put, the motivations to establish rural cemeteries in Baltimore were not the same as those in Charleston or Cincinnati or Louisville; just as there was (and is) no monolithic "American" culture, the rural cemetery was itself a malleable concept that could be adapted anywhere in the nation and still be regarded as an inherently "American" cultural institution reflective of universally shared values.

With the ruptures of secession and civil war, the nation's rural cemeteries, especially those in the South and loyal border states, continued to serve the needs of urban residents who sought respite from the city, and they further became the repositories for the bodies of the soldier dead from both sides of the conflict. The importance placed upon using the cities of the dead as the proper homes for the sacred dead, a principle established during the antebellum period, would carry over in the aftermath of war, as many of the preexisting and new rural cemeteries established during the 1860s would encompass Confederate soldier sections where, in some cases, burials numbered in the thousands, as well as national cemeteries established under the auspices of the federal government. The experiences of war and reconstruction would ultimately have a transformative effect on many of the nation's rural cemeteries, as they became spaces of contest over loyalty and identity where Americans from both the North and the South would shape the public history and public memory of the Civil War era.

"Consecrated in a Nation's Heart"

Rural Cemeteries in Civil War and Reconstruction

"Sometimes I took a Sunday afternoon stroll with Papa to Rose Hill Cemetery at the other end of College Street, a three-mile round trip. Papa, at his conversational and forensic best, would read me the tombstone inscriptions and discourse on the dead with considerable pomp and oratory. This was a wild and wonderful treat on Sunday."[1] This was but one feature of Dolly Blount Lamar's life as a young girl in Reconstruction-era Macon, Georgia, home to the Cotton South's first rural cemetery established in 1840. Born in the late 1860s, Lamar did not experience the Civil War herself, but as a girl she witnessed the efforts of her mother as a leader of the local Ladies' Memorial Association (LMA) to have the bodies of Confederate soldiers from area battlefields reburied at Rose Hill, and she experienced the cemetery as both a pleasure ground and a site for Confederate memory. Established only seventeen years following its city charter, Rose Hill Cemetery was granted its name by the city council in honor of the landscape designer Simri Rose (1799–1869), who oversaw "the clearing out and improvements" of the cemetery grounds along the Ocmulgee River.[2]

Like so many other rural cemeteries established throughout the antebellum period, Rose Hill Cemetery was a symbol of the city's development, and it was regarded as "the pride of Macon."[3] Nevertheless, when the Civil

War ensued, the cemetery came under duress in terms of both maintenance of the landscape and interment of the bodies of Confederate and Union soldiers who died in area hospitals and battlefields. Writing to the *Macon Telegraph* in 1864, one soldier complained bitterly to the editor about the lack of care and attention given to the soldier dead, whose coffins were cheaply made and often not buried until after a day or more exposed to the elements. "The fact is, no man of common decency can visit the 'soldiers burying ground' in Rose Hill Cemetery without having the finer feelings of his nature shocked," declared the writer, who pointed out that it was "not our enemies" whose bodies had thus been treated but "our own noble soldiers— the sons, brothers, husbands of the Confederacy, to whom we owe all of safety and of comfort we now enjoy."[4] As reflected in this soldier's letter, the Civil War did much to shatter traditional patterns of caring for the dead, which involved the proper preparation and viewing of the deceased prior to a funeral involving family and members of the community, followed by burial. Once the war ended in 1865, it then became a priority for communities across the nation to honor those on both sides who had perished in the bloody conflict. Rural cemeteries like Rose Hill were central to this process.

Indeed, the years encompassing the Civil War and Reconstruction proved to be a transformative era for the rural cemetery in America. Those established from the 1830s through the 1850s reflected new developments in taste and aesthetics even as they also responded to the extraordinary needs of society in the face of so much loss of life in four short and devastating years of military conflict. Not only did the nation's rural cemeteries in both the North and the South become repositories for the soldier dead, but they further reflected the major social and political developments that took shape during this time. During the war, rural cemetery managers throughout the country set aside space in their burying grounds for the burial of the soldier dead either out of necessity, as in the case of the South, or as acts of patriotism, as was the trend in the North. In a number of cases, those wartime lots designated strictly for the burial of the Union dead later became national cemeteries, connected to their original host rural cemetery but managed by the federal government. Beginning in 1868, local posts of the Grand Army of the Republic (GAR) along with members of the community ventured out to decorate the soldiers' graves on Memorial Day. National cemeteries also became bastions of racial liberalism, as any soldier who served in the Union army, whether white or in the United States Colored Troops (USCT), was buried equally and, for the most part, without segregated sections.[5] Nevertheless, the racial policies of the nation's rural cemeteries, despite Black emancipation and the vesting of freed people with citizenship and civil rights during Reconstruction, largely remained the same from prior to the war. Many of the federal dead who had been buried in the southern rural cemeteries were disinterred and relocated to the closest national cemetery if it was not already within the grounds of a preexisting rural cemetery. Further, rural cemeteries across the Confederate and loyal border South established lots for the burials and postwar reburials of the Confederate dead. These spaces, separate from the national cemeteries, continued to be cared for by the rural cemeteries, with the individual burials decorated annually in Confederate Decoration Day ceremonies organized by southern LMAs beginning in 1866.[6]

Because so many Union and Confederate soldiers shared burial space within the same rural cemeteries, these burying grounds ultimately became highly contested performative spaces in which civilians, through their care for and decoration of graves, exhibited their loyalty to one side or the other. The city of the dead, which before the Civil War had been regarded as an apolitical, if not an entirely uncontested, social space, through war became politicized *and* contested.[7] Especially in border states such as Kentucky and Maryland, where sympathies were deeply divided, outward shows of loyalty—especially to the Confederacy—illustrated the extent to which civilians were willing to rebuff federal and military dictates against supporting the Southern rebellion.[8] Across the nation, regardless of locality, the presence of the war's dead and the erection of large monuments in the rural cemeteries further enhanced and entrenched community identities, especially with regard to the white South's embrace of the mythology of the Lost Cause. Fundamental to the postwar fashioning of how communities regarded themselves within the wartime narrative and how they envisioned their place as they moved forward in a postwar, post-emancipation landscape, rural cemeteries across the nation ultimately became central locales for the formation and performance of the public history and memory of the Civil War. No longer strictly "pleasure grounds of death," rural cemeteries transformed into politicized landscapes where the cultural battles over public memory continue to be waged even in the twenty-first century.

At the time when the first shots of the Civil War rang out over Fort Sumter, South Carolina, on April 12, 1861, Americans were by no means unacquainted with death on both the individual and the catastrophic scale. Indeed, it specifically had been due to the pervasiveness of death from everyday causes in addition to epidemic disease that the rural cemetery movement had begun in the first place. Nevertheless, nothing had prepared the populace for the overwhelming loss of life that would be wrought within just four years of war. The worst nationwide epidemics during the antebellum era were cholera in 1832 and 1849, and the total combined estimated mortality across the country numbered 150,000 dead.[9] The Mexican-American War, fought from 1846 to 1848, resulted in the loss of 16 percent (12,640) of the 79,000 men who served, due in large part to disease and infection.[10] Despite such a high mortality rate in Mexico, however, the number of soldiers who lost their lives was miniscule compared to the human cost of the Civil War, in which upwards of 750,000 Union and Confederate soldiers and sailors perished.[11] Such numbers could not be conceived of at the start of the conflict, and even following the first battle of Bull Run on July 21, in which 387 Confederate and 460 Union soldiers were killed, there was as yet little notion on either side that the war would be anything other than relatively short with minimal loss of life.[12]

Nevertheless, it was not long before rural cemetery companies, especially those in the South, began to allot portions of their land for the burial of the war's dead. In the days following Bull Run, a number of Confederate officers wrote to the *Charleston Daily Courier* that "the State, the city, or, perhaps, the Fourth Brigade, should secure a suitable lot in Magnolia Cemetery, and have it dedicated to the use of those sons of South Carolina who have or may fall in the defence of her honor and liberties in the present struggle against Northern fanaticism." Not only should the city's largest and most elaborate cemetery dedicate space for the Confederate dead, they asserted, but the city should also plan to eventually erect a "proper monument" that would "recount to future generations their gallant deeds—of these already fallen—now deeply engraven upon the hearts of sympathizing fellow citizens."[13] Magnolia Cemetery had already become a site associated with martial romanticism in the aftermath of the Mexican-American War—a young soldier who had bid farewell to his mother before departing for Mexico was buried under the tree where he supposedly had kissed her goodbye.[14] The Civil War only magnified public sentiment that the rural cemetery became even more sanctified by the presence of the martial dead. On July 26, Charleston held a massive citywide funeral for Generals Barnard E. Bee and Francis S. Bartow and Lieutenant Colonel B. J. Johnson of the Confederate army. A "very large concourse of our citizens and a number of ladies" met the bodies at the train depot, after which hearses transported the dead to city hall to lie in state, at which point "between four and five thousand people" ventured a last look at the deceased before burial. Along the way, the "sidewalks, windows and piazzas of private residences, hotels and public buildings were packed with men, women and children anxious to pay the sad mark of respect due to the occasion." Stores remained closed, flags flew at half-mast, and the bells of the churches throughout the city tolled "at different intervals during the day." During the funeral at the Episcopal church, "every available foot of space" was occupied by mourners. The public's grief culminated in a massive display upon arrival at Magnolia Cemetery, where mourners heaped the coffins with wreaths of "laurel, palmetto and cypress."[15]

As the war wore on, such impressive funeral displays were primarily reserved for "the most prominent figures" while rank-and-file soldiers' bodies mostly ended up in hastily dug battlefield graves or, if they died in an urban military hospital, equally hastily dug graves in the local rural cemeteries, public burying grounds, or potter's fields.[16] Regardless of the rank of those interred, however, southern rural cemeteries like Magnolia became pilgrimage sites both during and after the war where white southerners, especially women, honored the rebel dead by decorating their graves and raising subscription funds for the erection of imposing monuments that would stand at the center of soldier burial sections. However, the mounting number of soldiers' graves meant that, despite the rural cemetery continuing to attract visitors for daily outings, the "pleasing, though melancholy reflection" that they had once evoked evaporated; instead, Magnolia and other rural cemeteries brought into stark relief the everyday realities of the human toll of this devastating war.[17] In the course of the Civil War, Magnolia became the resting place for approximately three thousand soldiers (between burials in the soldiers' lot and in private family lots), five Confederate generals, and fourteen signers of the Ordinance of Secession.[18] The LMA laid the cornerstone for the "Defenders of Charleston" monument at Magnolia Cemetery at the 1870 Decoration Day ceremony. Before the unveiling of that monument in 1882, the Washington Light Infantry dedicated its own memorial, and as noted by historian Thomas Brown, "Other monuments erected at Magnolia honored German soldiers, Irish soldiers, the Charleston Light Dragoons, Confederate generals from South Carolina, Confederate sailors, and the ironclads, forts, and batteries engaged in the defense of Charleston harbor. Markers for individual soldiers proliferated even more rapidly as Confederate veterans passed from the scene."[19] Interspersed throughout its landscape along with the private monuments to Charleston's elite, Magnolia evolved into a site where Charlestonians mourned the defeat of the Confederacy while they commemorated the dead and entrenched their postwar Confederate identity. The pattern thus established at Magnolia Cemetery went on to be repeated in rural cemeteries across the Confederate South, and through the experience of war and mass casualties, these elite burial grounds transformed into shrines to those whom white southerners regarded as the martyrs of the Lost Cause.

In Mobile, Alabama, the city's municipally owned New Burial Ground (established in 1836 and later renamed Magnolia Cemetery in 1867 by the city's mayor, who felt a distinguished name was necessary), which consisted of thirty-six acres and was laid out with rectilinear carriage and footpaths similar to the reform cemetery model, set aside a section of the cemetery in 1862 for Confederate burials.[20] This area would later become known as "Soldier's Rest" or "Confederate Rest." The soldiers' monument overlooking the 1,110 burials, funded by Mobile's Confederate Memorial Association, was unveiled on April 27, 1874. As described by one visitor in 1879, the "beautiful monument of Alabama granite gracefully rises from a heavy granite base to a height of over 30 feet and is surmounted by a Confederate soldier with his gun pointing down, mutely keeping watch over those who are resting in their last sleep below. Each grave has a large head board, with name and company of each soldier as far as known."[21] The burial in 1876 of Confederate general Braxton Bragg at Mobile's Magnolia Cemetery further elevated the reputation of the site as a shrine to Confederate memory.[22] At Elmwood Cemetery in Memphis, Tennessee, the cemetery association also provided ground for the Confederate dead "and made no charge for services rendered by their employees." In a pamphlet published by the cemetery in 1874, plans were in place for the erection of a monument, "hereafter to be reared in the middle of this bivouac of the dead . . . on whose sides will be inscribed recitals of gallant deeds done by those who began here an eternal march." As in Mobile's Magnolia Cemetery, Elmwood Cemetery eventually came to hold the bodies of about one thousand Confederate soldiers.[23] In its announcement inviting the public to participate in the city's first Decoration Day observance in April 1866, the *Memphis Daily Argus* beckoned the living to deck "the graves of our brave and illustrious dead . . . with garlands of roses . . . in the sacred precincts of Elmwood."[24] Such rural cemeteries, which offered daily reminders of the toll on human life during the war, became the central gathering places during Reconstruction where ex-Confederate men and women could focus their grief as well as fashion their collective memory of the war and give it meaning.

While the allotment of grounds for military burials during the war and the erection of sizable soldiers' monuments after 1865 were significant priorities in rural cemeteries across the Confederate South, there were outliers, albeit few in number. Most notable was Savannah's "far-famed" Bonaventure Cemetery.[25] Celebrated during the antebellum period for the seeming wildness of its landscape and imposing live oaks, it became the last resting place for over five hundred Confederate soldiers; yet, no particular section of the cemetery was allotted for the purpose of soldier burials.[26] Instead, "the neglect of four years of war caused the cemetery to appear wilder, and Bonaventure became a stop on post-Civil War disaster tours of the South."[27] Many other cemeteries and burying grounds across the South suffered similar fates of neglect and disrepair, but Bonaventure continued to draw visitors. Its unique trees and atmosphere, unlike any other rural cemetery anywhere, made it a continuously popular spot for tourists in the postwar period, but the graves of the Confederate dead were never the centerpiece of public attention as in cemeteries elsewhere.

One such tourist was the naturalist John Muir, who spent a week camping in Bonaventure Cemetery after the war in 1867. His account of the place particularly highlights how the trees and other plants, not the graves, arrested the attention of the visitor. "I gazed awe-stricken as one new-arrived from another world," he wrote. "Bonaventure is called a graveyard, a town of the dead, but the few graves are powerless in such a depth of life."[28] In Muir's estimation, the human endeavor to mark graves with stone and enclose lots with iron palings amounted to nothing more than folly. Casting man and Nature at odds with each other in the precincts of the cemetery, he mused,

> It is interesting to observe how assiduously Nature seeks to remedy these labored art blunders. She corrodes the iron and marble, and gradually levels the hill which is always heaped up, as if a sufficiently heavy quantity of clods could not be laid on the dead. Arching grasses come one by one; seeds come flying on downy wings, silent as fate, to give life's dearest beauty for the ashes of art; and strong evergreen arms laden with ferns and tillandsia drapery are spread over all—Life at work everywhere, obliterating all memory of the confusion of man.[29]

Several years after Muir's visit, the LMA of Savannah raised funds for the erection of a Confederate soldiers' monument. Their choice of Forsyth Park in the city's southern suburbs as the location for the $40,000 monument that would be dedicated in 1875 reflects further how Bonaventure diverged from the pattern exhibited in rural cemeteries elsewhere across the South.[30] Rather than become a dedicated shrine to the Confederate dead like so many rural cemeteries in the postwar South, Bonaventure retained its own unique character and reputation as a cherished local landmark.

Nevertheless, all across the South, the pattern of allotting grounds for the burial of the war's dead, marking and decorating those graves, and later erecting a central monument within the soldiers' section was remarkably consistent. The major differences lay in the degree to which the local rural cemeteries experienced the strain of managing the dead, especially in the principal theaters of war. As cemetery companies in cities across the South dedicated portions of their grounds for the burial of soldiers, arguably no city struggled more to bury the war's dead than Richmond, Virginia. Hollywood Cemetery continued to be the city's preeminent elite white rural cemetery. Nearby Oakwood Cemetery, another rural cemetery established and operated as a municipal burying ground in 1854, served the needs of the white working, middling, and elite classes as well as white paupers and both free and enslaved Black residents.[31] In August, the *Richmond Dispatch* noted with approval that the Hollywood Cemetery Company "generously gave a section for the burial of our soldiers dying in Richmond and its vicinity." By this time, there were still fewer than one hundred soldiers buried at Hollywood, but this would not remain the case for long.[32] Within the year, it was necessary to extend the boundaries of the portion of the cemetery dedicated to soldier burials, as the original portion had been filled, and by June 1863 a correspondent from Vermont who visited Richmond marveled how across the city there were "*thirty thousand burials within two years, and of these nearly all are from the hospitals!*"[33]

Even as Hollywood and Oakwood Cemeteries increased the amount of space available for the burial of soldiers, the matter of securing enough labor to bury the dead remained a chronic problem. The *Richmond Dispatch* chastised the lack of attention given to the corpses piling up at Oakwood in July 1862, where "no less than forty or fifty coffins with their ghastly contents [were] exposed to the sweltering rays of the July sun, the lids in many instances being forced off by the swollen bodies, emitting a most offen-

Graves of Confederate soldiers in Oakwood Cemetery in Richmond, Virginia, with board markers, 1865. (Courtesy Library of Congress Prints and Photographs Division)

sive effluvia."[34] William Henry Hurlbert, a northern traveler to Richmond, employed similar language when he witnessed in Hollywood Cemetery "piles of reeking coffins left lying in the summer sun for hours together, till the scanty force employed by these ghouls of the Government could find time to shovel their human spoil decently out of sight."[35] At Oakwood Cemetery, at least several of the gravediggers were enslaved African Americans, and in the face of struggles to keep up with the burial of the war's dead, their labor was at times supplemented by Union prisoners of war.[36] Cherished rural cemeteries they may have been, but the everyday sights at Hollywood and Oakwood were grim reminders of the realities of the ongoing war. Ultimately, between wartime burials and postwar reburials from battlefields, Hollywood Cemetery and Oakwood Cemetery held among the highest concentrations of Confederate dead in the South, with eighteen thousand eventually interred at Hollywood and seventeen thousand at Oakwood. Overflowing, as they were, with both buried and unburied corpses during the war, it was nearly impossible for these cemeteries to maintain their appeal to casual visitors as places of respite and exercise, yet Hollywood especially continued to beckon visitors with its high-profile wartime burials.

With Hollywood already a cemetery of national significance following the reburial of President James Monroe's remains in 1858, its reputation as a Mecca of the South intensified over the course of the war. Before his death in January 1862, former president John Tyler sided with the Confederacy and was elected to the Confederate House of Representatives. Upon his death, those who attended his funeral at Hollywood Cemetery included "President [Jefferson] Davis, members of Congress, the Governor of the State, members of the Legislature, the heads of the various Departments, and an immense concourse of citizens and strangers," and Tyler's body was laid to rest near that of James Monroe.[37] The May 1863 funeral for General Thomas J. "Stonewall" Jackson completely eclipsed that for Tyler, for at the time of Jackson's death, he was the South's great Christian hero-martyr.[38] Thousands, including the Confederacy's top leadership, attended the two-day-long proceedings that culminated in Jackson's burial in Lexington, Virginia, on May 15, per the general's wishes. The managers of Hollywood Cemetery had offered Jackson's family a plot for the sainted Confederate hero, and when Jackson's wishes for burial in Lexington were respected, there were those who lamented the decision, as they already hoped to make Hollywood "the heart of mourning for the Confederate dead."[39]

Even so, the funeral held in Richmond before moving Jackson's body on to its final place of interment was considered truly magnificent, especially considering conditions in the midst of war. Of the funeral train, Richmond clerk John Beauchamp Jones wrote,

> The grief is universal. . . . The pall bearers were generals. The President [Jefferson Davis] followed near the hearse in a carriage, looking thin and frail in health. The heads of departments, two and two, followed on foot—Benjamin and Seddon first—at the head of the column of young clerks (who ought to be in the field), the State authorities, municipal authorities, and thousands of soldiers and citizens. The war-horse was led by the general's servant, and flags and black feathers abounded.[40]

The *Richmond Dispatch* bemoaned the fact that Jackson would not be buried at Hollywood Cemetery and, though respectful of his wishes to be buried in Lexington, did not fail to note that it was in Richmond where "every breeze wafts his renown."[41]

A similar outpouring of public grief attended the 1864 funeral of Jefferson Davis's young son, Joseph, who died after falling from the balcony of the Confederate president's residence in Richmond. The child was buried in what would become the Davis family circle lot at Hollywood, and his funeral evidently drew "one of the largest gatherings of the citizens of Richmond that any of the events of the last three years have called together."[42] The addition of Confederate general J. E. B. Stuart's body on a hillside at

Hollywood Cemetery in May 1864 further added to the increasingly shrine-like quality of Richmond's most hallowed burial ground. The press reported upon how, following the funeral, in which once again the Confederacy's most notable figures turned out to express their grief, and during the burial at Hollywood, "the earth trembled with the roar of artillery and the noise of the deadly strife of armies—the one bent upon desecrating and devastating his native land, and the other, proudly and defiantly standing in the path and invoking the blessing of heaven upon their cause, to fight in better cheer for the memory of such as Stonewall Jackson and J.E.B. Stuart."[43] Despite the physical absence of Stonewall Jackson's body, his image and memory hung in the air around Hollywood Cemetery even as the remains of President Tyler, little Joe Davis, and J. E. B. Stuart further sanctified the grounds as hallowed to the cause of the Confederacy.

Such enormous funerals for the South's notable figures magnified Hollywood's role as a space in which southerners could regard the Confederate dead as martyrs to the cause of Southern independence and intensified the cemetery's reputation as a Mecca for loyal Confederate pilgrims; when the war ended and Confederates had to grapple with the reality of having been vanquished and give the war meaning, the cemetery then became a site for the concentration of white southern grief and memory. Reflecting upon the end of the war in her reminiscences published in 1903, Marta Lockett Avary of Virginia noted the despair that she and others felt as the Union army marched triumphantly through Richmond.

> Was it for this, I thought, that [General Stonewall] Jackson had fallen? For this that my brave, laughing [J. E. B.] Stuart was dead—dead and lying in his grave in Hollywood under the very shadow of that flag floating from the Capitol, in hearing of these bands playing triumphant airs as they marched through the streets of Richmond, in hearing of those shouts of victory? . . . I had to thank God that the kindly sod hid you from all those sights and sounds so bitter to me then. I looked toward Hollywood with streaming eyes and thanked God for your sake.

But it was not just the dead for whom Avary grieved. "Was it to this end we had fought and starved and gone naked and cold? To this end that the wives and children of many a dear and gallant friend were husbandless and fatherless? To this end that our homes were in ruins, our State devastated? To this end that Lee and his footsore veterans were seeking the covert of the mountains?"[44]

The living, however, could not grieve for the living, and so it remained the work of the living to give meaning to the war and to fashion the South's narrative of the Lost Cause by doing for the dead what could not be done except intermittently throughout the conflict. Devotion to the dead during the war had meant devotion to the cause of the Confederacy, and as Reconstruction began, the dead within the walls of the city's rural cemeteries remained critical to the fashioning of postwar southern identity. The mission of the Hollywood LMA that formed in the aftermath of the war was the same as countless LMAs that formed across the postwar South: it oversaw the burial and reburial of Confederate soldiers' bodies from battlefields (in 1866 it launched a campaign to have all Confederate bodies at Gettysburg transported to Richmond for reburial), it ensured that all burials were marked with headboards (later headstones) containing whatever identifying information could be gathered for each soldier, and it organized and directed the annual Decoration Day observances in the spring, when all shops and businesses closed so that the community could decorate the graves of soldiers and listen to speeches by religious and political leaders who further articulated the meaning of the war for the South.[45] The LMAs also raised funds for the erection of large central monuments within the Confederate section of their respective cemeteries. The fundraising efforts of the Hollywood LMA culminated in the construction by city engineer Charles Dimmock of a ninety-foot-tall pyramid dedicated to the Confederate soldiers, completed and dedicated in 1869.[46] This pattern would be repeated in the rural cemeteries throughout the South during Reconstruction and for years thereafter.

The wartime experiences of Richmond, as the capital of the Confederacy, and those of its cemeteries were striking, albeit reflective, of similar patterns and struggles elsewhere. Despite certain common themes, however—the allocation of burial space for the war dead by cemetery companies, the performative aspects of military funerals, and the efforts to decorate the graves of the fallen, for example—the wartime and postwar experiences of rural cemeteries elsewhere varied tremendously, especially in the contested border states of Maryland and Kentucky. When the war first commenced, Kentucky's political leadership had hoped to maintain a state of neutrality for the Commonwealth, but conservative unionists ultimately prevailed in keeping the state loyal to the Union in October 1861 while still remaining committed to maintaining the institution of slavery. This decision to remain within the Union immediately provoked questions regarding the burial of soldiers from both sides of the conflict as the public's sentiments concerning secession remained deeply divided.[47] Cemetery boards of trustees appear to have

Hollywood Cemetery, Richmond, Virginia: "Decorating the graves of the rebel soldiers, May 31, 1867." (*Harper's Weekly* [August 17, 1867, 524], drawn by W. L. Sheppard, courtesy Library of Congress Prints and Photographs Division)

maintained the policy that lot holders, regardless of political sympathies or even enlistment in the Confederate army, would be allowed to inter their dead; soldiers whose families already owned lots were buried throughout the war in their family lots regardless of sectional ties. As for the burial of soldiers who did not have family locally, the cities and cemeteries made preparations for military burials. In October 1861, Louisville's general council passed a resolution for the appropriation of "several acres of ground in Cave Hill Cemetery, for the purpose of burying such United States soldiers as may be buried in this vicinity," a resolution that was then adopted by the city's board of aldermen.[48] When Confederate prisoners began to die in Louisville's military prison and hospitals in the early months of 1862, local military authorities resisted the idea of burying the Confederate dead alongside Union soldiers. Elijah Huffman and Samuel Hamilton, local Confederate sympathizers who worked in the pork-packing business, resolved the issue when they purchased lots in Cave Hill that they then donated for the interment of rebel soldiers.[49] At the end of 1861, Lexington Cemetery set aside a lot for the burial of Union soldiers, and in the aftermath of the Confederate invasion of the city, the cemetery board established a section for rebel soldiers in the summer of 1862.[50] Similarly, when Confederates invaded Frankfort in the fall of that year, the state capital's rural cemetery began to be "filled with the new-made graves of the rebel dead," as the occupying Confederate forces buried soldiers wherever space could be had or taken.[51]

Loyal Bluegrass residents chafed at the prospect of Confederate burials in their hallowed rural cemeteries, especially those near the graves of the state's illustrious dead; in the case of statesman Henry Clay's burial spot in Lexington Cemetery, the proximity of the rebel dead caused particular consternation among unionists. For many, Clay's remains were a powerful reminder of preserving the Union. Similar to how the remains of Daniel and Rebecca Boone had been treated as civic relics with their reburial at Frankfort Cemetery in 1845 (see chapter 4), Clay's remains were arguably regarded with even greater reverence. The American public regarded the architect of the Compromise of 1850 following his death as a secular saint. The presence of Confederate bodies in the same ground as Clay represented an affront to the statesman's memory. When Clay's mausoleum, capped with a towering column surmounted by a larger-than-life statue of the statesman, was completed and dedicated on July 4, 1861, the event's Committee on Arrangements issued invitations to the military. The committee, which scheduled the event for "this glorious birth day of American freedom," intended the day to serve as "an occasion for the renewal of *national patriotic feelings* as opposed to the lamentable and mischievous *sectional prejudices* which have been so industriously propagated of late years with too much success by designing politicians." The monument would serve as a talisman, and Clay's remains as holy civic relics, through which "we may obtain a renewal of our love of country; and whilst in the immediate vicinity of his venerated ashes, we may more fully appreciate the benefits of that Union, to sustain which, his unrivalled powers of persuasion were so often wielded."[52] Throughout the war, the monument remained a major attraction for Union soldiers and civilians as well as an inspiration for them to continue to defend Kentucky from Confederate invaders. As one soldier wrote while stationed in Lexington in 1862, "Thus the tomb of the Sage of Ashland was consecrated to a perpetual Union, and by the help of the great God, it must so remain. Those who take their pilgrimage hither must not be compelled to ask the privilege of an alien foe."[53]

Even as the Federal army and loyal civilians begrudgingly accepted the reality of Confederate burials in Lexington Cemetery, as well as other rural cemeteries in the loyal border South, the cherished burying grounds became sites of contest over funerals and grave decoration as well as the performance of identity during the war. In Lexington, Union forces had no intention to permit overly lavish rebel funerals. Kentucky unionist Frances Dallam Peter wrote in her diary in March 1862 how it had been declared illegal for "secesh" funerals to include more than twenty carriages of people and how rebel efforts to hold an elaborate public procession and funeral ended in consternation with Federal troops turning away "eight or nine hundred rebels" at the cemetery gates, allowing in only the first twenty carriages carrying the principal mourners.[54] In a later entry, she wrote of a conversation she had with an unidentified federal soldier in June 1863 following his visit to Lexington Cemetery. On arrival, the soldier had encountered "several finely dressed ladies busy about them and the graves were adorned with a quantity of all kinds of fine flowers, arranged in every imaginable way." The soldier noted, however, that these ladies were not decorating the graves of Union soldiers. Rather,

> While he was looking at the graves of our soldiers which a[re] near those of the rebels, one of the ladies spoke to him and said "Only see what a difference there is between these two places; that one (pointing to our soldiers graves, which had no flowers or ornaments) so mean looking and this other so beautifully adorned with flowers." "Yes ma'am" he replied "I was just observing them, they are indeed beautiful flowers, in fact they are magnificent. But pray my dear lady[,"] he continued feigning ignorance[,] "can you tell me why there is so much difference made between the graves?" "Why" said she "don't you know these are the graves of the rebel soldiers?" "Rebel soldiers!" he said, "do they allow rebels to have a place of burial in a Christian cemetery?" The secesh lady retired.

The soldier went on to explain to Peter and her mother that he had encountered many "rebel ladies" during the war, having to guard them while submitting to verbal abuse and being spit on without retaliating. Faced with such open defiance to federal authority in this situation, concerning his remarks to the "secesh" women, he just "couldn't help it."[55]

As federal authorities took an increasingly hard line against rebel sympathizers, interference in the burial of the Confederate dead in the loyal border South states' most important burial grounds became more hotly contested and went beyond cutting remarks. In August 1863, following the Battle of

Gettysburg, a funeral was held in Baltimore's Green Mount Cemetery for the body of Confederate captain William D. Brown. During the ceremony, officials arrested eighteen people, among them the father of the deceased. Five, including Brown's father, were released shortly thereafter, while "the remainder were notified to appear before the Provost Marshal." The undertaker was likewise called in for questioning, and it was revealed that the cause for the arrests was the rumor that the deceased had been dressed in a new Confederate uniform before burial. The undertaker assured the court that Brown was buried in his original uniform, except that "a piece of gray cloth [was] laid on a portion of the body, on which the clothing had moulded." Everyone who had been arrested was released, but not before being asked "to take the oath [of allegiance]," to which "each and all declined," and "the declinations were noted opposite each name and kept." When the *Richmond Dispatch* reported on this incident, it concluded, "Such is Yankee rule in Baltimore."[56] Richmond may have struggled to have enough gravediggers on hand to bury its war dead, but it was clear from the perspective of the Confederate South that what was happening in rural cemeteries farther north was nothing more than political show that allowed federal authorities to terrorize mourners who wished to appropriately care for their dead. Adding insult to injury were the lavish funerals held in these contested cities for Union soldiers and officers, which local press reported upon as evidence of the strength of unionist sentiment.[57]

Nevertheless, as Federal efforts to crush any public—or even private—acts by rebel sympathizers to support the Confederate cause in loyal border states and occupied Confederate territory escalated, the rural cemetery increasingly became a cultural battleground upon which Confederates defied federal authority and made manifest where their allegiance lay. Such acts of defiance were largely accomplished with flowers and other grave decorations, as had been noted by the unnamed federal soldier in his conversation with Frances Dallam Peter in Lexington. During the war, flowers clearly conveyed to the living whose dead in the conflict were valued most within a community. Since the beginning of the rural cemetery movement in the 1830s, floral decorations had become standard in burial grounds across the country. Cemetery boards of trustees encouraged owners of family lots to plant flowers and shrubs to beautify their burial space even before any interments took place, and by the advent of the Civil War, the practice of leaving floral decorations on the burials and tombs of the deceased had become a common marker of affection and attention. Flowers were so integral to the antebellum cemetery landscape that they had become one of the most common symbols carved into headstones and monuments.[58] The absence of floral offerings to the Union dead during the war and the appearance of regular maintenance, including flowers, for the graves of Confederate soldiers in Union-occupied cities like Louisville, Lexington, New Orleans, and Baltimore spoke volumes about the private feelings of the cities' inhabitants.

Frustration over civilian aid to the Confederate cause in Kentucky reached such a height for federal military commanders that in 1863 General Ambrose Burnside issued General Orders No. 38, which declared, "All persons within our lines who harbor, protect, conceal, feed, clothe, or in any way aid the enemies of our country" will be "tried as spies or traitors; and if convicted, will suffer death." As Burnside asserted, there would be no further lenience shown to rebel sympathizers: "The habit of declaring sympathies for the enemy will no longer be tolerated in this department. Persons committing such offenses will be at once arrested, with a view to being tried as above stated, or sent beyond our lines into the lines of their friends." Any overt action or behavior that could be deemed supportive of the rebel soldiers or their cause would be regarded as treason and punishable as such. Within the civilian population, pro-Confederate white women had been regarded as most troublesome to federal authorities, and for their actions, "the so-called she-Rebels faced investigations, arrests, imprisonment, and exile for their devotion to the secessionist cause."[59] Even seemingly innocuous shows of support for the rebels became targeted as prosecutable offenses. For example, at a theater in Louisville, a number of ladies in attendance "flirted out of the room" during intermission when the band began to play some "national airs." The following night, the manager announced that the band would repeat its performance from the night before, "and all those who were too much opposed to the government to listen to them had now an opportunity to leave." The same ladies once again "got up and flirted out of the room but at the door they were met by the Provost guard who marched them off to jail."[60] Lizzie Hardin, a "die-hard rebel" from Harrodsburg, Kentucky, wrote privately of her Confederate sympathies, but when she and the other women in her family waved their handkerchiefs and cheered raider John Hunt Morgan and his men as they rode through town, she found herself targeted by authorities and ultimately expelled from the state until the end of the war.[61]

Grave decoration was an altogether different matter, for how can someone be prosecuted for aiding the enemy if the enemy involved is already dead? As observers during the war made evident, displays of loyalty to the rebel dead and their cause within the cemetery landscape represented perhaps the only overt expression of devotion that would *not* result in imprisonment or exile from the state. A Confederate chaplain who visited Cave Hill in 1863 observed, "A proper burial [has been given] to every Confederate soldier that has died in the city. Here, on the Northern border of Kentucky, [was] a sight that should put to shame many who inhabit cities further South. The grave of every Confederate was raised, sodded, and not a few surrounded with flowers. The name of the soldier, his State, and regiment, was lettered in black on a neat white headboard around which hung a wreath of myrtle, the Christian offering of the true Southern ladies of Louisville to the noble dead." By contrast, "in the grounds allotted to the burial of the Federal dead," the chaplain "found the graves sunken and uncared for; but few having stones or boards or marks of any kind."[62] Such a contrast in the treatment of Confederate versus Union graves in the cemeteries of occupied cities manifested elsewhere as well. In New Orleans, a city occupied by Union forces since 1862, All Saint's Day prompted citywide grave decoration activities. As the *Shreveport (LA) Semi-Weekly News* reported, "All the people . . . were allowed the privilege of visiting the city cemeteries." The paper noted, "All the graves of the Confederates were beautifully decorated, while those of the Yankee soldiers were neglected and not respected."[63] One lady in attendance wrote in confirmation of this statement, "The Confederate graves were beautifully decorated, not one neglected. They presented a glorious contrast to the graves of the Federals, some of which were covered with weeds, that made it almost impossible to see the head boards." Adding with no little amount of snark, she concluded, "Where the Union ladies were we should like to know."[64] While the graves of federal troops suffered the indignity of being ignored in these cities, the residents of Charleston, South Carolina, went even further in adding insult to injury by having the body of a Marine Corps lieutenant, C. H. Bradford, disinterred from Magnolia Cemetery and reburied in the city's potter's field.[65] In an "imposing demonstration" in March 1865, the body was once against disinterred, this time by federal troops, and reinterred back into Magnolia Cemetery with the hope that such action would "end the practice so long and universally adopted in the slave States of dishonoring the loyal dead."[66]

Matters concerning the burial of the war's dead and the treatment of their graves were nowhere near as fraught in the rural cemeteries of the North as they were in the contested loyal border states or in those of the

Confederacy, but, then, the allotment of grounds specifically dedicated to the burial of the war's dead within the northern cemeteries, while widespread, was not as universal as it was in the South. Two of the nation's most notable early rural cemeteries, Mount Auburn and Laurel Hill, eventually contained substantial numbers of the war's dead—over nine hundred at Mount Auburn while at Laurel Hill there were forty generals and approximately fifteen hundred soldiers—yet these cemeteries did not set aside lots for military burials during the war.[67] Rather, soldiers and officers killed in action, whose families could afford the cost of retrieval and transportation of the bodies home, were buried in their own private family lots. Because arterial embalming was still a new and therefore expensive practice during the war, relatively few bodies actually returned to the North.[68] In the case of Mount Auburn, only "about thirty bodies of the Civil War dead were shipped home for burial . . . by private initiative."[69] In some cases where bodies were not retrieved, cenotaphs within the cemetery memorialized the dead.[70] Such was the case for Colonel Robert Gould Shaw of Boston, who became notable in the Civil War for his leadership of the 54th Massachusetts Regiment, the Union army's first all-Black regiment in the war. When Shaw perished in the Union assault on Fort Wagner in South Carolina in July 1863, Confederates buried his body in a mass grave with his enlisted soldiers. A large central monument already stood in the center of the Shaw family lot near the Bigelow Chapel in Mount Auburn Cemetery, erected in 1832 by Shaw's grandfather (who bore the same name), a wealthy Boston merchant. Following the younger Shaw's death in 1863, the family added a bronze plaque dedicated to his service and sacrifice. By the addition of the plaque, the family monument was transformed into a cenotaph of national significance.[71] While no soldiers' lot was ever established at Mount Auburn, cemetery founder and board president Dr. Jacob Bigelow designed and funded the completion of a monumental Sphinx dedicated to the Union soldiers. Sculpted by Irish-born artist Martin Milmore, Bigelow intended his Sphinx to be a symbol for the nation moving forward beyond the war, one that was reunited and fully free. Bigelow highlighted what he envisioned as the new blended (albeit racially unequal) nation by adding Americanizing elements to the traditional Egyptian figure from antiquity, such as an Anglo-American woman's face, a bald eagle emerging from the pharaonic headdress, and a six-pointed star-shaped medal of honor. Unveiled in 1872, the Sphinx rests in a prominent location at Mount Auburn, facing the Bigelow Chapel.[72] In the case of Laurel Hill Cemetery in Philadelphia, while no soldiers' monument was ever erected, the Meade Post No. 1 of the Grand Army of the Republic purchased a lot two decades after the end of the war for the burial of veterans.[73]

Whereas cemeteries in the Confederate South and the border states allotted space for soldier burials in the early months of the war, mainly because of their proximity to the military actions that were unfolding, many of the northern rural cemeteries that did set aside land for that purpose did not do so until 1862 or even later. Simply put, so few soldiers' bodies were shipped back north in the early stages of the war that the need for a designated soldiers' space was not an immediate priority. Nevertheless, as increasing numbers of soldiers and officers perished and more bodies were transported away from the battlefields, cemetery companies increasingly allotted space for military burials. In some places, the proximity of prisoner-of-war camps meant that space for the burial of Confederate prisoners was required. Such was the case in Indianapolis, where Crown Hill Cemetery, established in 1863 during the war, contained dedicated grounds for both Union soldiers and Confederate prisoners who died in nearby Camp Morton (the Union section later went on to become a national cemetery). In many northern rural cemeteries, the decision to set aside grounds for soldier burials was an act of patriotism. For instance, at Green-Wood Cemetery in Brooklyn, the board of trustees voted to appropriate ground for the free interment of the state's deceased soldiers in June 1862. Reporting upon this decision, the *Brooklyn Daily Eagle* remarked with approval, "This action on the part of the Board reflects the utmost credit upon the patriotism and humanity of the managers of the institution, and will not fail to be appreciated by the public generally. It is but a fitting tribute of respect to the brave fellows, who, irrespective of party distinctions or the suggestions of personal interest, hurried *en masse* to the defence of their imperiled country."[74] The Albany Rural Cemetery Company acted similarly and set aside 0.16 acres within the grounds of Albany Rural, also in June 1862, for the burial of soldiers. In contrast to Green-Wood, however, when the soldiers' lot was established at Albany Rural Cemetery, the company promptly donated that portion of the cemetery to the federal government on June 17, a month prior to the passage of the National Cemetery Act by Congress.[75] When Ohio's governor purchased lots in Cincinnati's Spring Grove Cemetery for the burial of the state's soldiers in 1863, the *Semi-Weekly Wisconsin* in Milwaukee urged that "every State, and every city in every State, should make like provision for the burial of their dead heroes."[76]

Offering rural cemetery grounds for the burial of the Union dead was ultimately one of two patriotic impulses; the other was to erect substantial monuments on the cemetery grounds to commemorate the war's dead. The trend to memorialize the war's participants began during the war and proliferated nationwide during and after Reconstruction. As Thomas Brown has observed, the rage for erecting monuments for the Civil War dead represented an about-face from the iconoclastic views of the American public of the Revolutionary era and Early Republic. For Americans of these periods, monumentalization, especially of a nation's leadership, smacked of monarchy, something the nation hoped to avoid. Of the large-scale monuments erected in honor of the American Revolution, many of them were nonrepresentational, such as the monumental obelisks at Bunker Hill in Boston and at Groton, Connecticut. Further, the United States of the Early Republic was not regarded as a militaristic nation, and its people did not idolize the military or its soldiers. Even in the aftermath of the Mexican-American War, public monuments dedicated to the soldiers of that conflict were few in number. The avoidance of commemorating the nation's martial dead underwent a complete reversal during and after the Civil War, however, as the most immediate sentiment expressed by communities was to commemorate not the officers and generals but the rank-and-file citizen-soldiers.[77] As in the South with the postwar activities of the LMAs, northern rural cemeteries led the way as sites for these monument projects, and this was a reflection of the sepulchral character given to commemoration of the war's dead during the 1860s and 1870s. It generally was not until later, after the Reconstruction years, that commemorative monuments increasingly appeared beyond the precincts of the cemetery, with many dedicated in civic spaces such as courthouse lawns, public parks, and street intersections.

The earliest soldiers' monuments to be erected in northern rural cemeteries were those in Bangor, Maine, at Mount Hope Cemetery and in Cincinnati at Spring Grove Cemetery. Prompted by the death in Kentucky of Colonel Stephen Decatur Carpenter of Bangor on December 31, 1862, the managers of Mount Hope resolved to establish a memorial to the war's dead on a lot that could also be used for military burials. A central monument bearing the names of fifty-five fallen troops from the city was dedicated on June 17, 1864, following a successful subscription drive to raise the necessary $3,500. The Mount Hope Soldiers' Monument was thus the very first Civil War memorial of its kind in the nation. On the lot, a small number of soldiers were buried, while later in the 1890s another much larger lot was granted by the cemetery to the GAR for the burial of veterans. It was on this larger GAR lot that the Hannibal Hamlin and H. H. Beal Posts constructed a Grand Army of the Republic Fort, which included a crenellated masonry tower, canons, and flag.[78] Cincinnati's Spring Grove Cemetery acted similarly, raising subscriptions for the erection, also in 1864, of a "bronze statue on a granite pedestal, representing a Union soldier standing upon guard" and overlooking the soldiers' graves in the immediate vicinity.[79]

In most places, however, erecting and dedicating soldiers' monuments was a postwar activity, as the wartime focus remained on burying the dead. In Brooklyn, upon reporting on the appropriation of grounds in Green-Wood for military burials, the *Daily Eagle* expressed the hope "to see at no distant day an appropriate monument marking the resting place of our gallant dead in the delightful shades of Greenwood."[80] Green-Wood Cemetery eventually became the final resting place of over five thousand of the war's dead, contained within the soldiers' lot as well as scattered throughout the cemetery in private family lots.[81] A substantial soldiers' monument measuring thirty-five feet tall, consisting of a central shaft with soldier statues on each of the four corners of the base, was erected and dedicated in 1869.[82] In the decade following the war, around 1873, the GAR erected a fifteen-foot-tall soldiers' monument bearing plaques with the names of the fallen from Albany along with a bas-relief portrait of Abraham Lincoln on the front of the base in the Albany Rural Cemetery Soldiers' Lot.[83] Wartime monuments, such as the one in Bangor, were few in number, but with the war's end, lofty soldiers' monuments increasingly became central markers in the soldiers' sections established in northern rural cemeteries, just as they would be in the postwar southern rural cemeteries. Such activities persisted for decades. For instance, the sculpture known as the "Lion of Atlanta," dedicated to the unknown Confederate soldiers buried in the city's Oakland Cemetery, was not dedicated until 1894.[84] Ex-Confederates in Chicago funded the construction of a sizable monument dedicated in 1895 to the four thousand rebel prisoners of war from Camp Douglas whose bodies, originally buried in the swampy grounds of one of the city's potter's fields, were reinterred at Oakwood Cemetery.[85] In Rochester, New York, the soldiers' monument depicting a soldier with flag and a boy with bugle, was not installed in that city's Mount Hope Cemetery until 1908.[86]

Even as the war's dead increasingly took center stage in many of the nation's rural cemeteries, they nevertheless continued to be frequented daily by local visitors and tourists who rode carriages and strolled the grounds much as they had during the antebellum period. Newspapers con-

Albany Rural Cemetery, Soldiers' Lot, Cemetery Avenue, Menands, Albany County, New York. (Historic American Landscape Survey, 2000, courtesy Library of Congress Prints and Photographs Division)

tinued to publish articles and travelers' accounts with regularity throughout the period, signifying that the value of rural cemeteries as important cultural institutions whose presence was intimately tied to the reputation of the city with which they were associated had not diminished in the face of war. The *Boston Evening Transcript* wrote glowingly of Massachusetts's rural cemeteries in June 1862, noting that they "were never so attractive to visitors as they are at the present time," being as they were "under the charge of persons of large experience and fine taste in horticultural matters."[87] An Iowan visiting Philadelphia in June 1863 reported back to his newspaper in Muscatine on the "public institutions" he visited, including Laurel Hill Cemetery, the grounds of which, he noted, "are justly celebrated as the finest in the country."[88] Despite damage to the landscaping and monuments at Louisville's Cave Hill Cemetery when Union forces under the direction of General William Nelson built defensive fortifications in anticipation of Confederate invasion, the *Louisville Daily Democrat* nevertheless confidently asserted, "There is not, we venture to say, a more sublimely beautiful burial place in the United States than Cave Hill Cemetery, situated near this city."[89]

So beloved was Cave Hill, well beyond the confines of Louisville, that when Nelson died late in 1862, the press in the Confederate South regarded his demise as divine justice for "tearing open the graves and overturning costly monuments" with his fortifications through "the beautiful Cave Hill Cemetery. . . . Death has since avenged this ruthless invasion of his domain, by seizing the vile heart of the invader."[90] Writing about the nation's cities of the dead in 1864, the *Times-Picayune* (New Orleans) noted how "village competes with village, city with city, in the selection and improvement of the most beautiful and appropriate grounds in the still and quiet country, as the resting places of our dead." Listing such major rural cemeteries as Mount Auburn, Green-Wood, Laurel Hill, Green Mount, and Cave Hill, the newspaper went on to claim, "We . . . know of none in this country more beautiful" than those in New Orleans. In the city's contributions to the rural cemetery movement, including Cypress Grove, Greenwood, and Odd Fellows' Rest, "never did devotion consecrate its best offerings to the memory of the departed in pleasanter places."[91] Regardless of situations or challenges presented by war, the rural cemeteries remained the pride of their communities.

Civilians continued to frequent the cemeteries regularly as the war proceeded, and even soldiers who were encamped near major metropolitan areas noted in their diaries and correspondence how they visited the local rural cemeteries and toured the grounds when given the time. For example, while stationed in Louisville in October 1862, Samuel Patton, of the First Illinois Light Artillery Regiment, wrote to his wife, Nellie, about Cave Hill Cemetery. Having attended the funeral of two men from his regiment who were killed in an accidental explosion, Patton then explored the cemetery. "I saw more of the Cave Hill cemetery than I did the last time I was there and it is even hansomer [*sic*] than I thought it was," he wrote. "I cannot do justice to the taste displayed in monuments and decoration of the ground, by a description it would have to be seen to be appreciated."[92] Jenkin Lloyd Jones, of the 6th Wisconsin Artillery Battery, visited Elmwood Cemetery while stationed in Memphis, Tennessee. Venturing out on a February day in 1863 with two of his fellow artillerymen, Jones later wrote in his diary that it was "certainly a beautiful 'City of the Dead,' handsomely divided off by evergreen shrubbery, with spacious vaults of solid marble. From the white obelisk to the little lambs at the heads of once sparkling innocent babes, all was beautiful." Like other visitors to the rural cemeteries during the war, Jones also observed the rapid changes then underway. "But on one side were four hands busily piling up the rounded graves in close compact. They held the bodies of the unfortunate soldiers, averaging twelve a day. On the other side were the like victims of the Confederate States of America."[93] In these instances, military service and tourism intermingled. Everywhere, regardless of region, the areas dedicated to the war's dead, including individual burials of soldiers, officers, and even chaplains killed in the war, arrested the attention of passersby. Among the notable burials listed by one visitor to Mount Auburn in 1864 was "the fresh grave of Chaplain Arthur Fuller, who fell near Fredericksburg while assisting to lay the pontoon bridges. His memory will be cherished in New England as is the memory of General [Joseph] Warren."[94] Mixing tourism with reverence for the hallowed dead, visitors' accounts attested to the ways in which the nation's rural cemeteries continued to be valued as picturesque landscapes exhibiting taste and refinement even as they were transformed by war into shrines for the martyrs of the Union and the Confederacy.

With the close of the war in April 1865, proper care for the dead, many of whom remained in hastily dug battlefield graves, became a national priority, and campaigns were launched to have soldiers' bodies exhumed and reburied within formal cemetery landscapes across the country. Congress had passed the National Cemetery Act on July 17, 1862, which authorized the Lincoln administration "to purchase cemetery grounds and cause them to be securely enclosed, to be used as a national cemetery for the soldiers who shall die in the service of the country."[95] Soldiers' lots established during the war in Albany Rural Cemetery, Crown Hill Cemetery in Indianapolis, Cave Hill Cemetery, and Lexington Cemetery were added to the growing list of national cemeteries that would be cared for by the federal government. In some instances where federal soldiers had been buried in southern rural cemeteries such as Hollywood in Richmond or Magnolia in Charleston, their bodies were removed to the nearest national cemetery after 1865, thus leaving only the Confederate dead within the confines of the local rural cemetery. Southern LMAs launched reburial campaigns to gather the Confederate dead from the battlefields where their identities largely remained unknown to the living. Such was the case with the Hollywood LMA in Richmond, whose efforts involved the exhumation and reburial of 2,935 Confederates—"all the southern dead at Gettysburg except for 40 soldiers who had been buried where they fell in the Reverend Joseph Sherfy's peach orchard."[96] That their bodies would rest at home in southern soil was the preeminent priority.

Elsewhere, such as in Cave Hill Cemetery and Lexington Cemetery, the Union and Confederate dead remained in close proximity after the end of the war, which meant that the observance of competing Memorial Day ceremonies laid the groundwork for the cultural battles of the postwar era. Ex-Confederates across the South began observing their own Decoration Days beginning in 1866, with dates varying from the end of April into June. Communities decorated the graves of Confederate soldiers based upon dates of local significance, such as the birth or death dates of certain Confederate leaders or local heroes, but always during these months when appropriate flowers were most readily available. When the federal government established the national Memorial Day holiday, first observed on May 30, 1868, there were those in the ex-Confederate (and even loyal border) South who regarded the new national holiday as an affront and a paltry imitation of *their* holiday dedicated to *their* dead. In Kentucky, former Confederate cavalry officer William Jonathan Davis encapsulated the disparate emotions wrought by the memorial performances in letters to his wife in the spring of 1869. Concerning the Confederate grave decoration ceremony, Davis wrote,

> The best people turned out by thousands to visit Cave Hill. . . . The flowers strewed the graves in richest profusion; and all were decorated—some beautifully. The cemetery is a lovely spot, and, being laid out in an artistic and picturesque manner, would well repay a visit even on a less interesting occasion. I was delighted with the general good order and subdued gentleness of the vast concourse of people assembled to pay their annual tribute to the patriot dead of the South, whose cause, like themselves, though it now sleepeth—being of God—shall yet live.

In a subsequent letter, Davis expressed far less generous thoughts on the national Memorial Day services, which were nearly identical to those held earlier for the Confederates: "Yesterday at the cemetery the yankee preacher had just closed his sacrilegious prayer and the females, appointed for that purpose, had just begun their unholy rite of imitating Confederate sentiment, when a violent storm of wind and rain caused them to scatter in every direction, and the storm lasted so long that the whole ceremony, under Providence, proved a failure."[97] In Davis's estimation, the so-called Yankees, even though they were fellow Kentuckians, received their just desserts for daring to imitate what he regarded as a sacred Confederate ritual within the hallowed precincts of Cave Hill Cemetery.

Despite the sectional conflicts that split the nation and resulted in a bloody civil war, Americans continued to regard their rural cemeteries with pride as among their most important and valuable cultural institutions. While cemeteries across the North and the South answered the need to provide grounds to accommodate the burial of the war's dead, they persisted as attractive spaces to which the living could retreat for an afternoon stroll. Nevertheless, the Civil War had a transformative effect on these burial grounds because at a fundamental level, the war complicated the function of the rural cemetery. Still regarded as a community's most beautiful landscape, dotted with monuments to the notable and wealthy and containing views that evoked the picturesque and the sublime, rural cemeteries became vested with the additional qualities of serving as sites of collective memory and mourning for the war's dead. Not an overly militaristic nation before the Civil War, the United States increasingly embraced the image of soldiers, sailors, and other members of the armed forces as heroes whose courage and martial valor were to be idolized by the public. The ongoing annual ritual performances involving grave decorations and the erection of monuments, as shrines to those the public regarded as the heroes and martyrs of the Union and Confederacy, allowed the sectionalism of the past to persist well after the close of military hostilities. Further, throughout this period, as rural cemeteries became shrines dedicated to the sanctification of the war's dead, their managers sought to modernize their institutions to maintain relevance with a public whose tastes were rapidly changing in the postwar years. It would be in the final decades of the nineteenth century, then, that rural cemetery managers found themselves in the position to face their own novel challenges separate from the war—to expand and adapt with the changes of the times or to sink into obscurity like the churchyards and public burying grounds of an earlier age.

6

"Carpeted with a Green, Verdant Mantle"

Modernization and the Transformation from Rural to Landscape Lawn

The Civil War and Reconstruction era witnessed a significant amount of development for the nation's rural cemeteries and the rural cemetery movement, of which the changes wrought by the war itself were only one part. Even as rural cemetery managers east of the Mississippi River and within the main theaters of war dedicated space to accommodate the bodies of the war's dead and communities utilized these spaces in the postwar years to commemorate the dead and fashion their public history and memory of the war, numerous other important developments took shape during these years. The war, while seemingly ubiquitous in arresting the public's attention, did not bring urban planning and cultural developments like the rural cemetery movement to a halt; rather, rural cemeteries continued to spread westward into Kansas, Iowa, Wisconsin, Minnesota, Oregon, and California, as newer towns and cities exited their frontier stages and their residents sought to vest themselves with the same trappings of civilized refinement as their eastern counterparts. The expectation that any major metropolitan area ought to have such an institution meant that to go without could be regarded as a mark of shameful inattention to modernization and culture.

As communities in the Midwest and West laid out and dedicated new rural cemeteries, those who managed the eastern rural cemeteries labored to expand and modernize their landscapes, purchasing acreage and integrating new technologies and architectural and design elements that would continue to make their institutions attractive to lot holders and visitors alike. Keeping up with the march of improvement became a major priority for cemetery superintendents, an emerging professional class of cemetery managers whose multifaceted roles included landscape gardening, maintenance, and lot sales, in addition to the day-to-day operations of the burial grounds. Their challenge was to ensure that the nation's aging rural cemeteries would not be left behind as relics of a less advanced age, like the churchyards and public burying grounds before them. The new cemeteries were managed by professionals who, like undertakers, transformed care for the dead into an industry by century's end. Mount Auburn Cemetery, for example, had been in operation for thirty years by the beginning of the Civil War, and with newer rural cemeteries in New England and the Midwest showcasing such modern elements as macadam roads for carriages, fountains, and running water, there was motivation to maintain relevance and appeal for visitors and potential lot holders. By the 1890s, in response to progressive reformers' support for cremation, a number of cemeteries began integrating crematories on-site.

Cemetery managers and superintendents everywhere increasingly felt the pressure to modernize their rural cemeteries, primarily due to the expanding celebrity of Cincinnati's Spring Grove Cemetery. Spring Grove's original landscape design, when it opened in 1845, was based, like all other rural cemeteries of the era, on the picturesque aesthetics exhibited by Mount Auburn, Laurel Hill, and Green-Wood. Adolph Strauch, a Prussian-born landscape gardener, took charge as superintendent and in 1855 introduced what would be known as the "landscape lawn plan" at Spring Grove, a design aesthetic that, like Mount Auburn in 1831, once again upended the public's notion of what a cemetery landscape should look like and how visitors might engage with a landscape so dedicated to the care of the dead. Shirking the picturesque in favor of the beautiful—an aesthetic that favored "gently flowing lines, roundness and regularity, balance and symmetry, perfection and repose"—Strauch advocated the "dispensing with unsightly fences, hedges, head and foot stones, and other useless appendages" so that lot holders might instead erect a single, central family monument "which would be the admirations of generations to come."[1] Strauch further criticized the tendency of older rural cemeteries to have a wild, unrefined atmosphere that was overcrowded with trees, bushes, and flowers, many of which were planted by the lot holders themselves. Instead, his new landscape lawn plan meant fashioning sweeping vistas with strategically planted trees and other greenery that would create a cleaner, more open and parklike environment. By the 1870s, older rural cemeteries were adding new landscape lawn sections so that potential lot holders could choose for themselves which aesthetic they preferred for their final resting place, while new cemeteries, such as Woodlawn Cemetery (est. 1863) in the Bronx, Philadelphia's West Laurel Hill (est. 1869), and Pittsburgh's Homewood Cemetery (est. 1878), integrated Strauch's principles from the time of their establishment.

Even as the landscape lawn plan increasingly overtook the picturesque aesthetics embraced by antebellum Americans, cemeteries established through the 1880s that were designed according to the landscape lawn method continued to be referred to as "rural cemeteries." By the 1890s, however, virtually every new cemetery was self-consciously referred to either as a landscape lawn cemetery or simply as a "lawn cemetery." Nevertheless, despite the waning influence of rural cemeteries and the rural cemetery movement, which had dominated much of the nineteenth century, neither rural cemeteries nor their guiding principles disappeared. In the age of the landscape lawn cemetery, there were other newer cemeteries, particularly African American, that remained truer to the original ideals of the rural cemetery movement with the emphasis on groupings of family monuments and more naturalistic landscaping, even as white Protestant cemeteries became increasingly rigid in terms of landscaping and what lot holders were permitted to do with monuments and planting. In order to retain cultural relevance and attract lot holders, preexisting rural cemeteries—especially the larger ones—added acreage to which the new landscaping aesthetics could be applied and constructed new buildings for the comforts of the living and aboveground entombment of the dead. As cemetery superintendents embraced cleaner landscaping and new technologies with which to manage their landscapes, burial grounds at the end of the nineteenth century reflected the burgeoning sensibilities of the progressive movement, with its emphasis on cleanliness, sanitation, order, and control. Such a shift away from the attraction to romantic, naturalistic landscapes, with power in the hands of the lot holders to do as they saw fit with their lots, paved the way for the streamlined memorial parks that were introduced in the early twentieth century, and still prevail in the twenty-first century, in which death and nature alike became virtually invisible, their landscapes a well-ordered, parklike environment controlled by cemetery professionals.

While the rural cemetery movement began as a northeastern phenomenon in the 1830s, spreading throughout the South and Midwest during the 1840s, there was no singular path of westward expansion for the movement; by the 1850s rural cemeteries could be found from coast to coast with great pockets of space throughout the nation that had not yet established a modern burial ground, mainly because so many of the western territories were still very much within a frontier stage of development or used Spanish-derived burial patterns, such as those territories acquired from the Mexican Cession.[2] Even before the onset of the Civil War, the influence of the Gold Rush had meant the influx of Anglo-Protestant Americans to the West Coast, with accompanying rapid development of towns and cities. Among the first rural cemeteries established on the Pacific coast was that formed by the Chemeketa Lodge No. 1 of the Independent Order of Odd Fellows (IOOF) in Salem, Oregon, known originally as Odd Fellows Rural Cemetery when it opened in 1854. Much smaller than its eastern counterparts, Odd Fellows Rural Cemetery (today known as Salem Pioneer Cemetery) consisted of only five acres, though further land purchases in 1861 and 1890 increased the cemetery to its current size of just over seventeen acres. As described by its website, the cemetery embodied the hallmark characteristics of the rural cemetery movement ideal. The surrounding vistas of the Willamette Valley, including "the snow-capped peaks of Mt. Hood and Mt. Jefferson," added to the overall qualities of the picturesque and the sublime.

> The elevated site overlooks the city to the northeast in which the Capitol dome and Methodist Church spire are prominent features. . . . The regularity of the narrow, elongated gridiron of burial plots was relieved by curvilinear carriage turn-arounds and side lanes that gave access to sections lying on either side of the central driveway. A scattered cover of native oaks, madrones, and conifers and thousands of monuments both stately and humble make up a funerary landscape that exemplifies the historic Rural Cemetery movement in Oregon's mid-Willamette Valley.[3]

Elsewhere west of the Mississippi River, growing communities sought to expand and improve preexisting pioneer cemeteries according to the rural cemetery aesthetic or to establish new rural cemeteries to replace over-crowded frontier burying grounds. In Topeka, Kansas, the former was the case, as Elnathan Trask, undertaker and superintendent of Topeka Ceme-tery, urged lot holders in February 1861 to each "do a part towards making these grounds a credit to Topeka; a place in which her citizens may feel a legitimate pride, whose tendency may be to improve the taste, to soften the manners, and purify the morals of the people." In short, Trask hoped that by transforming Topeka Cemetery into a more genuine rural cemetery, it would have the civilizing and uplifting effects that had been the goal of many of the founders of the original rural cemeteries of the 1830s and 1840s. Exiting the frontier stage, residents of expanding communities like Topeka looked to vest themselves with the trappings of taste and refinement like their east-ern counterparts, as well as a more finely honed religious sensibility. "Let us here cultivate Nature's beautiful products," wrote Trask, "beautiful flowers, ornamental trees, and shrubs, to recall to imagination that paradise lost by transgression, and with it that lovelier, glorious paradise prepared for the good beyond the grave. The kind affections and pious thoughts awakened by the sight of tasteful rural cemeteries, are aids in the education of the heart, of which it is a misfortune to any community to be deprived." Eschewing all sense of gloom and even the pleasures of melancholy that were such a hall-mark feature of the romanticism of the antebellum era, Trask urged instead that the cemetery "should partake more of the character of a cheerful park or garden, than of a common grave yard" and should "form the most inter-esting of all places for contemplative recreation, and everything should be tasteful, classical, and poetical."[4]

Similar sentiments appeared in newspapers elsewhere across the coun-try, as civic-minded residents of younger cities sought to imbue their com-munities with what they considered to be the principal features of civilized society, just as the older eastern cities had endeavored during the first half of the century. As one newspaper in Independence, Iowa, expressed in 1862, "One of the most pleasing and attractive, and certainly one of the most prized improvements, connected with a city or town, is that of a tasteful ceme-tery. . . . We should have a burial place that it would be our pride to show and our pleasure to visit."[5] In Winona, Minnesota, the trustees of the Wood-lawn Cemetery Association moved ahead with the improvement of the new cemetery grounds in 1863. Lots were not yet available for sale though the grounds were open to visitors, and the Winona Daily Republican reported that "the impression forces itself upon us that Woodlawn Cemetery, because of its beautiful natural location, the absolute necessity which exists for a place of this character, and the good taste which has marked the operations of the Association hitherto, will soon become an object of pride and regard with the people of Winona."[6] That same year, in a letter signed "Publiola" to the local newspaper in Viroqua, Wisconsin, the author lamented the sorry state of their village graveyard and urged, "We owe it to ourselves as a Christian Community that we have large Cemetery Grounds well laid off into lots, carriage ways, and walks, and properly beautified and adorned."[7] Just as the colonial churchyards and burying grounds of the Northeast had become overcrowded and unkempt by the early nineteenth century, the same patterns of development leading to burial overcrowding spread throughout these younger regions of the country as they matured beyond the frontier stage of development and sought to claim their place as respectable modern communities. For many communities still without a rural cemetery by the 1860s, it had become a point of embarrassment and the mark of neglect to progress. The city of Nashville, Tennessee, still lacked a rural cemetery in 1866, for which one local newspaper lamented, "Shall Nashville continue the barbarous and abandoned practice of burying the dead within the growing marts of the city? Shall Nashville alone continue to lag in the path of civilization by exhibiting a carelessness in regard to the dead?"[8]

In Kansas, a "company of twenty gentleman" in Leavenworth engaged in a venture that would combine the burgeoning public parks movement with the rural cemetery movement, as they proposed the construction of a "Central Park" for their city, to which would be abutted an expanded and improved Mount Aurorie (originally Pilot Knob) Cemetery.[9] New York City's Central Park, designed by Frederick Law Olmsted and Calvert Vaux, which opened to the public in 1858, had been an immense success in satisfying the public's need for a strictly recreational environment and launched an entirely new parks movement that, like the rural cemetery movement, expanded across the country during the 1860s. The rural cemeteries of the 1830s and 1840s had been multipurpose institutions that blended together the functions of burial grounds, public parks, *and* experimental gardens. Critics like Olmsted regarded the pleasure ground aspect of cemeteries as having a degrading effect on their principal function as sacred spaces dedicated to the proper care for and burial of the dead. "The rural cemetery," wrote Olmsted, "which should, above all things, be a place of rest, silence, seclusion, and peace, is too often now made a place not only of the grossest ostentation of the living but a constant resort of mere pleasure seekers, travellers, promenaders, and loungers; and this indicates, as much as any thing else, the need that exists in every town and village for a proper pleasure ground."[10] Thus in Leavenworth, the two cultural movements blended together in what was anticipated to be an impressive public venue that would meet the needs of everyone in the community. The chief priority within this endeavor was to execute their project in the most modern and elegant manner. "The Park will be laid out and ornamented in the most skillful and elegant style," noted the *Leavenworth Bulletin*, "and the Cemetery will be laid off into alleys and fine carriage avenues, surpassed only by the broad public avenue that surrounds it. It will also be ornamented, at an early day, with a massive stone gate-way and a residence for the superintendent." To ease public access to the park and cemetery, the company intended to first construct and improve "two or three graded and macadamized roads," which when completed would "afford the most splendid drive from the City to the Park."[11] Leavenworth would thus have its pleasure ground and its cemetery side by side, the two institutions together the crown jewel of the burgeoning city's landscape.

Before Olmsted would go on to design other famous parks, such as Brooklyn's Prospect Park and Boston's Emerald Necklace, his reputation for Central Park earned him a commission in 1863 to design Mountain View Cemetery in Oakland, California.[12] As much as the cemetery association desired a beautiful rural cemetery that could be regarded as a jewel of the West, Olmsted, like cemetery designers before him, recognized that each region of the country presented its own challenges and opportunities when envisioning how best to organize and ornament the cemetery landscape. Writing to the president of the board of trustees, Major R. W. Kirkham, Olmsted urged caution in trying to simply copy the eastern cemeteries. This was due not only to considerations of cultural differences in the West but, more importantly, to the climatic conditions of the region. "Nowhere else is the danger of dilapidation from the alternation of Summer drought and Winter torrents, of stormy winds, and of vermin, so great; nowhere is dilapidation so inappropriate and offensive, and therefore so much to be guarded against, as in a cemetery," Olmsted warned.[13] In his view, the cemetery ought to be deliberately organized in such a way that it would, first and foremost, serve the necessary purpose of providing a spacious and respectable venue for the burial of the dead and *then* be ornamented with plantings that might enhance the beauty of the space.

> If, then, you desire to manifest respect for the remains of the dead, you will be likely to accomplish your purpose better, if you start with that

purpose directly in view, and not with the purpose of first making a beautiful landscape, and then finding a place where your dead may be buried without great injury to its beauty. Not only marble, but trees and earth and everything else should be treated in such a manner as (consistently with the nature of these materials) will best serve your purpose.[14]

In short, for Olmsted, form should follow function and not the other way around at Mountain View Cemetery. In Olmstead's prioritization of burial as the cemetery's principal function, even though he was contracted to design it as a rural cemetery, his words were consistent with his view that cemeteries should be cemeteries and parks should be parks.

Given Olmsted's view on the matter, it is with no small degree of irony that the 1860s and 1870s witnessed a dramatic expansion in the efforts of rural cemetery superintendents to make their institutions more parklike and less naturalistic and picturesque. This was primarily due to the expanding influence of Prussian landscape gardener Adolph Strauch's landscape lawn plan at Spring Grove Cemetery in Cincinnati, which he implemented in the mid-1850s. Like other new rural cemetery associations during the 1840s, responding to the public's excitement over Mount Auburn, Laurel Hill, and Green-Wood, those who first organized Spring Grove Cemetery in 1844 sought to follow the precedent of the eastern cemeteries. As such, they originally hired architect John Notman, who had designed Philadelphia's Laurel Hill Cemetery, to develop a plan for Spring Grove. What readily became apparent, as many subsequent rural cemetery founders discovered—and as Olmsted rightly pointed out when he designed Oakland's Mountain View Cemetery—was that differences of topography, climate, and local flora had to be taken into account. In Notman's plan for the laying out of Spring Grove, he did not do this, and the cemetery's founders, displeased with Notman's plan for the site, instead asked local architect Howard Daniels to produce a design that would better fit with the topography of the land they had purchased. What Daniels created was a rural landscape with complex carriage and footpaths that "formed a maze with a continuous series of reverse curves, which still disorient visitors." As historian Blanche Linden observed, "Even with a map, one can easily get lost in this landscape—by design."[15] Daniels left Cincinnati in 1850 to pursue other projects, and in 1852, Adolph Strauch arrived and shortly thereafter became superintendent of Spring Grove, where he transformed the concept of the rural cemetery.

Using plantings "to create a sequence of spaces and a sense of landscape

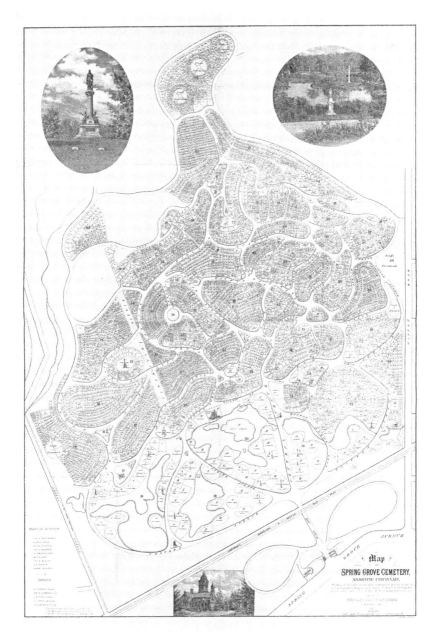

Map of Spring Grove Cemetery, adjoining Cincinnati: "Showing all burial lots with their numbers and sections, as laid out to date, together with about two thousand names of owners of the largest sized lots, and location of a number of the principal monuments, etc." (Robert Clarke & Co. and M. & R. Burgheim [1883], courtesy Library of Congress Geography and Map Division)

unity," Strauch sought to reform the rural cemetery landscape using "scientific management" to "reflect the neat, park-like naturalism of English Gardens such as Stourhead and Stowe."[16] Strauch's ideal was to incorporate sweeping vistas with strategically planted trees and shrubs and family lots dominated by a single monument with little or nothing else to disrupt the visual experience. By the 1860s, under Strauch's management, Spring Grove had expanded to encompass 412 acres, making it the largest cemetery in the nation and one of the premier destinations for visitors to the Midwest. As the cemetery included both the older section from the 1840s designed by Daniels that was more in accordance with the eastern rural cemetery aesthetic and new portions designed according to Strauch's plan, visitors could easily compare the differences in the landscape even as they appreciated the effect conveyed by the whole, with many in agreement that Spring Grove could rightfully claim its place among the preeminent institutions dedicated to the care for the dead. Concluding her 1859 description of Spring Grove as "this monumental home of the departed dead," visitor Juliet M. Hirst declared, "Like the sainted Mecca of Arabia, it must ever retain an enchanted celebrity to attract with devotional feelings of admiration millions yet unborn."[17] In 1860 the *Cincinnati Daily Press* claimed, "Disinterested gentlemen who have seen all the famous necropolii of Europe and America, do not hesitate to pronounce our Spring Grove superior in attractiveness to the best of them, though inferior to several in extent and costliness of decoration." Identifying Strauch as the principal force behind Spring Grove's ascent to supremacy among rural cemeteries, the newspaper thus described his approach:

> It has evidently been the aim of Mr. Strauch not to cover up, but to interpret Nature—to bring Art to aid her in the expression of her own idea; and while keeping in view the especial purpose to which the spot is devoted, to prevent the execution of that purpose from giving it a mechanical aspect, and destroying the unity which Nature had established. Indeed, the beauty of Spring Grove consists in the fact that we are able to view it as a whole. Unlike the other rural cemeteries of the country, its subdivision into parts, the subjects of individual ownership, has been kept from attaining such prominence as greatly to mar the general affect. To this end the most irksome of the labors of Mr. Strauch have been directed; but before his zeal and his assiduity, the obstacles have one after another given way—the ugly stone posts and grim iron rail-

ings, with which lot-owners, suffering under excellent intentions, but afflicted with terrible tastes, sought to *ornament* their property, are coming down; and there is reason to hope that, before long, Nature, set loose from her impediments, will be permitted to speak out with comparative freedom, in testimony of her own loveliness.[18]

Strauch had banned lot holders from erecting fences and chains around their lots, and preexisting enclosures were in the process of being removed in the effort to make the cemetery's older section more closely resemble the newer portions. His reasoning for this was that enclosures "in a well-governed cemetery, detract from the sacredness of the scene, by supposing it possible that such a place would be visited by persons incapable of conducting themselves properly, or that the grounds were pastured by cattle."[19] Indeed, these were *exactly* the reasons why lot holders had begun erecting cast-iron fences around their lots during the 1830s and 1840s, in the hope that unruly visitors would be dissuaded from stealing flowers or damaging monuments (see chapter 2). Misbehavior within the confines of the rural cemetery had not disappeared by Strauch's time—transgressions ranged from picking flowers and damaging trees to hunting and, the most egregious offense, committing sexual assault—but in his and other critics' estimation, enclosures muddied the visual quality of the landscape, and this was increasingly regarded as of greater importance by cemetery superintendents than the private wishes of lot holders who sought to protect and ornament their lots as they saw fit.[20]

In a further effort to curb lot holders' tendencies to over-ornament their lot with monuments of varying types and sizes, Strauch regulated that any individual stones—such as those labeled "Father," "Mother," "Son," and "Daughter"—could not rise more than eighteen inches from the ground, while the principal family monument ought to be a work of art or a specimen tree. He particularly favored the idea of planting a tree from the deceased's place of birth in lieu of erecting a monument. Strauch wrote,

Cemeteries in the vicinity of large cities invariably contain the remains of persons from many parts of the world, over the graves of whom the trees of their respective countries might very appropriately be planted, thereby forming an arboretum, which, in the course of time, would afford valuable information to our succeeding generations, and be of far more use than a collection of dilapidated marble slabs and toys. Thus, the sturdy Briton might rest under the shade of his native oak, while the northern man would find a place of repose beneath the leafy canopy of the mountain maple, or the pine, and the southerner rest in peace at the foot of his favorite cypress.[21]

In the case of monuments, Strauch urged an adherence to tasteful and classical designs. The problem here, however, was the same as it had been since the start of the rural cemetery movement—that is, that taste was, and remains today, highly subjective. With new developments in stone quarrying and carving, along with the explosion in popularity of white marble, which lent itself to greater variety of sculptural designs, critics since the 1830s had weighed in on what they regarded as tasteful and appropriate for sepulchral monuments. Nevertheless, lot holders, especially those with money, had proceeded to follow their own personal preferences regardless of the pronouncements made by so-called tastemakers. Thus, eclecticism became a hallmark feature of the nineteenth-century rural cemetery landscape as lot holders had erected all manner of monuments reflective of the vogue for architectural revivalism as well as more romantic iconography involving flowers, angels, lambs, doves, allegorical figures, and portraits of the deceased. While rural cemeteries had always included within their bylaws language concerning the removal of offensive monuments, it was under Strauch's oversight that the erection by a lot holder of a proposed monument was outright refused. The offending monument in question included the carving of a steam fire engine to mark the burial lot of its inventor.[22] Baffled by such a decision, the Cincinnati Daily Press pointed out the seeming absurdity of how "figures of heathen gods, and imitations of the architecture of heathen temples, and all sorts of mythological devices are allowed, but exceptions are made to the enshrining of a steam fire-engine, a feature peculiar to our city and most honorable to the inventor."[23] Strauch's vision for a beautiful, well-regulated cemetery meant regulating the lot holders as much as the landscape itself, and as his approach to cemetery design took hold elsewhere in the country, so too would the regulatory power of superintendents expand.

By the early 1860s, increasingly it became clear that the original landscaping ideals that had made early rural cemeteries such attractive retreats for urban dwellers who sought to escape the noise and smells of the city for an afternoon were falling out of favor. After years of lot holders being encouraged to plant their own flowers, bushes, and even trees on their lots, in addition to erecting all manner of headstones and monuments, observers began to regard the rural cemetery landscape as altogether too crowded with greenery and marble, to the point that some critics considered the cemetery landscape as chaotic and, ironically, lacking taste and refinement. The individuality and cultivated wildness of the picturesque were, for many postwar Americans, increasingly antithetical to emerging views of what constituted the great civilizing forces in society—technology and order.

It took time for Strauch's landscape lawn plan to really take hold, but elements of his major design principles—such as removing lot fences, constructing wider carriage paths, and fashioning more open vistas—began to be integrated into preexisting rural cemeteries as early as 1861. For superintendents of older rural cemeteries, this often meant undertaking significant construction projects to modernize the grounds to be more open and parklike while expanding into new acreage with the newer landscape gardening ideas in mind. At Mount Auburn Cemetery, in his annual report for the board of trustees in 1861, Dr. Jacob Bigelow described current construction and beautification projects that were in keeping with what other modern rural cemeteries were doing. "The introduction into the grounds of fresh running water, and the construction of fountains in suitable parts of the cemetery, has long been thought a desirable object by the trustees," he asserted. "Such fountains exist in various cemeteries in the United States, and are among the highest ornaments in landscape gardening." As such, the cemetery trustees had made appropriations in the amount of $8,000 for the construction of "one or more fountain jets at Mount Auburn." In order to complete this project, this further necessitated digging a new well to provide water to the fountains, a reservoir at the top of the hill near Washington Tower, and installation of a steam engine pump to carry water throughout the cemetery, to the fountains, and back into the well.[24] In addition to modernizing the cemetery's infrastructure, Mount Auburn also embraced Strauch's prohibition on lot fences. One visitor from Pennsylvania noted in 1864 how many lots were now bordered by granite curbing and that iron fences would no longer be permitted, even as older ones were being removed. "When they are all gone," he noted with approval, "the cemetery will look a hundred per cent better than it now does."[25] Within the space of another two decades, even the granite curbing would no longer be permitted at Mount Auburn as the cemetery embraced the transition to the landscape lawn plan.[26]

At Green-Wood Cemetery in Brooklyn, the efforts expended to maintain a pleasing atmosphere for pleasure seekers were evident, for by the 1860s, the cemetery's comptroller, J. A. Perry, estimated that between four hundred thousand and five hundred thousand visitors arrived annually within its gates.[27] One writer from Vermont noted how the carriage avenues "are graded and curved with much care," that "green grass borders them on either hand," and that the artificial lake's "refreshing loveliness is enhanced by a fountain in constant play." Nothing was overgrown or left to be directed by the whims of nature—visitors witnessed what had been meticulously planned and maintained in order to achieve such a perfect aesthetic. Urging others to see the cemetery for themselves, this writer concluded, "Greenwood can be easier seen than described. The visitor is charmed by its soothing quiet, its mingled beauties of art and nature." Such an admonition was hardly necessary, though, for the cemetery had become so extensive and such a popular attraction for non-mourners by the early 1860s that carriages were on hand within the gates to drive visitors "through its numerous and extensive avenues."[28] Not only were carriages ready on-site to bring visitors through the grounds, but enterprising business owners set up shop nearby the cemetery to provide services to those spending the day. "Near the entrance to the cemetery," wrote another tourist, "are several neatly built cottages, built for the sale of refreshments, called by such names as 'Green-Wood Saloon,' 'Greenwood House,' &c., &c. Persons who come to Greenwood to spend the day—and it takes a day to obtain a satisfactory view of the entire grounds, usually avail themselves of these conveniences for the purpose of saving a walk to the city to dine."[29] Frederick Law Olmsted may have wanted to separate the park from the cemetery, but for places like Green-Wood that had developed such a reputation as a popular resort, it was impossible to stem the tide of tourism (if the cemetery's board were even interested in such a thing, which is unlikely), and so efforts continued within the cemetery itself and the surrounding neighborhood to make it an even more attractive destination.

It was during the 1860s, as western towns established rural cemeteries and eastern cities expanded and improved preexisting ones, that eastern cities also continued to establish newer rural cemeteries adopting the landscape lawn plan, first within certain sections and later as integral to their overall design. Eastern metropolitan areas had expanded well beyond what the original rural cemetery planners had envisioned during the 1830s and 1840s, and thus many of the earlier rural cemeteries that had originally sat from one to four miles beyond the city centers were by the 1860s surrounded by business and residential districts, thus making it impossible to further expand their boundaries to accommodate more burials. Even in places with massive rural cemeteries that seemingly had an inexhaustible amount of burial space, such as Brooklyn with its Green-Wood Cemetery, there was the drive to develop new "modern" rural cemeteries set even further beyond the borders of urban development. This meant that from the 1860s through the 1880s, a whole new generation of rural cemeteries emerged that also illustrated the transition from the rural to the landscape lawn aesthetic. Such a transition reflected several major developments during these decades, among them a reaction against the intensification of industrialization and the seeming disorder it engendered within the cities and the distancing by century's end of Anglo-Protestant Americans' relationship with death and care for the dead. Among the notable new burying grounds that marked the transition in favor of the landscape lawn design but that were still referred to as "rural cemeteries" were Woodlawn Cemetery (est. 1863) in the Bronx; West Laurel Hill Cemetery (est. 1869) in Philadelphia; Cedar Grove Cemetery (est. 1869) near Boston; and Homewood Cemetery (est. 1878) in Pittsburgh.

Incorporated in 1863 with its first burial in 1865, Woodlawn Cemetery in the Bronx drew immediate comparisons to the older rural cemeteries, most notably Green-Wood. In September 1865, the *New York Times* reprinted an extract of a letter written by the secretary of Laurel Hill Cemetery after having visited the new burying ground. Impressed by the progress made in the landscaping since his visit to the site the previous year, he declared, "Woodlawn Cemetery is, I think, destined to become, in time, the principal rural burying-ground of the City of New-York." Noting that the land upon which the new cemetery was situated—somewhere between three hundred and four hundred acres—possessed "extensive and picturesque views in every direction," his letter indicated that the most important quality of Woodlawn by far was its location for ease of access.

> The great advantages of this location, especially for those citizens of New-York who reside in the upper part of the island, are obvious, when one takes into account the difficulties which interpose more seriously every year against the access to Greenwood. That beautiful spot, the pioneer of the rural cemeteries of New-York, and justly the pride of its citizens, is not only on the other side of a wide and sometimes difficult sound, whose ferries are always crowded with vehicles and passengers,

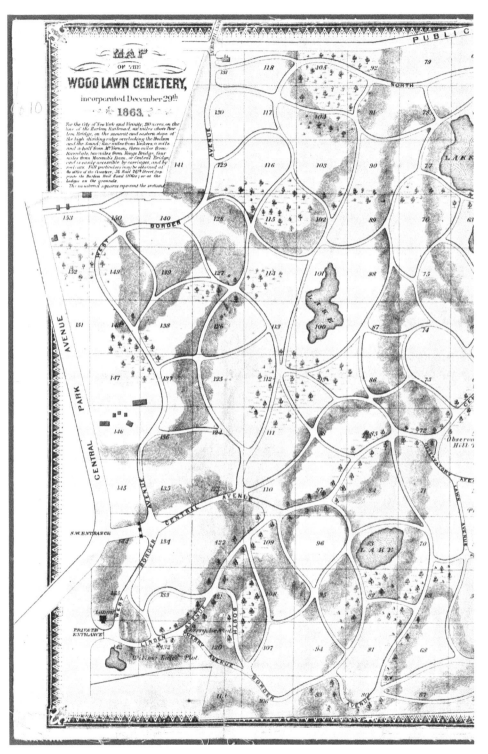

Map of the Woodlawn Cemetery. (Courtesy Lionel Pincus and Princess Firyal Map Division, New York Public Library Digital Collections)

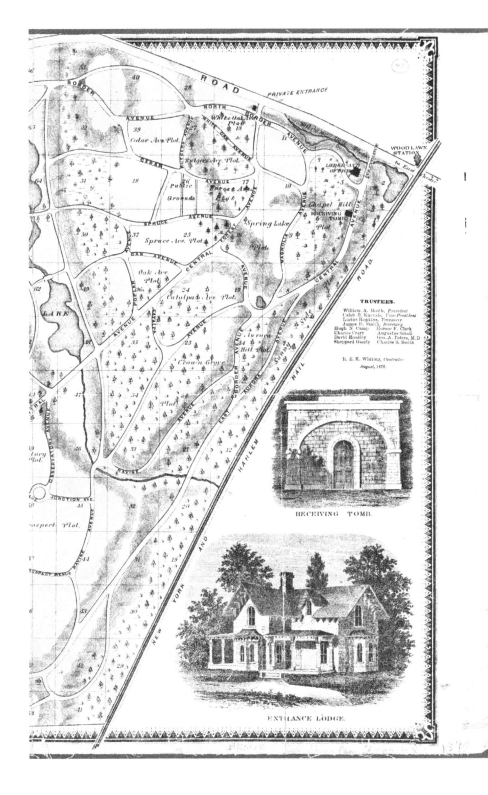

RECEIVING TOMB.

ENTRANCE LODGE.

but the lots, according to the report of the trustees for 1861, are nearly all sold; so that the preparation of a new resting place . . . was a duty not to be put off.

In short, even the magnificent Green-Wood, the pride of Brooklyn, was becoming antiquated, mainly due to space and accessibility issues. Among the notable features that would help ease public access to Woodlawn was the construction of a wide new road that would lead to the southwest entrance of the cemetery, while arrangements had been made with the Harlem Railroad Company to transport special funeral trains to the northeast entrance. As the cemetery was still in the process of being developed, with comptroller "Mr. Clift" overseeing the work of fifty laborers "constantly employed" at accomplishing the "substantial and tasteful improvements" to put the ground in order, Woodlawn was at this early stage still a work in progress.[30]

Nevertheless, by the following year, the *New York Times* reported with great satisfaction on the "rapid development" of Woodlawn Cemetery and that "the gentlemen who have it in charge have accomplished wonders." Among the wonders added by "a liberal expenditure" were "buildings, bridges, catacombs, avenues and lakes." Noting its comparative remoteness from the bustle of the city, the *Times* declared, "It is essentially a rural cemetery, and must remain so for generations to come."[31] The cemetery officers and trustees themselves regarded Woodlawn as a rural cemetery, and in a promotional pamphlet published in 1864, they specifically thanked John Jay Smith, founder of Philadelphia's Laurel Hill Cemetery, for his advice on cemetery design, as well as acknowledged Green-Wood and Mount Auburn as sources of inspiration for "hints of improvements."[32] Albeit Woodlawn was a rural cemetery by name and deeply indebted to the earliest rural cemeteries for much of its design, Strauch's landscape lawn aesthetic was nevertheless an integral part of its landscaping from an early stage, with one portion developed according to the older rural aesthetic and another developed according to Strauch's plan. Proprietors thus had the choice, in purchasing lots, of which section they preferred. However, a number of Strauch's most fundamental ideals associated with the landscape lawn applied throughout the whole cemetery. As reported by the *Boston Evening Transcript* in 1868, at Woodlawn, "soon to rival Greenwood in beauty, the ornamentation of undivided lots is held subordinate to the general effect, thus avoiding the excessive adornment of particular spots, and securing a pleasant harmony throughout." Lot holders were forbidden from erecting any "visible boundaries," such as fences or curbing, around their lots; graves were "levelled even with the lawn," instead of mounded as they traditionally had been; and they were marked "by a small slab laid flush with the sod."[33]

Philadelphia followed suit in 1869, establishing West Laurel Hill Cemetery in that year. Philadelphia had become home to several rural cemeteries during the antebellum period, including first the famed Laurel Hill (which would come to be known as Laurel Hill East to differentiate it from West Laurel Hill), followed by Monument Cemetery (est. 1837), Mount Moriah Cemetery (est. 1855), and Mount Vernon Cemetery (est. 1856). Philadelphia's African American community, which was excluded from burial within these rural cemeteries, established Lebanon Cemetery in 1849 according to the same design principles of the rural cemetery movement. Driven by the same hope that resulted in the establishment of Woodlawn Cemetery, West Laurel Hill's promoters, among whom were men "who were the pioneers in the present Laurel Hill Cemetery," sought to add a new cemetery on the west side of the Schuylkill River that would be "convenient of access to the city" while also "not likely to be disturbed by the march of improvements."[34] Despite decades of urban development and expansion, the men who planned and executed the new batch of rural cemeteries in the years after the Civil War continuously held out the very same hopes as those of the 1830s and 1840s that their new cemeteries would remain beyond the reach of businesses, factories, and residential neighborhoods. That the older rural cemeteries, once situated beyond major development, were increasingly engulfed on all sides by roads and construction was a source of consternation, not least for Philadelphia. As *Lippincott's Magazine* observed in 1870, "The rapid expansion of this city, while a matter of just pride to Philadelphians, is not without its attendant embarrassments. Many suburban burial grounds, which had been considered secure from invasion by streets, either are, or threaten to be, enveloped by buildings." Laurel Hill Cemetery was the exception, as it was bounded on three sides by Fairmount Park and on the fourth by Ridge Avenue. Mount Vernon Cemetery, located directly across from Laurel Hill Cemetery on Ridge Avenue, provided a further buffer against development encroaching upon the older rural cemetery.

West Laurel Hill Cemetery, across the river, was therefore intended to function as an extension of Laurel Hill, comprising about 150 acres and accessible by Belmont Avenue and the Reading Railroad. West Laurel Hill's founders hoped that, as in the Bronx, Philadelphians would increasingly turn to modern methods of mass transit—particularly the trains—to access the new cemetery for funerals and outings.[35] The press regarded using the railroad to access the cemetery as a positive innovation that likewise saved money otherwise expended on carriages. "This new arrangement is a great saving to the relatives of deceased persons, who have heretofore been taxed heavily in hiring carriages for themselves to attend funerals at the cemeteries near the city," reported the *Reading (PA) Times* in 1870.[36] The press further marveled at another funeral innovation at West Laurel Hill—a movable chapel "to protect mourners from the rain during service at the grave." Such a novelty led the *San Francisco Chronicle* to declare, "Philadelphia funerals are luxuries. . . . As a contemporary says, why, because one man has died, should all the mourners catch bad colds? Bereavement should be made as comfortable as possible."[37] The *Atchison Daily Champion* in Kansas observed that such a structure, presumably moved "upon wheels," would also be a "protection against excessive heat."[38]

For its location over the Schuylkill River, its landscaping, which incorporated both the older rural and newer landscape lawn aesthetics, and its innovations, West Laurel Hill, like Woodlawn Cemetery, received much praise. The *Philadelphia Inquirer*, in reviewing West Laurel Hill and comparing it to Laurel Hill East in 1877, noted how the collective experience of the management of the older rural cemetery, men including Laurel Hill's founder, John Jay Smith, was the source of the new cemetery's success. "As the management is in the hands of those who have had an experience in the care of a cemetery of forty years duration it is no wonder that West Laurel Hill should be, as it really is, a worthy successor to the older one on the east bank of the river, and that, having been started during an era of enlarged views and grander proportions, it should receive the patronage of the wealthy."[39] However much experience led to innovation at West Laurel Hill, however, Smith and the other managers maintained certain older policies found at its predecessor. Like Laurel Hill East before it, West Laurel Hill upheld the color line in Philadelphia by selling burial lots only to white people, thus leaving Lebanon Cemetery to become increasingly overcrowded and plagued by body snatchers until its closure in 1903.[40] Neither Laurel Hill East nor West Laurel Hill allowed Black interments until 1973.[41]

Even in Boston, the very heart of the rural cemetery movement, the democratic principles of choice in matters of personal bereavement and commemoration of the dead became subordinate to the new landscaping ideology. Commenting upon the emerging popularity and success of the landscape lawn plan in 1873, the *Boston Evening Transcript* reflected what by then was becoming a widely shared attitude concerning modern cemeteries—that they "should partake of the park character, and should, as much as possible, be carpeted with a green, verdant mantle; that they should be tasteful, classical and poetical, surrounded by the soothing influences of nature, and fitted for shade, repose and the comfort of the living as well as for the interment of the dead." To achieve this effect meant allowing cemetery superintendents to wrest control over the entirety of the landscape at the expense of lot holders' personal wishes. Requiring "unity of design and demand[ing] uniformity of grade," cemetery authorities needed to be able to grade sections "without listening to the private fancies or caprice of the individual proprietors." Mount Auburn and Forest Hills Cemetery (est. 1848), as Boston's principal rural cemeteries, had begun implementing the landscape lawn plan in newly added sections while removing lot fences and stone coping in the older sections to be more in line with the new tastes. Cedar Grove Cemetery, established in nearby Dorchester in 1869, had "to a considerable extent been laid out on the landscape-lawn plan" and, according to the *Evening Transcript*, "differs widely" from the older rural cemeteries "in its general appearance."[42] Like at Woodlawn and West Laurel Hill, the railroad became a critical feature at Cedar Grove, with the Old Colony Railroad actually building a station on the cemetery grounds, its line bisecting the cemetery in half.[43] The original rural cemeteries had been situated at a distance from urban centers, requiring extensive walking or the use of carriages to escape the city into the confines of a seemingly antimodern, naturalistic environment; despite their continued function as a getaway from the industrialized city, the newer rural cemeteries like Cedar Grove embraced modern industry and technology, so much so that they became embedded features in a burial landscape that was itself becoming more visibly artificial and associated less with a vision of untouched nature.

Amid the general push during the early 1870s to modify existing rural cemeteries and establish new cemeteries designed according to the landscape lawn model, the managers of Pittsburgh's Allegheny Cemetery stood out in urging caution against making cemeteries more parklike and stripping lot holders of their authority over their own burial spaces. Most vocal among the cemetery's leadership was Dr. James R. Speer, among Allegheny's founders. In 1873, Speer, then acting as cemetery secretary and treasurer, authored an essay included in a book about the cemetery, part of which was reprinted in the *Pittsburgh Weekly Gazette*. Speer first explained the nature of what was meant by landscape lawn—with its various prohibitions against excessive

decoration, mounded graves, enclosures, and headstones and footstones—
before proceeding with his concerns about what such policies would ultimately do to the sepulchral character of the cemetery. Echoing Frederick
Law Olmsted, he wrote, "It is obvious . . . that there is an essential difference
between the purposes and sentiments connected with the arrangements of
a cemetery and private graves, and those of a public park. . . . Any attempt to
introduce into the picture the gay and mirthful scenes and actors of parks
and pleasure grounds would be inconsistent with the rules of good taste and
propriety, and tend only to mar its intrinsic interest and beauty."[44] Not wanting to cause offense to the profession of landscape gardening or to parks and
pleasure grounds, Speer affirmed that the purpose of his remarks stemmed
from a desire "to suggest a caution against an excessive application to the
Cemetery, of tastes and arrangements appropriate only to parks and pleasure grounds, and in keeping with them."[45] Speer conceded that the idea
of banning enclosures and perishable materials (such as wood) from grave
plots was a good and necessary change, but this was really the only aspect of
the landscape lawn plan of which he approved.

Where Speer expressed his most severe critique of the turn toward the
landscape lawn plan was with regard to how it constrained lot holders in
making their own choices according to custom and taste. As he warned:

> It must be conceded that there is an individuality of ownership in the
> family lot, which the proprietor has bought and paid for, and for which
> he holds a deed in "fee simple," subject only to the rules and regulations
> of the Cemetery; and that there is also a personality of grief, affection
> and veneration connected with it, especially when it has become the last
> resting place of the once animated forms still dearer to him than his own
> life, that ignores the professional tastes and arrangements of the land-
> scape gardener and park engineer, when they conflict with the innate
> sentiments and feelings of his own nature.

Speer then proceeded to observe that the landscape gardener, whom he had
previously wished not to insult, "looks on the burial lot, with its solemn
surroundings, as a blemish in the picture of a beautiful consistent whole,"
whereas the bereaved "reveres it as a consecrated spot, on which the foot
of the stranger should scarcely be permitted to tread."[46] Invoking an imagi-
nary scenario of a son returning to his hometown following a long absence,
Speer described how dear would have been the graves of family and friends,

with "every object in and around the family lot in which they are buried . . . photographed on his memory. The inclosures, the monuments, the trees, the mounds that cover the remains of his father, mother, sister and brother, and distinguish them from each other, are fresh in his mind, and make up the vivid picture he has carried with him through storms and perils by sea and land." However, upon returning to the cemetery to visit his loved ones, he is shocked to find

> that new arrangements have recently been introduced into the Cemetery—that these inclosures must be removed—that this modest monument erected by his father, over the remains of his beloved mother, must be taken down, one monument only being permitted in each lot— that the head and foot-stones marking the spot where others of the family are laid, must be lowered to the level of the surrounding surface; that these mounds, identifying the remains of his honored parents, and all the other deceased members of the family, must be reduced to the same level—that they disfigure the grounds by their unsightly appearance, and mar the landscape effect, and park-like appearance of the Cemetery.

Having thus created this fictional scene in which the son faces the requirement to essentially dismantle and depersonalize his family's lot, Speer then imagines the young man's indignant protest: "Is this a modern park? A place for gayety and pleasure? Or is it a Cemetery, sacred to the repose of the dead, and thoughtful reflection to the living? Talk not to me of spreading the green carpet of nature over these graves. . . . Remove the inclosures of the lot if you please, but disturb not these mounds that tell me the precise spot where the remains of my revered father and mother and the rest of my kindred repose."[47] Like Olmsted before him, Speer concluded, in the version of his essay for the *Weekly Gazette*, with a general plea for the establishment of a public park for "our Smoky City, of two hundred thousand inhabitants," rather than any endeavor to make Allegheny, the city's major rural cemetery, more parklike. "We have a first-class cemetery of 280 acres. Let us have a first-class park of equal or greater interest."[48]

Despite Speer's exhortations on the matter, the tide of public opinion was already swept away with the enthusiasm for parklike landscape lawn cemeteries. Five years later, Pittsburgh's Homewood Cemetery on the city's eastern side opened to the public, while Allegheny, too, eventually succumbed to popular opinion and incorporated new landscape lawn sections.

Originally comprising 175 acres, the new cemetery was situated on elevated and "comparatively secluded" land that its proprietors hoped would be "forever free from the smoke and dirt of manufacturing establishments" while at the same time "convenient and easy of access."[49] In a publication made by the cemetery in 1905, the managers reflected upon the nineteenth-century debates concerning the laying out and ornamentation of cemeteries and looked upon the older rural cemeteries, which had not kept up with the times, with regret. "The older Cemeteries, which at first accepted the plan generally in use, of allowing lots to be inclosed with hedges and fences of all descriptions, are slow to admit they have made a mistake, or to favor the modern landscape system. This is not to be wondered at, because the adoption of the open and natural system is now beyond their power." Pointing to Green-Wood Cemetery as an example of such a situation, the Homewood managers cited the cemetery's annual report of 1876 and its description of how enclosing burial plots and allowing too much uncontrolled greenery had led to dilapidation of both the monuments and the sward.[50]

Anticipating the eventual shift to the memorial park ideal, in which all grave markers must be flush with the ground, the Homewood managers wrote glowingly of the benefits of an open, organized, and uncluttered landscape. "Grass—and trees, and ornamental shrubs, distributed with judgment and taste over a handsome, rolling surface—with good roads winding around in different directions, wherever they are absolutely needed, compose the principal features of a landscape which always gives true pleasure, and has a wonderfully calming and joyous effect upon the mind." Such an effect, they asserted, could be achieved in both the public park and the cemetery without "detracting from the sacredness and privacy of a true city of the dead."[51] Recognizing large forest trees as "sacred," the managers nevertheless believed that their presence should be restricted to ornamental and undeveloped sections of the cemetery and not allowed in any of the areas where burial sections were located. Toward the close of their discussion on cemetery design, the cemetery managers affirmed their support for the landscape lawn plan, but in a modified form. "We do not forbid all structures upon a lot except the central monument," they explained, "although we approve of it; but we discard inclosures, we keep the corner posts low, we commend the central monument, and we provide for the glorious grass carpet, free from litter and weeds, and for a judicious planting under the control of the Managers."[52] In their conclusion, the stress upon control and order over the landscape is particularly striking as well as reflective of the

Monuments at Homewood Cemetery, Pittsburgh. (Photograph by the author)

sentiments embraced by cemetery managers and superintendents elsewhere across the country.

> The smooth, shaven lawn; the proper distribution of small trees and
> ornamental shrubs, kept constantly pruned; the preservation or cultiva-
> tion of single trees, groups or thickets, in places set apart for such orna-
> mentation; the soft grassy walks between lots; the winding, well kept
> roads, and the more or less lofty and elaborate central monument, show-
> ing through the rich green foliage here and there, and all kept, every lot,
> in perfect order—this is our idea of what a Cemetery should be, and it is
> what we aim for in Homewood Cemetery.[53]

A major part of what allowed cemetery superintendents to exert greater
control over the entirety of the cemetery landscape was the widespread adoption by cemetery companies of perpetual care policies in the years following
the Civil War. In an 1885 guidebook to Rochester's Mount Hope Cemetery,
the cemetery managers urged perpetual care as an assurance that lots would

not fall into disrepair once living family or friends who cared about such lots were gone: "Many persons who invested in the perpetual repair fund have since died, leaving no relative or friend to look after their lots or graves. Yet they are cared for and the interest on investment expended on them and will continue to be."[54] A similar book published by the West Laurel Hill Cemetery Company expanded upon this language and asserted that perpetual care funds provided "the means by which the cemetery grounds might for all time be maintained in a condition becoming to their sacred purpose, and in order that the lot-owners and their descendants may have assurance that when they are deceased, or when in the process of time the cemetery is wholly occupied as a place of burial, that these resting places of the dead shall not suffer from neglect, either on account of the indifference of posterity, or the inability of the Cemetery Company to supply the moneys for their care."[55] Despite language concerning the fate of lots following the death of lot holders, the unwritten implication here was that even the lot holders themselves were neither expected nor even really encouraged to maintain—either with decorations or plantings—their own lots, which had been an integral aspect of lot ownership and the living's relationship with the rural cemetery and the dead buried within it during the antebellum period.

The adoption of perpetual care and superintendents' usurpation of control over lots were but small parts of the broader cultural transformations then occurring in the Anglo-Protestant relationship with death and the dead. As new cemeteries were even more far removed from the day-to-day sight of the living than their predecessors, despite the supposed ease of access by carriage and train, and undertakers assumed greater control over the processes involved in preparing the dead for burial, white Americans in particular became increasingly removed—both literally and figuratively—from traditional modes of mourning and care for the dead as the nineteenth century entered its final decades. In the years after the Civil War, white American families progressively outsourced care for their dead to professionalized undertakers, whose wartime experience honing the craft of arterial embalming gave them, in the postwar period, a greater air of specialized knowledge than they previously had in the antebellum era.[56] During the first half of the nineteenth century, death and the preparation and display of the dead took place in the home, where family members and neighbors were intimately involved. The undertaker was only necessary when it came time to rent a carriage hearse to carry the body from the home to the place of burial. In rural areas, where family burial grounds were located within

the bounds of the family's property, pallbearers were sufficient to remove
the body from the home to the grave and no hearse was necessary. The rural
cemetery movement had magnified the importance of the corpse itself, and
families maintained an intimate relationship with the dead within the picturesque burial landscape where they could erect monuments and fences
and plant trees, flowers, and shrubs according to their personal taste. The
purchase of a burial lot within a rural cemetery was a transaction that meant
the lot itself had become the personal property of the lot holder, to beautify
and do with as they wished. That it was incumbent upon the living to care for
the lots of their loved ones perpetuated the physical relationship between
the living and the dead—this had not been the case in older churchyards
and burying grounds, and it would also not be the case in lawn cemeteries
or memorial parks. The changing religious patterns wrought by the Second
Great Awakening of the antebellum era meant that there was an ideological
shift in favor of not only faith in eternal salvation—thus rejecting the Calvin-
ist doctrine of predestination—but also faith in the heavenly reunion of the
family.[57] A further antebellum trend was, despite cemetery reformers' views
of decomposing flesh as dangerous and the potential source of disease, the
elevation in importance of the corpse as precious and, subsequently, the
heightened desire to keep family members within close proximity of each
other within family lots. Thus the bonds of family remained strong after
death, the bodies of the dead regarded as both precious and sacred, their
place of burial to be visited and ornamented regularly.[58]

The professionalization of undertaking into a full-blown funeral industry, combined with the transformation of the American hospital into a place
of health and healing by the 1880s, meant that for an increased number of
Americans, their relationship to death, dying, and care for the dead experienced a seismic shift that fundamentally distanced the living from the
dead for much of the next century.[59] This shift was further connected to an
emerging consumerism in both healthcare and deathcare, in which Americans paid sizable fees to professional outsiders, trusting that they could care
for the ill, infirm, or dead as well as, if not better than, families had in the
antebellum era. Changes in the American hospital system and end-of-life
care thus ultimately led to an increasing number of Americans dying within
the hospital setting rather than in bed at home, surrounded by family and
friends. The traditional deathbed scene progressively gave way to a medi-
calized death. Family then called upon the newly professionalized undertaker to whisk the body away for preparation for the viewing and burial—a

preparation that now involved arterial embalming in addition to washing and dressing the dead. The undertaker—increasingly referred to, by century's end, as a funeral director—also sold the casket to the grieving family, provided the venue for the wake, and arranged for transportation to the church and place of burial. By the 1880s, to style themselves as serious professionals and alleviate any "customers' anxieties and concerns about giving over not only their deceased loved ones . . . but sizable fees as well," undertakers within the nascent funeral industry began to publish trade journals that were "focused on the business of death." As noted by historian Gary Laderman, "These journals catered to undertakers who interacted with consumers and offered information and advice about a range of issues related to death and the disposal of the dead." Among the earliest of these trade journals was one titled *The Casket*.[60]

In truth, by the end of the nineteenth century, Anglo-Protestants did not need to do more to care for the dead other than pay the hospital's and undertaker's fees and show up for the funeral. This is not to say that Americans stopped grieving for their loved ones. Quite the contrary, for Victorian mourning practices involved an expansive material culture associated with socially expected extended grief—especially for widows—and popular modes for communing with the dead, such as through spiritualism.[61] Rather, the physical care for the dead body and its burial site were integrated into the broader mourning culture that rested upon an increasingly transactional consumer culture. Since midcentury, mourning consumer culture had included the purchase of elaborate mourning attire (all black for full mourning, partially black for half mourning), mourning jewelry, and postmortem photographs (either of the deceased alone or as part of a family portrait).[62] By the late nineteenth century, monument companies issued catalogs with standardized styles that altogether streamlined the purchasing process.

The main characteristics of the landscape lawn cemetery further reinforced the late nineteenth-century process of depersonalizing death and making it more of a consumer-based industry. The value of the individual, with personalized grave markers and decorations, became subordinate to the collective family entity, with the modern rural cemetery's emphasis on an imposing central family monument surrounded by unobtrusive flush markers. Relinquishing control over the landscape to professional cemetery superintendents released lot holders from any sense of responsibility to physically care for the graves of their loved ones, as now doing so would in fact go against cemetery regulations. The poor and the working class, who had already long been marginalized and made invisible in life, became increasingly so in death. When it was established, among Mount Auburn's foundational principles was that anyone, regardless of monetary wealth, could be respectfully buried within the picturesque rural landscape. Others, such as Laurel Hill Cemetery, were more elitist from the start, but many rural cemeteries like Mount Auburn included public lots for single interments that were financially within the reach of working-class artisans and craftsmen and areas for the burial of paupers and strangers. Modern cemeteries established during the 1870s and 1880s still maintained the option for single interments, but the new business model of the landscape lawn cemetery pushed potential buyers to purchase lots measuring not three hundred square feet, as had been the standard at Mount Auburn, but in the thousands of square feet. The landscape lawn cemetery thus made society's marginalized dead even more invisible, as the visibility of the working class's or pauper's graves would mar the overall visual effect superintendents sought to achieve.

Responsive to the opportunity to purchase sizable burial lots within the newer cemeteries, members of the new industrial capitalist elite, multimillionaires who regularly looked for new ways to spend and display their wealth, sought to distinguish themselves in death as in life and erected impressive freestanding mausoleums that cost tens of thousands of dollars. Financier Jay Gould, who purchased a ten-thousand-square-foot lot at Woodlawn Cemetery, began construction in the 1880s of a neoclassical mausoleum on the model of the Parthenon that the press reported as costing upwards of $100,000. The construction of expensive and lavish mausoleums while still living became a cultural phenomenon among the nation's wealthiest citizens, and the press published extensive articles on the craze for mausoleum building, fashioning it into a competition between captains of industry.[63] Rural cemeteries had long been regarded by the public as repositories for the notable and the wealthy. One visitor to Mount Auburn in 1864 observed the cost and elegance of many of the monuments and thus concluded, "Death, it is said, levels all distinctions among men, in position, rank, wealth, etc., but this is true only to a certain extent. Wealth gives prominence in Mount Auburn, as really as in Boston Common or the Central Park."[64] The greater division of rich from poor during the last half of the nineteenth century merely amplified what had already been evident within the rural cemeteries for decades, and by century's end, no one could realistically claim that death was the great equalizer. The desire on the part of cemetery superintendents to establish a sense of order and control over their burial landscapes further illustrated the efforts on the part of urban progressive reformers to exert control over the modern city, which had become not only increasingly polluted and generally unhealthy to the living but also overcrowded and, to elites and the middle class, overrun by slums and impoverished immigrants.[65] The modern cemetery, molded by cemetery superintendents, became for the dead what middle-class and elite Americans desired, but could not fully achieve, in modern cities for the living—cleanliness, orderliness, calm, and altogether lacking in unwashed riffraff.

By the final decade of the century, the designs and guiding principles of new cemeteries—Kensico Cemetery (est. 1891) north of White Plains, New York; Druid Ridge Cemetery (est. 1896) near Baltimore; and Paxtang Cemetery (est. 1898) in Harrisburg, Pennsylvania, notable among them—were worlds away from the rural cemeteries that preceded them. These and others like them established around the country during the 1890s marked the triumph of the landscape lawn cemetery model, both as an aesthetic and as a business, over the rural cemetery. While cemeteries established during the 1870s and even into the 1880s still maintained certain ephemeral connections to the rural cemetery movement—for instance, by still employing the term "rural cemetery" despite the increasing dominance of the landscape lawn method—all new cemeteries by the 1890s were designed and explicitly labeled as landscape lawn cemeteries (or simply as "lawn cemeteries"), marking an era in cemetery development that possessed its own distinct characteristics while also serving as a bridge between the nineteenth-century rural cemetery and the twentieth-century memorial park. Run by cemetery professionals who endeavored to use technology and landscape gardening techniques to fashion parklike burial grounds for the enjoyment of the living, modern cemeteries by this time had become major businesses that offered services to the bereaved as consumers, with little attention paid to the mourning rituals that had been such an important part of American culture since the late eighteenth century.

Kensico Cemetery, established in 1891 in the village of Kensico, north of White Plains, New York, led the way in breaking all ties with the long-standing rural cemetery movement. Described by Moses King in *King's Handbook of New York City* in 1893, Kensico's primary features, all of which involved significant financial cost, were those that involved providing physical comfort to visitors and displaying the most advanced modern technology. These included, for example, the Queen Anne–style stone railroad depot, "costly and perfect in all its appointments," which functioned as the entrance to the cemetery in lieu of a gateway, and the public receiving tomb, containing 178 catacombs, "built of stone and granite . . . with a most perfect system for their interior ventilation." Noting the large fountain in front of the tomb and the garden within the nearby grounds, *King's Handbook* thus declared, "The artistic treatment of this building and its surroundings has made it a most beautiful and attractive spot." Noting the intent of the cemetery's founders and managers to make Kensico Cemetery "one of the most beautiful of American burial-places," the *Handbook* observed how "leading architects and landscape gardeners" were at that moment in charge of planning the buildings and laying out the grounds, which would include the construction of a chapel and conservatory to be located near the entrance for the greater convenience of the living. It further explained how wealthy lot holders were then in the process of ordering the erection of monuments and construction of mausoleums costing thousands of dollars.[66] *Appleton's Dictionary of New York*, published in 1898, further noted how the cemetery's buildings, including additional "temporary catacombs" near the entrance, would "introduce a custom to New York, of conducting full funeral services at the cemetery. Special funeral trains, making one or two trips daily, will render this possible."[67] Such services, emerging by the end of the century, foreshadowed the development of twentieth-century cemeteries into a "one-stop shop" experience where consumers could eventually arrange all necessary services for the dead—purchase a lot or mausoleum crypt or, increasingly, after the turn of the century, purchase an urn and mausoleum or columbarium niche to hold cremains (cremated remains) following cremation at the on-site crematory. All cemeteries by then would include perpetual care services, and many also went into the business of selling monuments as well.[68]

At the dedication ceremonies for Druid Ridge Cemetery in 1898, the Presbyterian reverend Madison C. Peters from New York City delivered the principal oration, which illustrated the changes in mourning patterns encouraged by not only religious figures like himself but those within the deathcare industry. "To do away with the excess of flowers, and, above all, with crepe veils," he said, "is what we want. Fashionable mourning is the greatest possible satire on grief. It expresses hopelessness instead of faith. . . . If you have flowers give them to your friends while they are alive. Avoid all unnecessary display and expense."[69] The caution against flowers especially

Monuments at Druid Ridge Cemetery, Pikesville, Maryland, including a mosaic monument of Christ the Shepherd by the Tiffany Company. (Photograph by the author)

was consistent with cemeteries' efforts to prevent lot holders from decorating graves. As for mourning attire, the expectation, especially for women, to wear nothing but black (full mourning) for an extended period of time had been a central characteristic of nineteenth-century mourning practices; in the open, parklike landscape lawn cemeteries, however, mourners bedecked in black gowns and veils would be incongruous with what cemetery managers intended as the pleasant atmosphere of the burial ground.[70]

The rural cemetery's design, in which visitors and mourners alike would be surrounded by nature and picturesque views that would enhance introspection and melancholic feelings, had become anathema to the cemetery industry by century's end, and the public's attitude toward death and mourning altered in parallel despite its attachment to elaborate funerary accoutrements (the flowers and clothing, for example, denounced by Reverend Peters) and expensive monuments. When Joseph Story delivered his address at the consecration of Mount Auburn in 1831, he opened with the words, "The occasion which brings us together, has much in it calculated to awaken our sensibilities, and cast a solemnity over our thoughts. We are met to consecrate these grounds exclusively to the service and repose of the dead."[71] In stark contrast to Story's sentiment, one New Jersey newspaper reported, after listing the full program of the afternoon's exercises for the opening and dedication of a new cemetery in Somerton Hills, Pennsylvania in 1899, "There is every reason to believe" that those present "will be well entertained." Rather than carrying with it the weight of enhancing the visitor's thoughts upon mortality and eternity, the new cemetery embodied "all the essential elements of the newer idea of burial reform, made possible only by means of unlimited capital and with no restrictions as to expense.... Our cemeteries, the burying grounds of America, are becoming more and more spots of adornment and lasting beauty."[72]

In the midst of such changes, the managers of many of the nation's rural cemeteries did not sit idly by and allow their institutions to fade into obscurity. Maintaining relevance was key, and this meant expanding acreage and keeping step with the march of what many believed was progress. The managers of Chicago's Rosehill Cemetery issued an extensive report to the *Tribune* on the efforts to improve and modernize their cemetery. Among these was the expansion of the receiving vault, capable of holding upwards of 250 bodies and extensive enough that "those desiring to have funerals there find it a very great convenience, as they can afterward examine and select lots and have interments made thereon at their leisure." Further, the managers had overseen the construction of an artesian well and water and sewer system, artificial lakes supplied with water from the well, and "handsome greenhouses and conservatories." Family lots were available measuring anywhere from ten by fifteen feet to one hundred by one hundred feet, while a new landscape lawn section was available with even larger lots in response to "the request of a number of the most prominent and wealthy citizens of Chicago, who desired to secure large and handsome lots for themselves and heirs." In responding to the desires of the city's elite, the managers expressed confidence that "this feature of the cemetery is rapidly meeting with favor, and will, in a short time, form one of the most pleasing and satisfactory as well as the handsomest and most desirable portion of the cemetery."[73] In Salem, Oregon, the Odd Fellows, who had established that city's rural cemetery, negotiated for the purchase of an additional twenty-two acres of land adjoining the cemetery in 1892 so that it could expand, and as the electric trolley line had now reached the cemetery, the *Statesman Journal* asserted that "there is no doubt but those grounds will hereafter be much better kept, since they are so easy of access."[74] In Louisville, Cave Hill Cemetery's managers, like those in Chicago, undertook major projects in the 1890s to modernize the infrastructure of their burying ground. These included the installation of thousands of feet of water and sewer pipe, hydrants for the use of lot holders throughout the cemetery, construction of an office building, a clock and bell over the gatekeeper's lodge, and beautification of the lake, "which covers about three acres and is now a charming feature of the landscape." Further reflective of how the superintendents of older rural cemeteries altered their landscapes according to changing cultural tastes and patterns, the management at Cave Hill determined to remove the cypress, willow, and cedar trees and replace them "with trees of a less melancholy significance and greater beauty."[75] In addition to their continuous projects to improve its grounds, in 1898, officials at Mount Auburn Cemetery responded to the expanding popularity of the cremation movement and submitted a petition before the state legislature for permission to erect a crematory on the cemetery grounds.[76]

By contrast, late nineteenth-century African American cemeteries, many of them established by burial associations, shirked the landscape lawn approach in favor of holding true to many of the principal features of the older rural cemetery. Black cemeteries in Richmond, Virginia, effectively illustrate this tendency, with the founding of Evergreen Cemetery in 1891 and East End Cemetery in 1897. As noted by historian Ryan K. Smith, both cemeteries "were laid out in tight geometrical designs, with a few carriage lanes for access. Neither pursued the emerging lawn park model exemplified in Hollywood Cemetery's newest addition. Rather, both gave free rein to plot holders, with family sections typically measuring fifteen by fifteen feet to be bounded by stone curbing or metal fencing at the owners' direction."[77] In Baltimore, what began as the African Burying Ground evolved and changed locations over time until in the early twentieth century it became the thirty-four-acre Mount Auburn Cemetery. Described by historian Kami Fletcher, Baltimore's Mount Auburn Cemetery illustrated African Americans' "demand for citizenship during Jim Crow segregation with the creation of a lawn/park cemetery to showcase African Americans' historical legacy to the city."[78] Albeit Mount Auburn was not explicitly designed as a rural cemetery, the naming of it in Baltimore bore with it the cultural weight of the nation's first rural cemetery, its name denoting hope for future success and stability.

❖ ❖ ❖

Designed according to antebellum ideals concerning taste, refinement, and proper care for the dead, the rural cemetery had become, in the opinion of many Americans and cemetery professionals, an antiquated institution that did not reflect the progressive values of turn-of-the-century America. Increasingly during the last forty years of the nineteenth century, the picturesque gave way to the beautiful, while the power of lot holders to ornament their lots and care for their dead as they saw fit succumbed to the rules of perpetual care instituted by cemetery superintendents who increasingly sought to wield total control over the landscapes of the dead. Where there had been at one time the movement to separate the pleasure ground from the cemetery with the emergent parks movement of the 1850s and 1860s, one of the most influential aspects of the landscape lawn plan was the very opposite—to transform the cemetery into a more parklike institution, dedicated to the comfort and pleasure of the living. Adolph Strauch was instrumental in effecting such a transformation in cemetery landscape aesthetics, and by the end of the 1870s, one cemetery publication declared, "America is as yet unaware how much she owes to this large-hearted, and accomplished Prussian, who has devoted his talents for many years, to the achievement of results unequalled in this country, and scarcely surpassed in the old world."[79] Care for the dead, which had always been the responsibility of the family, came under the authority of funeral directors and cemetery professionals, and while Americans, especially members of the elite, poured untold thousands into the erection of grand monuments and mausoleums, the ties that bound the living and the dead became nearly invisible by 1900. Rural cemeteries as operational burying grounds survived because of the labor of managers and superintendents to expand and develop the grounds according to modern preferences, but they no longer wielded the same national cultural influence as they had at midcentury. Nevertheless, many of the foundational principles fashioned for rural cemeteries dating back to the 1830s remained influential even as the landscapes transformed over time. Removing the place of burial away from urban development in the interest of public health and sanitation, establishing codes of conduct for visitors, and transforming the place of burial into a space to be enjoyed by the living were among the features of the rural cemetery that persisted for decades, even as the values associated with picturesque landscapes and the intimate relationship between the living and the dead fell away.

Conclusion

In the early decades of the twentieth century, it appeared as though the rural cemetery as the ideal model for the disposition of the dead and as a central cultural institution was itself dead, an artifact of a less developed time in American history. Forest Lawn Cemetery opened in Glendale, California, in 1906 and under the direction of Hubert Eaton was transformed in 1917 into the nation's first memorial park, which represented a complete rejection of the nineteenth-century rural—and even landscape lawn—cemetery. Rejecting the vertical family monument, Forest Lawn allows as grave markers only flush to the ground bronze plaques. Speaking to the press in 1921, Eaton declared, somewhat ironically, "We are doing something that no other cemetery in the country has ever attempted. In all history nature has made death the most beautiful episode of mortal's careers, while men have made it the most gruesome. We are going to stick by old Dame Nature and make Forest Lawn one of the real beauty spots of southern California."[1] The irony of Eaton's assertion is that the rural cemetery movement had sought to create a burial environment reminiscent of untouched nature, a space where mourners could grieve, contemplate mortality and eternity, and find solace within an environment that rejected the modernism of the emerging industrial city. Eaton's ideal landscape meant subduing nature in the effort to create a beautiful park where neither death nor nature is present in any obvious way. Scattered throughout Forest Lawn are sculptural works placed by the memorial park, while trees and other plantings—already diminished in the landscape lawn plan—are sparsely interspersed. The overall environment favors an aesthetic of wide-open lawns in a setting that avoids all references to death and mourning. Forest Lawn's website declares proudly, "Our original Forest Lawn location has been a Southern California landmark since 1906. It has a world-renowned art museum, extraordinary statuary, and the Hall of the Crucifixion-Resurrection which is home to two of the largest religious paintings in the Western hemisphere."[2] According to Jessica Mitford, in *The American Way of Death*, Forest Lawn "pioneered the current trend for cemeteries to own their own mortuary and flower shop, for convenient, one-stop shopping."[3] Today, there is even a gift shop on-site.

Like Mount Auburn Cemetery when it opened in 1831, Hubert Eaton's Forest Lawn Memorial Park became a cultural phenomenon, and the memorial park model spread cross-country throughout the twentieth century to become the dominant type of burial ground for Americans, both for inhumation and for the disposition of cremated remains. The broad acceptance of the memorial park went hand in hand with modern Americans' further distancing of themselves from death and the dead, to the point that scholars and social commenters have long noted the intensification of Americans' fear and even denial of death during the last century. Worlds away from Americans' intimate daily interaction with mortality during the eighteenth and nineteenth centuries, much of this changed attitude toward death can be directly connected to advances in medicine and surgery leading to longer life expectancies in the West, along with the medicalization of end-of-life care, with death largely occurring outside the home.[4] As part of the increased disassociation between American society and death, the natural processes of grief and bereavement have become pathologized as abnormal behaviors if they persist for more than a few weeks or months.[5] In the United States, private companies are not held to any federally mandated standards for bereavement leave, though most offer between three and seven days—in short, enough to hold a funeral and dispose of the remains.[6]

The last quarter century, however, has witnessed a resurgence among the general population of finding novel ways to maintain meaningful connections with the dead and express their grief both publicly and privately. Twenty-first-century Americans have had to contend with all manner of "traumatic deaths" on an everyday basis—as a result of gun violence, the opioid crisis, the COVID-19 pandemic, rising suicide rates—in addition to health conditions leading to premature death, including heart disease, diabetes, and cancer.[7] Memorial parks continue to maintain the facade of a denial of death, but through social media memorial pages, RIP T-shirts, memorial decals for automobiles, and memorial tattoos, Americans have developed a rich material culture of what I term "traveling cenotaphs"—the memorial moves with the mourner rather than residing over the body of the deceased. Other types of "everyday memorials," as David Charles Sloane calls them, include RIP murals, ghost bikes (bicycles painted white and displayed on streets where bicyclists have been killed by motorists), and road-side shrines.[8] Taken altogether, such objects function as modern memento mori for people, very much like those in the nineteenth century, coming to grips on a daily basis with the reality of death and loss.

Further, despite what might be regarded as the century-long disap-pearance of death from mainstream American society, the rural cemeteries that stood as such cherished and important cultural institutions during the nineteenth century did not simply fade into oblivion. Most of the largest and oldest rural cemeteries now bear National Historic Landmark desig-nation and also continue to function as active burial grounds. There were those, on the other hand, that for a variety of reasons did not survive to the present day or are no longer in operation. Philadelphia's African American Lebanon Cemetery (est. 1849), for instance, was regularly beset by body snatchers, and by the end of the century was overcrowded. When the ceme-tery was condemned in 1899, the bodies were relocated to the newly estab-lished Eden Cemetery (est. 1903), where they remain today, many of them unidentified.[9] Other rural cemeteries, due to mismanagement and even-tual abandonment, have become overgrown and subject to vandalism. In these cases, individuals and nonprofit charitable friends associations have undertaken the labor and fundraising efforts to rehabilitate these historic burying grounds by clearing away overgrowth and repairing and resetting grave markers. Such has been the case with Philadelphia's Mount Vernon and Mount Moriah Cemeteries, both of which now have active volunteer associations trying to undo decades of damage and neglect.[10]

The march of time and the demands of urban development in the twen-tieth century also meant that rural cemeteries occupying prime real estate within developed or developing areas, especially smaller ones and those serving marginalized communities, were especially at risk for demolition. Philadelphia's Monument Cemetery (est. 1838), which had been established after Laurel Hill Cemetery as an alternative for elite Philadelphians at a more walkable distance from the city center, and Baltimore's African American Laurel Cemetery (est. 1851) offer two of the most jarring cases of cemetery destruction. Laurel Cemetery's (est. 1851) decline began in the early twen-tieth century, beginning first with the relocation of the remains of buried United States Colored Troops to Loudon Park National Cemetery "to accom-modate the expansion of Belair Road." Portions of the property continued to be sold through the 1920s and 1930s, while the portions of the cemetery occupied with graves became "overgrown and garbage-strewn." Laurel

Cemetery declared bankruptcy in 1952, and in 1958 the sole shareholder sold the cemetery to the McKamer Realty Company for $100. Before the company leveled what remained of the cemetery, a few hundred remains were reinterred elsewhere (nowhere near the actual number originally buried at Laurel Cemetery), and the site became home to a Two Guys Department Store in 1962.[11] In Philadelphia, Monument Cemetery comprised fifteen acres of land directly across the street from Temple University, and by the time of its final burial in 1929, it held the bodies of twenty-eight thousand individuals, including the university's founder, Russell Conwell, who died in 1925. As early as 1928, Temple University attempted to purchase the cemetery, not to preserve it but to level it for campus expansion. By the 1950s, no longer generating income from burials, the cemetery had begun to fall into disrepair and was subjected to vandalism. The university, now wishing to use the space as a parking lot, successfully lobbied the city government to have Monument Cemetery condemned, after which it was able to seize control of the cemetery through eminent domain and proceed with demolition in 1956. Families were contacted to claim the bodies of their loved ones for reinterment elsewhere, and only several hundred did so. According to photographer Ed Snyder, who documented Monument Cemetery's destruction on his *Cemetery Traveler* blog and photographed the cemetery's grave markers and monuments, nearly all of which were unceremoniously dumped into the Delaware River, over twenty thousand unclaimed bodies ended up in a mass grave in nearby Lawnview Cemetery. Intrepid wanderers can see the grave markers if they descend to the banks of the river at low tide.[12]

In many of the nation's historic rural cemeteries, however, professionalized cemetery managers were able to expand upon the success of their institutions by adding acreage that conformed to society's changing tastes and continue to operate in the twenty-first century as successful businesses. Like Forest Lawn Memorial Park, many of these operational rural cemeteries have embraced vertical integration into their business model, providing cremation services, monument and urn sales, grave decorations, and complete funeral packages, all on-site. Cincinnati's Spring Grove Cemetery, for example, is now part of an entire deathcare suite of businesses bearing the Spring Grove name, including multiple funeral homes across the state of Ohio, the Spring Grove Cremation Society, and Oak Hill Cemetery (est. 1910).[13] Visitors to rural cemeteries today can easily observe the transformations over time of landscaping aesthetics, as they traverse through the original rural into the later landscape lawn, memorial park, and, in an increasing number now, green burial sections. In a number of rural cemeteries, such as Mount Auburn, Green-Wood, and Cave Hill Cemeteries, the green burial options—burial without embalming and inside a biodegradable container—mean burial within the original historic sections of the cemetery. Community mausoleums, which were first introduced in the late nineteenth century as an alternative to in-ground burial, became increasingly common in both rural and modern cemeteries after the 1920s, so in addition to in-ground casket and urn burial options, operational rural cemeteries generally have community mausoleum entombment and columbarium niches for urns available as well.

Just as many Americans during the nineteenth century regarded rural cemeteries as the final resting places of the elite, those searching for burial space at a rural cemetery in the twenty-first century face magnified expenses of burial or mausoleum interment, often beyond the reach of only the wealthiest. While some rural cemeteries, such as Mount Hope Cemetery in Bangor, Maine, maintain affordable prices because they still primarily cater to locals, others among the most famous historic cemeteries are prohibitively expensive.[14] For instance, those interested in purchasing space at Mount Auburn Cemetery have several options available, none of which are cheap. According to the cemetery's website, Mount Auburn "is committed to providing elegant, tranquil, and environmentally sensitive burial space now and well into the future. Current options include conventional casket graves, natural burial graves, and space for the burial of cremated remains, and accommodate a wide range of memorial styles. With features like reflection pools, woodland gardens, or scenic overlooks, today's offerings reflect the Cemetery's founding principle that nature helps to console the bereaved and inspire the living." The price for casket graves, which can accommodate the burial of both casketed bodies and cremated remains, begins at $25,000; for cremation burials and niches in the Story Chapel Columbarium, prices start at $3,000 for an individual space and $15,000 for spaces that accommodate two or more; natural burial graves, "available largely in the historic areas of the Cemetery and . . . intended for unembalmed bodies buried in biodegradable containers," begin at $9,000.[15] At Brooklyn's Green-Wood Cemetery, the sky's the limit as far as pricing is concerned. Entombment in a community mausoleum ranges from $31,000 to $55,000, while urn niches range from $2,300 to $19,000. In-ground burials start at $21,000 per standard grave plus foundation costs ($1,633–2,042), while premium lots cost $35,000 per grave. A 378-square-foot sarcophagus site is $250,000, while a

756-square-foot mausoleum site can be had for $450,000. These, of course, are the prices for just the real estate. There are further charges for opening graves or vaults, for cremation, and, in the case of in-ground burials, the excavation and foundation charges.[16] Just as it had during the nineteenth century, burial or entombment within a culturally significant cemetery—many of which are now also historically significant and are located on prime real estate within the nation's major metropolitan areas—often comes with a hefty price.

Even as rural cemeteries have continued to operate as attractive burial grounds, many have managed to maintain themselves as multifunctional institutions, just as they had been when they were first established. Mount Auburn Cemetery hosts regular walking tours as well as speakers, artists workshops, bird watching, and performances, all of which are posted on their online events calendar.[17] Laurel Hill Cemetery engages the public with regular programming, including both virtual and live cemetery tours, a monthly book club, and major annual events, including the Market of the Macabre, the Gravediggers' Ball, which raises money for the Friends of Laurel Hill nonprofit charitable organization, and the Rest in Peace 5K race on Halloween.[18] Other rural cemeteries also take advantage of the popular connection between cemeteries and Halloween to host themed events, such as Atlanta's "Run Like Hell 5K" and "Capturing the Spirit" tour at Oakland Cemetery.[19] Louisville's Cave Hill Cemetery offers a host of themed tours, available on foot or in a golf cart, including a historical tour; a twilight horticultural tour; tours focusing on literary figures, notable women, musicians, and even bourbon distillers; and a Civil War–related tour.[20] In the wake of Muhammad Ali's death and burial at Cave Hill Cemetery in 2017, the cemetery hosted a civil rights leaders tour that year.[21]

Among the founding principles of the rural cemetery movement was the creation of picturesque landscapes situated beyond the realm of urban development to provide a retreat for the living where they could escape the noise, smells, and hubbub of the city for an afternoon. That mission remains just as relevant if not more so in the twenty-first century as climate change has made devastating summer heatwaves in major metropolitan areas increasingly common. The marriage between burying ground and horticulture remains strong, as many rural cemeteries are also arboretums and provide critical green space amid the urban landscapes that grew around them over the past century or more. Rural cemeteries encompassing hundreds of acres often provide some of the largest areas with tree cover and green space for the cities where they are located, such as Green-Wood Cemetery in Brooklyn.[22] In an ironic twist, even many landscape lawn cemeteries, which were originally landscaped with minimal tree cover at the time of their founding, have experienced tree growth to the effect that they appear more as rural, rather than lawn, cemeteries today. Such has been the case at Pittsburgh's Homewood Cemetery, where staff are considering tree *removal* to bring the landscaping aesthetics back to what they were originally.[23] The important function of cemeteries as green spaces is not just restricted to the United States—in their study of cemeteries in Bristol, England, Katie McClymont and Danielle Sinnett of the Centre for Sustainable Planning and Environments at the University of the West of England have argued that cemeteries have an important role "within a multifunctional network of green infrastructure" in their "potential to contribute both to climate change mitigation, and to increasing quality of life for urban residents."[24]

On November 5, 2022, I traveled to Pittsburgh for the fall meeting of the Pennsylvania Chapter of the Association for Gravestone Studies. I was there as both chapter co-chair and presenter, and following the morning presentations, our group headed to Allegheny Cemetery for a tour led by my friend and colleague Dr. Elisabeth Roark, who teaches art history at Chatham University and specializes in cemetery sculpture. This was only my second visit to Allegheny, my first having been back in 2008 when I was hunting for Egyptian Revival monuments for my dissertation. Driving through the massive gateway, with the Gothic Revival office to the left and the gatehouse to the right, on this occasion I was less focused on individual monuments and was able to take in the totality of the site. Whereas Allegheny Cemetery, like so many rural cemeteries, was originally situated several miles beyond the city's major development when it was established in the 1840s, today it is entirely engulfed by residences and businesses, and across the street along one entire side of the cemetery is the UPMC Children's Hospital. As we walked, I noticed a group of Cub Scouts working on a project, joggers, families sitting at picnic tables opposite the office building, and couples strolling hand in hand. Then there was our excited little group of cemetery nerds, bustling from monument to monument, taking photographs and listening to Beth's explanations of different symbols, monument designs, and histories. Later, I drove through the grounds to find the Winter mausoleum—an Egyptian Revival confection, complete with large-breasted guardian sphinxes—which I had

Members of the Pennsylvania Chapter of the Association for Gravestone Studies being led on a tour of Pittsburgh's Allegheny Cemetery by Dr. Elisabeth Roark, November 5, 2022. (Photograph by the author)

written about in my dissertation. On my way, I passed an artificial pond and was struck by the profusion of leaves scattered on the ground and over the monuments. When I arrived at the Winter mausoleum after getting turned around a few times by the curving avenues, I was disappointed to find a group of young adults dressed all in black, lounging on the sphinxes and on the steps of the mausoleum, who looked as though they would not take too kindly to me asking them to move so I could take a photograph. In retrospect, they may have wanted to *be* in the photograph, had I asked. Had I asked them why they were in Allegheny, why they were hanging out at that mausoleum, they may very well have answered, as well as anyone else who was there that day, that it was because it is there. Despite all of the debates and contests during the nineteenth century over what cemeteries should look like, where they should be located, how they should function, how the public should behave, and matters of taste, choice, control, representation, and identity, at the end of the day, in the twenty-first century, the rural cemetery is still with us, its most fundamental ideals intact. In the center of the city, the rural cemetery as a sacred space dedicated to the burial of the dead is somewhere for the living to go as well—whether it is a place to lounge, to walk, to eat, to grieve, or to enjoy nature, it remains now, as it ever was, an oasis for all who visit, a pleasure ground of death that is brimming with life and the living.

Notes

INTRODUCTION

1. James Deetz and Edwin Dethlefsen, "Death's Heads, Cherubs, and Willow Trees: Experimental Archaeology in Colonial Cemeteries," *American Antiquity* 31, no. 4 (April 1966): 502–10.

2. While today scholars refer to rural cemeteries without quotation marks, because of this potentially confusing label of "rural," a number of researchers during the 1970s and 1980s persistently wrote "rural" cemetery in their published works (either in the title of articles or in the body of their discussions), denoting the fact that "rural" in this instance meant style rather than location. For instance, see Stanley French, "The Cemetery as Cultural Institution: The Establishment of Mount Auburn and the 'Rural Cemetery' Movement," *American Quarterly* 26, no. 1 (March 1974): 37–59; Thomas Bender, "The 'Rural' Cemetery Movement: Urban Travail and the Appeal of Nature," *New England Quarterly* 47, no. 2 (June 1974): 196–211; Blanche Linden-Ward, "Strange but Genteel Pleasure Grounds: Tourist and Leisure Uses of Nineteenth Century Rural Cemeteries," in Richard E. Meyer, ed., *Cemeteries & Gravemarkers: Voices of American Culture* (Logan: Utah State University Press, 1989), 293–328.

3. C. L. V. Meeks, "Picturesque Eclecticism," *Art Bulletin* 32, no. 3 (September 1950): 227–28.

4. Aaron Sachs, *Arcadian America: The Death and Life of an Environmental Tradition* (New Haven: Yale University Press, 2013), 28. See also Bender, "The 'Rural' Cemetery Movement."

5. French, "The Cemetery as Cultural Institution," 59.

6. Blanche M. G. Linden, *Silent City on a Hill: Picturesque Landscapes of Memory and Boston's Mount Auburn Cemetery* (Amherst: University of Massachusetts Press, 2007), 11.

7. Jeffrey Smith, *The Rural Cemetery Movement: Places of Paradox in Nineteenth-Century America* (Lanham, MD: Lexington Books, 2017), xi; James R. Cothran and Erica Danylchak, *Grave Landscapes: The Nineteenth-Century Rural Cemetery Movement* (Charleston: University of South Carolina Press, 2018), xiii.

8. Dell Upton, *Another City: Urban Life and Urban Spaces in the New American Republic* (New Haven: Yale University Press, 2008), 221–22.

9. Ryan K. Smith, *Death and Rebirth in a Southern City: Richmond's Historic Cemeteries* (Baltimore: Johns Hopkins University Press, 2020), 158.

10. For a history of Baltimore's Laurel Cemetery, see Isaac Shearn and Elgin Klugh, *A Place for Memory: Baltimore's Historic Laurel Cemetery* (Lanham, MD: Rowman & Littlefield, 2023).

11. Ryan K. Smith, *Death and Rebirth in a Southern City*, 217.

12. For general studies of the rural cemetery movement, see Richard V. Francaviglia, "The Cemetery as an Evolving Cultural Landscape," *Annals of the Association of American Geographers* 61 (September 1971), 501–9; Stanley French, "The Cemetery as Cultural Institution"; Bender, "The 'Rural' Cemetery Movement"; David Schuyler, "The Evolution of the Anglo-American Rural Cemetery: Landscape Architecture as Social and Cultural History," *Journal of Garden History* 4 (July–September 1984), 291–304; David Charles Sloane, *The Last Great Necessity: Cemeteries in American History* (Baltimore: Johns Hopkins University Press, 1991); Blanche Linden-Ward, "Strange but Genteel Pleasure Grounds: Tourist and Leisure Uses of Nineteenth-Century Rural Cemeteries," in *Cemeteries & Gravemarkers: Voices of American Culture*, ed. Richard E. Meyer (Logan: Utah State University Press, 1992), 293–328; Aaron Sachs, "American Arcadia: Mount Auburn Cemetery and the Nineteenth-Century Landscape Tradition," *Environmental History* 15 (April 2010), 206–235; Jeffrey Smith, *The Rural Cemetery Movement*; and James R. Cothran and Erica Danylchak, *Grave Landscapes: The Nineteenth-Century Rural Cemetery Movement* (Columbia: University of South Carolina Press, 2018). For studies of specific rural cemeteries, see Barbara Rotundo, "Mount Auburn Cemetery: A Proper Boston Institution," *Harvard Library Bulletin* 22 (July 1974): 268–79; R. Kent Lancaster, "Green Mount: The Introduction of the Rural Cemetery into Baltimore," *Maryland Historical Magazine* 74 (March 1978): 62–79; Margaretta J. Darnell, "The American Cemetery as Picturesque Landscape: Bellefontaine Cemetery, St. Louis," *Winterthur Portfolio* 18 (Winter 1983): 249–69; Barbara Rotundo, "Mount Auburn: Fortunate Coincidences and an Ideal Solution," *Journal of Garden History* 4 (July–September 1984): 255–67; Blanche Linden-Ward and Alan Ward, "Spring Grove: The Role of the Rural Cemetery in American Landscape Design," *Landscape Architecture* 75 (September/October 1985): 126–31; Ruth L. Bohan, "A Home Away from Home: Bellefontaine Cemetery, St. Louis, and the Rural Cemetery Movement," *Prospects* 13 (October 1988): 135–79; chapter on Laurel Hill Cemetery in Colleen McDannell, *Material Christianity: Religion and Popular Culture in America* (New Haven: Yale University Press, 1995), 103–31; Mary H. Mitchell, *Hollywood Cemetery: The History of a Southern Shrine* (Richmond: Library of Virginia, 1999); Blanche M. G. Linden, *Silent City on a Hill: Picturesque Landscapes of Memory and Boston's Mount Auburn Cemetery* (Amherst: University of Massachusetts Press, 2007); and Ted Phillips, *City of the Silent: The Charlestonians of Magnolia Cemetery* (Columbia: University of South Carolina Press, 2010).

CHAPTER 1

1. Dell Upton, *Another City: Urban Life and Urban Spaces in the New American Republic* (New Haven: Yale University Press, 2008), 207–8.

2. Erik R. Seeman, *Death in the New World: Cross-Cultural Encounters, 1492–1800* (Philadelphia: University of Pennsylvania Press, 2010), 237–39, 251–52.

3. "Yellow Fever and Mosquitoes," *Science* 12, no. 305 (November 2, 1900): 692–93.

4. George Browning, "On Yellow Fever," *British Medical Journal* 1, no. 168 (March 17, 1860): 209 (208–10).

5. World Health Organization, "Yellow Fever," https://www.who.int/news-ro om/fact-sheets/detail/yellow-fever

6. Henry H. Townshend, *The Grove Street Cemetery: A Paper Read before the New Haven Colony Historical Society, October 27, 1947* (Printed for the Society, 1948), 5–6.

7. Ezra Stiles, *The Literary Diary of Ezra Stiles, edited under the authority of the corporation of Yale University* (New York: C. Scribner's Sons, 1901), 551. Stiles notes that another 12 of the town's residents "died at sea," bringing the total dead for 1794 to 191, but presumably these were not buried in New Haven and so I've not added them to the total of bodies that went into the old burying ground.

8. Townshend, *The Grove Street Cemetery*, 6–10.

9. Townshend, *The Grove Street Cemetery*, 11.

10. David Charles Sloane, *The Last Great Necessity: Cemeteries in American History* (Baltimore: Johns Hopkins University Press, 1991), 32.

11. Upton, *Another City*, 222.

12. Upton, *Another City*, 222.

13. Catherine E. Kelly, *Republic of Taste: Art, Politics, and Everyday Life in Early America* (Philadelphia: University of Pennsylvania Press, 2016), 7.

14. Timothy Dwight, *A Statistical Account of the Towns and Parishes in the State of Connecticut, Published by the Connecticut Academy of Arts and Sciences* (New Haven: Walter and Steele, 1811), 54–55.

15. Theodore Chase and Laurel K. Gabel, *Gravestone Chronicles I* (Boston: New England Historic Genealogical Society, 1997), 6.

16. Regarding Colonial New England gravestone styles and iconography, see Harriet Merrifield Forbes, *Gravestones of Early New England and the Men Who Made Them, 1653–1800* (Boston: Houghton Mifflin, 1927); Allan Ludwig, *Graven Images: New England Stonecarving and Its Symbols, 1650–1815* (Hanover, NH: University Press of New England, 1966); Dickran Tashjian and Ann Tashjian, *Memorials for Children of Change: The Art of Early New England Stonecarving* (Middletown, CT: Wesleyan University Press, 1974); James Deetz, *In Small Things Forgotten: An Archaeology of Early American Life* (New York: Anchor Books, 1996), 89–124; and Chase and Gabel, *Gravestone Chronicles I and II*.

17. Timothy Dwight, *A Statistical Account*, 55.

18. Joy M. Giguere, *Characteristically American: Memorial Architecture, National Identity, and the Egyptian Revival* (Knoxville: University of Tennessee Press, 2014), 60.

19. Timothy Dwight, *A Statistical Account*, 55.

20. Nehemiah Cleaveland, *Green-Wood Illustrated, in Highly Finished Line Engraving, from Drawings Taken on the Spot by James Smillie* (New York: R. Martin, 1847), 45.

21. Timothy Dwight, *A Statistical Account*, 55.

22. John M. Duncan, *Travels through Part of the United States and Canada in 1818 and 1819* (New York: W.B. Gilley, 1823), 100–101.

23. Duncan, *Travels*, 102–4.

24. Blanche M. G. Linden, *Silent City on a Hill: Picturesque Landscapes of Memory and Boston's Mount Auburn Cemetery* (Amherst: University of Massachusetts Press, 2007), 64–65.

25. Linden, *Silent City on a Hill*, 75–76.

26. Caroline Elizabeth Wilde Cushing, *Letters, Descriptive of Public Monuments, Scenery, and Manners in France and Spain, Vol. I* (Newburyport, MA: E. W. Allen, 1832), 120–21.

27. Emma Hart Willard, *Journal and Letters from France and Great Britain* (Troy, NY: N. Tuttle, 1833), 108.

28. James Stuart, *Three Years in North America, Volume I* (Edinburgh: John Stark, 1833), 365.

29. Theodore Dwight, *Things as They Are: Or, Notes of a Traveller through Some of the Middle and Northern States* (New York: Harper & Brothers, 1834), 79–80.

30. Theodore Dwight, *Things as They Are*, 80–81.

31. "Population of the 61 Urban Places: 1820," https://www.census.gov/populati on/www/documentation/twps0027/tab05.txt

32. James Hardie, *An Account of the Yellow Fever, Which Occurred in the City of New-York, in the Year 1822, to Which Is Prefixed a Brief Sketch of the Different Pestilential Diseases, with Which This City Was Afflicted, in the Years 1798, 1799, 1803 & 1805, with the Opinion of Several of Our Most Eminent Physicians, Respecting the Origin of the Disease, Its Prevention and Cure, to Which Is Added, a Correct List of All the Deaths by Yellow Fever during the Late Season, Taken from Official Documents* (New York: Samuel Marks, 1822), 6. Stanley French, "The Cemetery as Cultural Institution: The Establishment of Mount Auburn and the 'Rural Cemetery' Movement," *American Quarterly* 26, no. 1 (March 1974): 42.

33. Upton, *Another City*, 210.

34. Cheryl J. La Roche and Michael L. Blakey, "Seizing Intellectual Power: The Dialogue at the New York African Burial Ground," *Historical Archaeology* 31, no. 3 (1997): 84–85; Upton, *Another City*, 210.

35. Upton, *Another City*, 210.

36. "Grave Yards," *National Advocate* (New York), March 18, 1822, 2.

37. "Trinity Church Yard," *New York Spectator*, March 19, 1822, 1.

38. Thomas A. Apel, *Feverish Bodies, Enlightened Minds: Science and the Yellow*

Fever Controversy in the Early American Republic (Stanford: Stanford University Press, 2016), 70–71, 78.

39. *Report of the Select Committee in Relation to the Quarantine Laws of the Port of New York* (New York State Legislature, 1846), 32.

40. *A History of the Proceedings of the Board of Health, of the City of New-York, in the Summer and Fall of 1822; Together with an Account of the Rise and Progress of the Yellow Fever, Which Appeared During That Season, and the Several Documents in Relation to It, Which Were Laid before the Board* (New York: Board of Health, 1823), 50.

41. *New-York American for the Country* (September 21, 1822), 3.

42. "Trinity Church Yard," *New York Evening Post*, October 11, 1822, 2.

43. For example, see Benjamin Romaine, *Observations, Reasons and Facts, Disproving Importation: And Also, All Specific Personal Contagion in Yellow Fever, from Any Local Origin, Except That Which Arises from the Common Changes of the Atmosphere* (New York: J. C. Spear, 1823); Sloane, *The Last Great Necessity*, 37–38.

44. Francis D. Allen, *Documents and Facts Showing the Fatal Effects of Interments in Populous Cities* (New York, 1822); F. Pascalis-Ouvrière, *Exposition of the Dangers of Interments in Cities* (New York, 1823).

45. "Allen's Pamphlet," *National Advocate* (New York), November 21, 1822, 2.

46. *New York Evening Post*, April 5, 1823, 2.

47. "The Danger of Interments in Cities," *New York Evening Post*, April 11, 1825, 2; "Review of the Report Concluded," *New York Evening Post*, September 23, 1825, 2.

48. "Church-Yards," *Charleston Mercury*, November 22, 1822, 1 (reprinted from the *Statesman* [New York]).

49. Sloane, *The Last Great Necessity*, 40; Mary French, New York City Cemetery Project: Public Burial Ground, Bryant Park, https://nycemetery.wordpress.com/2019/05/30/public-burial-ground-bryant-park/

50. "Burying Ground," *New York Evening Post*, June 12, 1823, 2. With regard to the reference here to Albany, New York, in 1800, the town established the State Street Burying Ground, which consisted of four large sections allotted to the various churches as well as space set aside for strangers, African Americans, and nondenominational burials. The whole was surrounded by a fence, and by the time Albany Rural Cemetery was dedicated in 1844, this burying ground was in major disrepair, and most of the burials and gravestones were relocated to the new cemetery. See "The State Street Burying Grounds," *The Church Grounds—Albany Rural Cemetery*, https://albanychurchgrounds.wordpress.com/the-state-street-burying-grounds/

51. J. St. George Joyce, *Story of Philadelphia*, Philadelphia, 1919, 218.

52. Upton, *Another City*, 223.

53. Upton, *Another City*, 224.

54. "The Philadelphia Cemetery," *National Gazette* (Philadelphia), April 11, 1827, 1.

55. Regarding the fate of Ronaldson's Cemetery, it was closed and the land was transformed into Palumbo Playground in 1954. Remains were relocated to Forest

Hills Cemetery, while the gravestones "of seven Revolutionary War heroes . . . were taken to the burial ground of Gloria Dei (Old Swedes)." See "Ronaldson's Cemetery," *Philadelphia Inquirer*, April 25, 1957, 10.

56. "For the National Gazette," *National Gazette* (Philadelphia), December 29, 1826, 1.

57. "Grave-Yards," *National Gazette* (Philadelphia), January 5, 1827, 2.

58. *Laws of the General Assembly of the Commonwealth of Pennsylvania* (Harrisburg: J. M. G. Lescure, 1848), 233–34.

59. Linden, *Silent City on a Hill*, 117–18 (quote on 118).

60. K. David Patterson, "Yellow Fever Epidemics and Mortality in the United States, 1693–1905," *Social Science & Medicine* 34, no. 8 (1992): 857–58.

61. "Neglected Grave Yards," *New England Farmer & Horticultural Journal* 7, no. 39 (April 17, 1829): 307.

62. Linden, *Silent City on a Hill*, 122.

63. John Gorham Coffin, *Remarks on the Dangers and Duties of Sepulture: Or, Security for the Living, with Respect and Repose for the Dead* (Boston: Phelps and Farnham, 1823), 17, 11.

64. Coffin, *Remarks on the Dangers and Duties of Sepulture*, 20–22.

65. Coffin, *Remarks on the Dangers and Duties of Sepulture*, 60.

66. Coffin, *Remarks on the Dangers and Duties of Sepulture*, 61.

67. Coffin, *Remarks on the Dangers and Duties of Sepulture*, 64

68. Regarding the development of the "Boston Brahmin" class and its influence in forming institutions such as the Boston Athenaeum, see Ronald Story, "Class and Culture in Boston: The Athenaeum, 1807–1860," *American Quarterly* 27, no. 2 (May 1975): 178–99.

69. The phrases "useful arts" and "mechanical arts" were used during the eighteenth and nineteenth centuries to denote what later would collectively be termed "technology." See Jacob Bigelow, *Elements of Technology, Taken Chiefly from a Course of Lectures Delivered at Cambridge, on the Application of the Sciences to the Useful Arts, Now Published for the Use of Seminaries and Students* (Boston: Hilliard, Gray, Little, and Wilkins, 1829).

70. Regarding the Sphinx at Mount Auburn, see Joy M. Giguere, "The Americanized Sphinx: Civil War Commemoration, Jacob Bigelow, and the *Sphinx* at Mount Auburn Cemetery," *Journal of the Civil War Era* 3, no. 1 (Spring 2013): 62–84; Giguere, *Characteristically American*, 127–62.

71. Jacob Bigelow, *A History of the Cemetery of Mount Auburn* (Boston: James Munroe, 1859), 1–4 (quotes on 1, 2); *The Picturesque Pocket Companion, and Visitor's Guide, through Mount Auburn: Illustrated with Upwards of Sixty Engravings on Wood* (Boston: Otis, Broaders, 1839), 5–6; Linden, *Silent City on a Hill*, 134–36.

72. Aaron Sachs, *Arcadian America: The Death and Life of an Environmental Tradition* (New Haven: Yale University Press, 2013), 24.

73. Erik Seeman, *Speaking with the Dead in Early America* (Philadelphia: University of Pennsylvania Press, 2019), 219.

74. Linden, *Silent City on a Hill*, 139–40.

75. "Report of a Committee of the Massachusetts Horticultural Society, on the Expediency of Measures Being Taken for the Establishment of an Experimental Garden, and Rural Cemetery," *New-York Farmer & Horticultural Repository* 4, no. 6 (June 1, 1831): 142–43.

76. Townshend, *The Grove Street Cemetery*, 14; Sloane, *The Last Great Necessity*, 45.

77. "Report of a Committee of the Massachusetts Horticultural Society," 178.

78. "Mount Auburn," *Boston Traveler*, September 20, 1831, 3.

79. Edward Everett, "The Proposed Rural Cemetery," in Bigelow, *A History of the Mount Auburn Cemetery*, 138.

80. For an explanation of public lots and cemetery bylaws, see Jacob Bigelow, *A History of the Mount Auburn Cemetery*, 22 (quote on 233).

81. Regarding some of these new options in grave marker styles and symbolism, see June Hadden Hobbs, "Say It with Flowers in the Victorian Cemetery," *Markers XVIIII* (2002): 240–71; Elise Madeleine Ciregna, "Museum in the Garden: Mount Auburn Cemetery and American Sculpture, 1840–1860," *Markers XXI* (2004): 100–147; Elisabeth L. Roark, "Embodying Immortality: Angels in America's Rural Cemeteries, 1850–1900," *Markers XXIV* (2007): 56–111; Joy M. Giguere, "Variety There Must Be: Eclecticism, Taste and the Nineteenth-Century Rural Cemetery Landscape," *Markers XXXIII* (2017): 82–104.

82. For more on fencing, see Blanche Linden-Ward, "'The Fencing Mania': The Rise and Fall of Nineteenth-Century Funerary Enclosures," *Markers VII* (1990): 34–58.

83. "Mount Auburn Cemetery," *New England Farmer & Horticultural Journal* 10, no. 5 (August 17, 1831): 38; "Mount Auburn Cemetery," *Boston Medical & Surgical Journal* 5, no. 6 (September 20, 1831): 99–100.

84. Joseph Story, "An Address Delivered on the Dedication of the Cemetery at Mount Auburn, September 24th, 1831," in Bigelow, *A History of Mount Auburn Cemetery*, 144.

85. Concerning the modern "denial of death," see, for example, Shai Lavi, "How Dying Became a 'Life Crisis,'" *Daedalus* 137, no. 1 (Winter 2008): 57–65. The medicalization of death (that is, death in the hospital environment), combined with the changes occurring in the twentieth-century deathcare industry, hastened the removal of death as an everyday reality from people's lives. The development of the modern memorial park further encouraged the disappearance of reminders of death, with its emphasis on manicured lawns and flush, rather than vertical, grave markers. See Sloane, *The Last Great Necessity*, 159–244; David Charles Sloane, *Is the Cemetery Dead?* (Chicago: University of Chicago Press, 2018).

86. Regarding modern trends for grappling with death and new ways of memorialization, see Sloane, *Is the Cemetery Dead?*; and Candi K. Cann, *Virtual Afterlives: Grieving the Dead in the Twenty-First Century* (Lexington: University Press of Kentucky, 2014).

87. For considerations of antebellum mortality, see Gary Laderman, *The Sacred*

Remains: American Attitudes Toward Death, 1799–1883 (New Haven: Yale University Press, 1996), 22–26; and Alan C. Swedlund, *Shadows in the Valley: A Cultural History of Illness, Death, and Loss in New England, 1840–1916* (Amherst: University of Massachusetts Press, 2010).

88. Regarding New England Puritan attitudes toward death and corpse disposal, see David Stannard, *The Puritan Way of Death: A Study in Religion, Culture, and Social Change* (New York: Oxford University Press, 1977).

89. Story, "An Address Delivered," 147–48.

90. Story, "An Address Delivered," 155.

91. Story, "An Address Delivered," 165–66.

CHAPTER 2

1. On the memento mori culture of colonial New England, see David E. Stannard, *The Puritan Way of Death: A Study in Religion, Culture, and Social Change* (Oxford: Oxford University Press, 1977).

2. "Mount Auburn Cemetery," *North American Review* 33 (October 1831): 405.

3. For broader discussions of this era, see David S. Reynolds, *Waking Giant: America in the Age of Jackson* (New York: Harper Collins, 2008); Daniel Walker Howe, *What Hath God Wrought: The Transformation of America, 1815–1848* (New York: Oxford University Press, 2007); Louis P. Masur, *1831: Year of Eclipse* (New York: Hill and Wang, 2001); and Charles Sellers, *The Market Revolution: Jacksonian America, 1815–1846* (New York: Oxford University Press, 1991).

4. "Mount Auburn Cemetery," *Mechanics' Magazine & Register of Inventions & Improvements* 2, no. 1 (July 1, 1833): 40.

5. "Cemetery at Mount Auburn," *New England Farmer* 10, no. 11 (September 28, 1831): 82.

6. "Mass. Horticultural Society," *New England Farmer* 11, no. 45 (May 22, 1833): 3.

7. For the early history of Bigelow's efforts, the Horticultural Society, and its eventual disengagement from the cemetery proprietors, see Jacob Bigelow, *A History of the Cemetery of Mount Auburn* (Boston: James Munroe, 1859), 1–5, 30–33.

8. Dell Upton, *Another City: Urban Life and Urban Spaces in the New American Republic* (New Haven: Yale University Press, 2008), 221–22.

9. According to Blanche Linden, the number of private monuments erected in Pere Lachaise "escalated annually from 51 in 1808 to 113 in 1812, 242 in 1813, 509 in 1814, and 645 in 1815. . . . By 1830, with over 31,000 monuments in place, the original look of the picturesque had been obliterated." See Linden, *Silent City on a Hill: Picturesque Landscapes of Memory and Boston's Mount Auburn Cemetery* (Amherst: University of Massachusetts Press, 2007), 76.

10. "Mass. Horticultural Society," *New England Farmer* (Boston) 11, no. 45 (May 22, 1833): 3.

11. As noted by Jacob Bigelow, single interments were located in the public lot called St. James's lot. Once this became full, a second public lot, St. John's lot, was

laid out in 1848. By this time, the cost for a single interment had risen to $12, and for an additional fifty-cent charge, a numbered marker could be placed over the burial that corresponded to the name of the deceased in the burial record. The cost for the three-hundred-square-foot family lots likewise rose in price, to $65 in 1834; $80 in 1836; $100 in 1844; and $150 in 1854. Even with these price increases, the cost for single interments and family lots remained reasonable compared to other cemeteries established later during the rural cemetery movement. See Bigelow, *A History of the Cemetery of Mount Auburn*, 22–23.

12. Edward Everett, "The Proposed Rural Cemetery," in Bigelow, *A History of the Cemetery of Mount Auburn*, 136.

13. David Charles Sloane, *The Last Great Necessity: Cemeteries in American History* (Baltimore: Johns Hopkins University Press, 1991), 53.

14. Sloane, *The Last Great Necessity*, 49.

15. "Cemetery at Mount Auburn," 82.

16. "Walks About Boston, Mount Auburn Cemetery," *Parley's Magazine*, January 1, 1835, 390.

17. Joseph Story, "An Address Delivered on the Dedication of the Cemetery at Mount Auburn, September 24th, 1831," in Bigelow, *A History of the Cemetery of Mount Auburn*, 156–57.

18. Jacob Bigelow, "A Discourse on the Burial of the Dead," in Bigelow, *A History of the Cemetery of Mount Auburn*, 195.

19. "Mount Auburn Cemetery," *North American Review* 33 (October 1831): 397–98.

20. Thaddeus William Harris, *Discourse Delivered before the Massachusetts Horticultural Society, on the Celebration of Its Fourth Anniversary, October 3, 1832* (Cambridge: E. W. Metcalf, 1832), 68.

21. "Mount Auburn," *American Quarterly Observer* 3 (July 1834): 171–72; regarding death as sleep, see Thomas W. Laqueur, *The Work of the Dead: A Cultural History of Mortal Remains* (Princeton, NJ: Princeton University Press, 2015), 216–17.

22. G. T. C., "Mount Auburn," *New-England Magazine* 7 (October 1834): 316.

23. Colonial gravestone images including winged skulls (death's heads), hourglasses, bells, crossbones, and the like may collectively be referred to as "mortality symbols." Regarding colonial New England attitudes toward death, see Stannard, *The Puritan Way of Death*. For studies on Puritan gravestones and iconography, see James Deetz and Edwin Dethlefsen, "Deaths Heads, Cherubs, and Willow Trees: Experimental Archaeology in Colonial Cemeteries," *American Antiquity* 31, no. 4 (April 1966): 502–10; Allan Ludwig, *Graven Images: New England Stonecarving and Its Symbols, 1650–1815* (Hanover, NH: University Press of New England, 1966); and Dickran Tashjian and Ann Tashjian, *Memorials for Children of Change: The Art of Early New England Stonecarving* (Middletown, CT: Wesleyan University Press, 1974).

24. Paul Binski, *Medieval Death* (London: British Museum Press, 1996), 134–38; Peter C. Jupp and Clare Gittings, eds., *Death in England: An Illustrated History* (New Brunswick, NJ: Rutgers University Press, 1999), 93–94.

25. "Mount Auburn," *American Quarterly* (July 1834): 160.

26. Stannard, *The Puritan Way of Death*, 76–79.

27. "Mount Auburn," *American Quarterly* (July 1834): 160.

28. G. T. C., "Mount Auburn," *New England Magazine* (October 1834): 316.

29. Ann Douglas, "Heaven Our Home: Consolation Literature in the Northern United States, 1830–1880," *American Quarterly* 26, no. 5 (December 1974): 496–515.

30. Poet John Keats was one of the more popular literary consumptives during this period, and his *Ode to a Nightingale* (1819) and *On Death* (1814) both reflected Keats's grappling with his own mortality. Edgar Allan Poe's *The Masque of the Red Death* (1842) portrays Prospero, who holds a grand party and endeavors to escape the grasp of the "Red Death" (consumption). Giuseppe Verdi's opera *La Traviata* (1853) centers on the life and death of a beautiful soprano who ultimately succumbs to the ravages of consumption (while singing all of the high notes, of course). See Helen Bynum, *Spitting Blood: The History of Tuberculosis* (London: Oxford University Press, 2015), 77–94.

31. William A. Brewer, *Recreations of a Merchant, or the Christian Sketch-Book* (1836), 165–66.

32. Brewer, *Recreations of a Merchant*, 167.

33. Brewer, *Recreations of a Merchant*, 167.

34. Brewer, *Recreations of a Merchant*, 169.

35. Brewer, *Recreations of a Merchant*, 170.

36. Zillah, "Mount Auburn," *Lowell Offering* (October 1840): 13–14.

37. *Report of the Garden and Cemetery Committee of the Massachusetts Horticultural Society, September 17, 1834*, in Bigelow, *A History of the Cemetery of Mount Auburn*, 199.

38. James R. Cothran and Erica Danylchak, *Grave Landscapes: The Nineteenth-Century Rural Cemetery Movement* (Columbia: University of South Carolina Press, 2018), 60.

39. Quoted in Trudy Irene Scee, *Mount Hope Cemetery of Bangor, Maine: The Complete History* (Charleston, SC: History Press, 2012), 25.

40. Cothran and Danylchak, *Grave Landscapes*, 60.

41. "Mount Hope Cemetery," *Bangor Daily Whig & Courier*, July 2, 1836, 2.

42. "Mount Hope Cemetery," *Bangor Daily Whig & Courier*, July 20, 1836, 2.

43. Quoted in Scee, *Mount Hope Cemetery*, 25–26.

44. "City Affairs," *Bangor Daily Whig & Courier*, October 26, 1836, 2.

45. It should be noted, however, that while some rural cemeteries took care in relocating older graves to the new burial grounds so that the old burying grounds could be overtaken by urban development, this was not a universal practice. In many locations, older burying grounds, churchyards, and reform cemeteries continued to be used or were left to decay, the graves overtaken and at times lost to the ravages of time and changes in the landscape. This was especially the case for African American cemeteries and potter's fields. In other cases, some, but not all, burials from older burying grounds were relocated. In her paper delivered at the 2023 annual meeting of the Association for Gravestone Studies held at the University of Denver, archaeologist Krista Horrocks described the history of Columbus, Ohio's North Graveyard,

which was established in 1813. Bodies from the North Graveyard were exhumed and relocated to the city's rural cemetery, Greenlawn Cemetery, established in 1847. Excavations of the North Graveyard site in 2023 have yielded nearly one thousand grave shafts containing human remains, which will be reburied at Greenlawn as were those during the 1840s. Krista Horrocks, "Burials under the Pavement: The History of Columbus, Ohio's North Graveyard and the 2023 Excavations at the North Market Parking Lot," Association for Gravestone Studies Annual Meeting, University of Denver, June 20–25, 2023.

46. "Senate," *Fall River (MA) Monitor*, February 20, 1836, 1.

47. Reprinted from the *Whig and Reporter* (Taunton, MA) as "Rural Cemetery at Taunton," *New England Farmer* (Boston), July 20, 1836, 8.

48. John Hayward, *A Gazetteer of the United States of America: Comprising a Concise General View of the United States; Also, Its Mineral Springs, Waterfalls, Caves, Beaches, and Other Fashionable Resorts* (Philadelphia, 1854), 593; Samuel Hopkins Emery, *History of Taunton, Massachusetts: From Its Settlement to the Present Time* (Syracuse, NY: D. Mason, 1893), 54.

49. "Rural Cemeteries," *North American Review* 53, no. 113 (October 1841): 400.

50. "Rural Cemeteries," *North American Review*, 385–412.

51. Colleen McDannell, *Material Christianity: Religion and Popular Culture in America* (New Haven: Yale University Press, 1995), 108–9.

52. The museum was short-lived. Dunn moved the entire collection to London in 1841. See "Nathan Dunn and His Museum of '10,000 Chinese Things,'" https://blogs.harvard.edu/preserving/2015/06/03/nathan-dunn-and-his-museum-of-10000-chinese-things/

53. "Who's Buried in Laurel Hill Cemetery? PCP Luminaries," https://usciencesblogs.typepad.com/experts/2011/04/whose-buried-in-laurel-hill-cemetery-pcp-luminaries.html

54. "Henry Toland, Jr.," https://www.findagrave.com/memorial/73102918/henry-toland

55. McDannell, *Material Christianity*, 111; *Regulations of the Laurel Hill Cemetery, on the River Schuylkill, near Philadelphia* (1837), 8.

56. *National Gazette* (Philadelphia), August 5, 1837, 2.

57. Allan Amanik, "A Beautiful Garden Consecrated to the Lord": Marriage, Death, and Local Constructions of Citizenship in New York's Nineteenth-Century Jewish Rural Cemeteries," in Allan Amanik and Kami Fletcher, eds., *Till Death Do Us Part: American Ethnic Cemeteries as Borders Uncrossed* (Jackson: University Press of Mississippi, 2020), 15–34.

58. "Entrance and Ground Plan of Laurel Hill Cemetery," *Atkinson's Casket*, no. 10 (October 1837): 2–3.

59. *Regulations of the Laurel Hill Cemetery*, 4.

60. "The Monument Cemetery," *Ladies' Garland and Family Wreath Embracing Tales, Sketches, Incidents, History, Poetry, Music, etc.*, August 1, 1839, 48.

61. *The Charter, By-Laws and Regulations of the Woodlands Cemetery Company, with a List of the Lot Holders, to August 1857* (Philadelphia: James B. Chandler, 1857).

62. Old Mortality was the central character in one of Sir Walter Scott's Waverly novels, *Old Mortality* (1816).

63. "Entrance and Ground Plan of Laurel Hill Cemetery," 2–3.

64. *Guide to Laurel Hill Cemetery, Near Philadelphia* (C. Sherman, 1847), 132.

65. Regarding the early developments of introducing sculpture in rural cemeteries, see Elise Madeline Ciregna, "Museum in the Garden: Mount Auburn Cemetery and American Sculpture, 1840–1860," *Markers XXI* (2004): 100–147.

66. Story, "An Address Delivered," 150–51.

67. Rev. Pharcellus Church, *An Address Delivered at the Dedication of Mount Hope Cemetery, Rochester, Oct. 2, 1838; and Repeated, by Request, before the Rochester Athenaeum and Young Men's Association* (Rochester, 1839), 12.

68. Levi Lincoln, *An Address Delivered on the Consecration of the Worcester Rural Cemetery, September 8, 1838, by Levi Lincoln* (Boston, 1838), 18–19.

69. *Address Delivered on the Consecration of the Spring Grove Cemetery, Near Cincinnati, August 20th, 1845, by the Hon. John M'Lean* (Cincinnati, 1845), 9.

70. On the early history of the English churchyard, see Laqueur, *The Work of the Dead*, 114–22.

71. Story, "An Address Delivered," 163.

72. Church, *An Address*, 17–18.

73. Lincoln, *An Address Delivered on the Consecration of the Worcester Rural Cemetery*, 14.

74. Lincoln, *An Address Delivered*, 24.

75. *Address Delivered on the Consecration of the Spring Grove Cemetery*, 14.

76. Bigelow, *A History of the Cemetery of Mount Auburn*, 26.

77. Jacob Bigelow, *Elements of Technology, Taken Chiefly from a Course of Lectures Delivered at Cambridge, on the Application of the Sciences to the Useful Arts, Now Published for the Use of Seminaries and Students*, 2nd ed. (Boston: Hilliard, Gray, Little, and Wilkins, 1831), 132.

78. Jacob Bigelow, *The Useful Arts, Considered in Connexion with the Applications of Science, with Numerous Engravings*, 2nd ed. (New York: Harper & Brothers, 1863), 23.

79. "Ancient Architecture," *North American Review* 88, no. 183 (April 1859): 343.

80. Bigelow, *A History of the Cemetery of Mount Auburn*, 26.

81. Giguere, *Characteristically American*, 82–84.

82. Giguere, *Characteristically American*, 87.

83. Green Mount Cemetery: Architecture, https://www.greenmountcemetery .com/greenmount-cemetery-features-architecture.html

84. James Gallier, "American Architecture," *North American Review* 43, no. 93 (October 1836): 380, 356.

85. Gallier, "American Architecture," 379. A more comprehensive discussion of these tensions between critics of the Egyptian Revival and other forms of architectural revivalism appears in my first book, *Characteristically American*, 72–76.

86. James R. Cothran and Erica Danylchak, *Grave Landscapes: The Nineteenth-Century Rural Cemetery Movement* (Columbia: University of South Carolina Press, 2018), 65; Historical Currency Converter, https://futureboy.us/fsp/dollar.fsp?quantity=134000&currency=dollars&fromYear=1839

87. Cothran and Danylchak, *Grave Landscapes*, 65.

88. *Exposition of the Plan and Objects of the Green-Wood Cemetery. An Incorporated Trust Chartered By The Legislature of the State of New York* (New York, 1839), 16.

89. *Exposition of the Plan and Objects of the Green-Wood Cemetery*, 18.

90. "The Greenwood," *Long-Island Star* (Brooklyn), June 22, 1840, 2.

91. "Rural Cemeteries," *North American Review*, 399.

92. "A Drive through Greenwood," *Brooklyn Daily Eagle*, September 20, 1844, 2. The last point about Père Lachaise serving as the model for Green-Wood is erroneous, as Mount Auburn actually served as the direct inspiration. However, such was the international fame of Père Lachaise that it received much of the credit for inspiring American rural cemeteries.

93. Andrew Jackson Downing, "Public Cemeteries and Public Gardens" (1849), in *Rural Essays* (New York: Leavitt & Allen, 1857), 155.

94. Downing, "Public Cemeteries and Public Gardens," 156.

95. *An Address Delivered on the Consecration of the Worcester Rural Cemetery*, 24.

CHAPTER 3

1. Regarding the social function and governing behaviors of the promenade, see Daniel M. Bluestone, "From Promenade to Park: The Gregarious Origins of Brooklyn's Park Movement," *American Quarterly* 39 (Winter 1987): 529–50; David Scobey, "Anatomy of the Promenade: The Politics of Bourgeois Sociability in Nineteenth-Century New York," *Social History* 17 (May 1992): 203–27; Patrick M. Malone and Charles A. Parrott, "Greenways in the Industrial City: Parks and Promenades along the Lowell Canals," *IA: The Journal of the Society for Industrial Archaeology* 24, no. 1 (1998): 19–40; Mona Domosh, "Those 'Gorgeous Incongruities': Polite Politics and Public Space on the Streets of Nineteenth-Century New York City," *Annals of the Association of American Geographers* 88 (June 1998): 209–26; and Catherine McNeur, *Taming Manhattan: Environmental Battles in the Antebellum City* (Cambridge, MA: Harvard University Press, 2014), 46, 55–61.

2. Henry Dearborn, "Report of June 18, 1831," in Thaddeus William Harris, *Discourse Delivered before the Massachusetts Horticultural Society, on the Celebration of Its Fourth Anniversary, October 3, 1832* (Cambridge, MA, 1832), 68.

3. For studies of behavior in antebellum public spaces of leisure and entertainment, see David Grimsted, *Melodrama Unveiled: American Theater and Culture, 1800–1850* (Chicago: University of Chicago Press, 1968), 65–67; Bruce A. McConachie, "'The Theater of the Mob': Apocalyptic Melodrama and Preindustrial Riots in Antebellum New York," in Bruce A. McConachie and Daniel Friedman, eds., *Theater for the Working-Class Audiences in the United States, 1830–1980* (Westport, CT: Praeger,

1985), 17–46; Lawrence W. Levine, *Highbrow Lowbrow: The Emergence of Cultural Hierarchy in America* (Cambridge, MA: Harvard University Press, 1988), 56–69; John F. Kasson, *Rudeness & Civility: Manners in Nineteenth-Century Urban America* (New York: Hill & Wang, 1990), 216–22; Richard Butsch, "Bowery B'hoys and Matinee Ladies: The Re-Gendering of Nineteenth-Century American Theater Audiences," *American Quarterly* 46 (September 1994): 374–405; and Paul E. Johnson, *Sam Patch, the Famous Jumper* (New York: Hill & Wang, 2004).

    4. Jacob Bigelow, "A Discourse on the Burial of the Dead," in Jacob Bigelow, *A History of the Cemetery of Mount Auburn* (Boston: James Munroe, 1859), 194–95.

    5. "Domestic Architecture," *New England Magazine* 2 (January 1832): 35.

    6. Theodore Dwight, *Things as They Are; Or, Notes of a Traveller through Some of the Middle and Northern States* (New York: Harper & Brothers, 1834), 162.

    7. Gideon Miner Davison, *The Traveller's Guide through the Middle and Northern States, and the Provinces of Canada* (Saratoga Springs, NY, 1834), 379.

    8. Bigelow, *A History of the Cemetery of Mount Auburn*, 29.

    9. "Mount Auburn," *New York American*, September 30, 1833, 2.

    10. "Mount Auburn," *Liberator* (Boston), April 27, 1833, 67.

    11. "Mount Auburn," *New York American*, 2.

    12. Bigelow, *A History of the Cemetery of Mount Auburn*, 29–30.

    13. Untitled, *American Traveller* (Boston), July 25, 1834, 2.

    14. Matthew R. Costello, *The Property of the Nation: George Washington's Tomb, Mount Vernon, and the Memory of the First President* (Lawrence: University Press of Kansas, 2019), 157–59.

    15. "Mount Auburn Cemetery," *Saturday Morning Transcript* (Boston), July 26, 1834, 186.

    16. "Mount Auburn," *American Quarterly Observer* 3 (July 1834): 171–72.

    17. "Reminiscences of Park Street by J. Collins Warren, M.D.," in Robert Means Lawrence, *Old Park Street and Its Vicinity* (Boston, 1922), 49, 103.

    18. "Regulations Concerning Visitors," in Bigelow, *A History of the Cemetery of Mount Auburn*, 252–54.

    19. Historical Currency Converter, https://futureboy.us/fsp/dollar/fsp

    20. Bigelow, *A History of the Cemetery of Mount Auburn*, 29–30.

    21. "Report of the Garden and Cemetery Committee of the Massachusetts Horticultural Society, September 17, 1834," in Bigelow, *A History of the Cemetery of Mount Auburn*, 201–2.

    22. Harriet Martineau, *Retrospect of Western Travel, Vol. 3* (London, 1838), 281.

    23. G. T. Curtis, "Mount Auburn," *New England Magazine* 7 (October 1834): 316–17.

    24. *Regulations of the Laurel Hill Cemetery, on the River Schuylkill, near Philadelphia* (1837), 8; Colleen McDannell, *Material Christianity: Religion and Popular Culture in America* (New Haven: Yale University Press, 1995), 108–11.

    25. "Entrance to Laurel Hill Cemetery," *Ladies' Garland and Family Wreath Embracing Tales, Sketches, Incidents, History, Poetry, Music, etc.* 1, no. 12 (January 1838): 196.

26. "The Monument Cemetery," *Ladies' Garland and Family Wreath Embracing Tales, Sketches, Incidents, History, Poetry, Music, etc.* (August 1, 1839): 48.

27. *Report of the Board of Managers to the Proprietors and Lot-Holders of Green Mount Cemetery* (Baltimore, 1840), 23.

28. *Rules and Regulations of the Green-Wood Cemetery; with a Catalogue of Proprietors, and Mr. Cleaveland's Descriptive Notices of Green-Wood Illustrated* (New York, 1851), 21–22.

29. Reprinted as "Curious Fulfillment of a Promise," *Southern Patriot* (Charleston, SC), April 18, 1845, 2.

30. "The Freedom Lots," https://green-wood.maps.arcgis.com/apps/MapJournal/index.html?appid=b550a7818cbd408d812755c5183bd619

31. Nehemiah Cleaveland, *Green Wood Illustrated. In Highly Finished Line Engraving, From Drawings Taken on the Spot, by James Smillie* (New York: R. Martin, 1847), 19–25. Cleaveland's description of Indian Mound and of Do-Hum-Me includes, at the end, a poem titled "The Forest Child" about the young Native American woman.

32. Gordon M. Sayre, *Les Sauvages Américains: Representations of Native Americans in French and English Colonial Literature* (Chapel Hill: University of North Carolina Press, 2000); Mary De Jong, ed., *Sentimentalism in Nineteenth-Century America: Literary and Cultural Practices* (Madison, NJ: Farleigh Dickinson University Press, 2013); Mary Louise Kete, *Sentimental Collaborations: Mourning and Middle-Class Identity in Nineteenth-Century America* (Durham: Duke University Press, 2000).

33. On P. T. Barnum, see Reynolds, *Waking Giant*, 224–25.

34. *Rules of the Laurel Hill Cemetery*, 3–4; *Rules and Regulations of the Green-Wood Cemetery*, 21–22; *Report of the Board of Managers to the Proprietors and Lot-Holders of Green Mount Cemetery*, 23; *Albany Rural Cemetery Association: Its Rules, Regulations, &c. with an Appendix* (Albany, NY, 1846), 33; Edward P. Humphrey, *An Address Delivered on the Dedication of the Cave Hill Cemetery near Louisville, July 25, 1848* (Louisville, KY, 1848), 28–31.

35. "Independence Hall—Girard College—Laurel Hill, &c.," *Washington (PA) Reporter*, July 4, 1849, 2.

36. "City News," *New York Commercial Advertiser*, July 11, 1845, 2; Andrew Jackson Downing, "Public Cemeteries and Public Gardens, July, 1849," in *Rural Essays* (New York, 1856), 157.

37. Martineau, *Retrospect of Western Travel*, 278.

38. Anne Henry Ehrenpreis, ed., *Happy Country This America: The Travel Diary of Henry Arthur Bright* (Columbus: Ohio State University Press, 1978), 118.

39. Thomas Chandler Haliburton, *The Clockmaker: The Sayings and Doings of Samuel Slick of Slickville* (Paris, 1841), 133.

40. Wilson Flagg, "Rural Cemeteries," *Magazine of Horticulture, Botany, and All Useful Discoveries and Improvements in Rural Affairs* 19 (1853): 487.

41. "Mount Auburn," *Columbus (MS) Democrat*, August 26, 1837, 2 (reprinted from the *Boston Mercantile Journal*).

42. Martineau, *Retrospect of Western Travel*, 282–83.

43. "Friday Evening," *Saturday Morning Transcript* (Boston), August 10, 1839, 199.

44. "Vandalism and Sacrilege," *New Bedford (MA) Register*, June 28, 1843, 2.

45. "Defacing Public Grounds," *National Aegis* (Worcester, MA), July 4, 1843, 2.

46. "Beauties of the Town of Springfield," *New York Commercial Advertiser*, September 8, 1846, 2.

47. Ryan K. Smith, *Death and Rebirth in a Southern City: Richmond's Historic Cemeteries* (Baltimore: Johns Hopkins University Press, 2020), 113; Daina Ramey Berry, *The Price for Their Pound of Flesh: The Values of the Enslaved, from Womb to Grave, in the Building of a Nation* (Boston: Beacon Press, 2017), 148–93; Kenneth C. Nystrom, "The Bioarchaeology of Structural Violence and Dissection in the 19th-Century United States," *American Anthropologist* 116, no. 4 (December 2014): 765–79.

48. "Greenwood Cemetery," *Evening Post* (New York), July 8, 1847, 2.

49. "The Whittling Propensity," *Centinel of Freedom* (Newark, NJ), December 19, 1854, 3.

50. Ehrenpreis, *Happy Country This America*, 162.

51. "An Example," *Daily Evening Transcript* (Boston), October 4, 1852, 2.

52. *Plan, Prospectus, and Terms, for the Establishment of a Public Cemetery, at the City of Baltimore, to Be Called the Green Mount Cemetery* (Baltimore, 1838), 9; regarding the cemetery's distance from the city, see *The Dedication of Green Mount Cemetery, July 13, 1839* (Baltimore, 1839), 30–31.

53. *Report of the Board of Managers to the Proprietors and Lot-Holders of Green Mount Cemetery* (Baltimore, 1840), 23.

54. Untitled, *The Sun* (Baltimore), September 2, 1840, 2.

55. Ann Douglas, "Heaven Our Home: Consolation Literature in the Northern United States, 1830–1880," *American Quarterly* 26, no. 5 (December 1974): 496–515.

56. Here I am applying the term "social geography" as discussed by Glenna Matthews, *The Rise of Public Woman: Woman's Power and Woman's Place in the United States, 1630–1970* (New York: Oxford University Press, 1992), 103–5.

57. John F. Kasson, *Rudeness & Civility: Manners in Nineteenth-Century Urban America* (New York: Hill & Wang, 1990), 117, 128–29.

58. Marise Bachand, "Gendered Mobility and the Geography of Respectability in Charleston and New Orleans, 1790–1861," *Journal of Southern History* 81 (February 2015): 42–44.

59. "Green Mount Cemetery," *The Sun* (Baltimore), May 18, 1841, 2. The first violent exchange actually resulted in a court case, which was reported in "The Troubles of the Cemetery," *The Sun* (Baltimore), May 31, 1841, 1. As the report describes, the gravediggers were Irish brothers, William and James Wier. The "rowdies" were William Morrison, Captain Robert Atkins, and George W. Moore. Judge Brice found everyone involved to be guilty on some level, so Morrison and Atkins were ordered to pay "a fine of fifty cents and costs," while the Wiers were required to pay the costs in the case of Moore, who was acquitted. Since it was determined that Morrison had

only assaulted William Wier and Atkins had assaulted James Wier, the Wiers were also forced to pay for the further acquittals (since Morrison and Atkins had been prosecuted for an assault on both brothers).

60. "Green Mount Cemetery—Ladies' Rights," *The Sun* (Baltimore), May 27, 1841, 2.

61. "Green Mt. Cemetery," *Baltimore Saturday Visiter*, April 30, 1842, 2.

62. "Green Mt. Cemetery," *Baltimore Saturday Visiter*, 2.

63. "Green Mount Cemetery—Second Report of the Board of Managers to the Lot Holders," *The Sun* (Baltimore), November 21, 1843, 1.

64. "Green Mount Cemetery," *The Sun* (Baltimore), September 17, 1844, 2.

65. Andrew Jackson Downing, "A Talk about Public Parks and Gardens," *Horticulturalist and Journal of Rural Art and Rural Taste* 3 (October 1848): 157.

66. Charles E. Beveridge, ed., *Frederick Law Olmsted: Writings on Landscape, Culture, and Society* (New York, 2015), 158.

67. Downing, "Public Cemeteries and Public Gardens, July, 1849," 158–59.

68. With regard to Downing's and Olmsted's intentions to use parks to shape the morals and behavior of the public, see Roy Rosenzweig and Elizabeth Blackmar, *The Park and the People: A History of Central Park* (Ithaca: Cornell University Press, 1992), 238–46; Dorceta E. Taylor, "Central Park as a Model for Social Control: Urban Parks, Social Class and Leisure Behavior in Nineteenth-Century America," *Journal of Leisure Research* 31, no. 4 (1999): 420–77; and David Wall, "Andrew Jackson Downing and the Tyranny of Taste," *American Nineteenth Century History* 8 (June 2007): 187–203.

69. *Regulations of the Laurel Hill Cemetery, On the River Schuylkill*, 9.

70. Blanche M. G. Linden, *Silent City on a Hill: Picturesque Landscapes of Memory and Boston's Mount Auburn Cemetery* (Amherst: University of Massachusetts Press, 2007), 180.

71. "Celebrating Indiana's Limestone History," https://www.visitbloomington.com/limestone/

72. Linda Smith Chaffee, John B. Coduri, and Ellen L. Madison, *Built from Stone: The Westerly Granite Story* (Westerly, RI: Babcock-Smith House Museum, 2011).

73. June Hadden-Hobbs, "Say It with Flowers in the Victorian Cemetery," *Markers XIX* (2002): 241.

74. Charles David Sloane, *The Last Great Necessity: Cemeteries in American History* (Baltimore: Johns Hopkins University Press, 1991), 77.

75. In my earlier work, I have contended that the most widespread and popular of the revival styles for the memorial context (both in cemeteries and public monuments) was the Egyptian Revival. See Joy M. Giguere, *Characteristically American: Memorial Architecture, National Identity, and the Egyptian Revival* (Knoxville: University of Tennessee Press, 2014). See also Peggy McDowell and Richard E. Meyer, *The Revival Styles in American Memorial Art* (Bowling Green, OH: Bowling Green State University Popular Press, 1994).

76. T. J. Jackson Lears, *No Place of Grace: Antimodernism and the Transformation of*

American Culture, 1880–1920 (Chicago: University of Chicago Press, 1994), 33. See also David Charles Sloane, *Is the Cemetery Dead?* (Chicago: University of Chicago Press, 2018), 178. Among the major critics against eclecticism in the late nineteenth century were Clarence King and Henry Van Brunt. See "Style and the Monument," *North American Review* 141, no. 38 (November 1885): 443–44; and Henry Van Brunt, "On the Present Condition and Prospects of Architecture," *Atlantic Monthly* 57, no. 341 (March 1886): 374.

77. This list represents the dominant iconographic themes of the colonial into the early national periods, and there were, of course, local and regional variations as well as folk designs that diverged from these popular images. Regarding eighteenth-century iconography, see James Deetz, *In Small Things Forgotten: An Archaeology of Early American Life*, rev. ed. (New York: Anchor Books, 1996); James Hijiya, "American Gravestones and Attitudes Toward Death: A Brief History," *Proceedings of the American Philosophical Society* 127, no. 5 (October 14, 1983): 339–63; Allan Ludwig, *Graven Images: New England Stonecarving and Its Symbols, 1650–1815*, 3rd ed. (Hanover, NH: University Press of New England, 1999); Dickran Tashjian and Ann Tashjian, *Memorials for Children of Change* (Middletown, CT: Wesleyan University Press, 1974); Peter Benes, ed., *Puritan Gravestone Art: The Dublin Seminar for New England Folklife Annual Proceedings, 1976* (Boston: Boston University Press, 1977); and James Deetz and Edwin Dethlefsen, "Death's Head, Cherub, Urn and Willow," *Natural History* 76, no. 3 (1967): 29–37.

78. "Mount Auburn Cemetery," *North American Review* 33 (October 1831): 405–6.

79. Quoted in Linden, *Silent City on a Hill*, 181.

80. Quoted in Linden, *Silent City on a Hill*, 181.

81. "Mount Auburn," *Saturday Morning Transcript* (Boston) (evening edition), September 21, 1833, 10. Regarding "the Trollopes, Fiddlers, and Hamiltons," the editor here was referring to what had become a tradition among European tourists to the United States to publish scathing narratives of their experiences, in effect to scoff at the absence of taste, culture, and refinement exhibited among the Americans. See, for example, Frances Trollope, *Domestic Manners of the Americans* (1832).

82. No title, *Saturday Morning Transcript* (Boston), September 21, 1833, 10. Antonio Canova (1757–1822) was an Italian sculptor, while Bertel Thorvaldsen (1770–1844) was a Danish sculptor and medalist, both of whom garnered major international reputations for their art.

83. G. T. Curtis, "Mount Auburn," *New England Magazine* 7 (October 1834): 319–20.

84. "Style and the Monument," *North American Review* 141, no. 38 (November 1885): 443–44.

85. James Gallier, "American Architecture," *North American Review* 43, no. 93 (October 1836): 356–57.

86. Gallier, "American Architecture," 378.

87. Gallier, "American Architecture," 378–80.

88. Regarding the Gothic supplanting the Egyptian Revival in popularity, the

case of Forest Hills Cemetery in Roxbury, Massachusetts, is instructive. The original gateway, in painted wood, was constructed at the time of the cemetery's establishment in 1848 in the Egyptian style. Its replacement in stone, constructed in 1865, is an example of Gothic Revival architecture. See Susan Wilson, *Garden of Memories: A Guide to Historic Forest Hills* (Forest Hills Educational Trust, 1998), 22.

89. "Mount Auburn," *Columbus (OH) Democrat*, August 26, 1837, 2.

90. "Miscellany from the Boston Courier," *Gloucester (MA) Telegraph*, August 18, 1838, 3.

91. "A Chaste and Beautiful Idea," reprinted in the *Salem (MA) Gazette*, September 4, 1838, 2.

92. Elise Madeleine Ciregna, "Museum in the Garden: Mount Auburn Cemetery and American Sculpture, 1840–1860," *Markers XXI* (2004): 113.

93. Cornelia Walter, *Mount Auburn Illustrated in Highly Finished Line Engraving, from Drawings Taken on the Spot, by James Smillie. With Descriptive Notices by Cornelia W. Walter* (New York: Robert Martin, 1847), 22.

94. Nathaniel Dearborn, *A Concise History of, and Guide through Mount Auburn* (Boston: Nathaniel Dearborn, 1843), 5.

95. "Rural Cemeteries," *North American Review* 53, no. 113 (October 1841): 405.

96. "Copp's Hill, Boston," *Norfolk Democrat* (Dedham, MA), June 27, 1845, 1.

97. No title, *National Aegis* (Worcester, MA), January 12, 1842, 2.

98. "Greenmount Cemetery," *The Sun* (Baltimore), August 9, 1844, 2.

99. Walter, *Mount Auburn Illustrated*, 14–15.

100. Nehemiah Cleaveland, *Green-Wood Illustrated, in Highly Finished Line Engraving, from Drawings Taken on the Spot by James Smillie* (New York: R. Martin, 1847), 44–52.

101. "Thoughts Connected with Rural Cemeteries," *Christian Review* (March 1848): 18–19.

102. "Cemeteries and Monuments," *The New Englander* 7, no. 28 (November 1849): 498–500.

103. Wilson Flagg, "Rural Cemeteries," *Magazine of Horticulture, Botany, and all Useful Discoveries and Improvements in Rural Affairs* 19 (1853): 486–498.

104. Downing, "Public Cemeteries and Public Gardens, July 1849," 156.

105. Flagg, "Rural Cemeteries," 498.

106. A. D. G., "Rural Cemeteries," *Horticulturalist and Journal of Rural Art and Rural Taste* (1855), 279.

CHAPTER 4

1. Andrew Jackson Downing, "Public Cemeteries and Public Gardens," in A. J. Downing, *Rural Essays*, edited by George William Curtis (New York, 1853), 154.

2. Charles Fraser, *Address Delivered on the Dedication of Magnolia Cemetery, on the 19th of November, 1850* (Charleston, SC, 1850), 18.

3. Ren Davis and Helen Davis, *Atlanta's Oakland Cemetery: An Illustrated History and Guide* (Athens: University of Georgia Press, 2012), xiv–xx.

4. Regarding the phrase "special dead," I am employing Thomas W. Laqueur's definition as he applies it both to the holy relics of Catholic saints and to the Protestant "anti-relic relics" of the United States, such as the remains of the Reverend George Whitefield. In the context of this chapter, I am using this phrase specifically in reference to the bones (e.g., relics) of individuals who bore national significance. See Thomas W. Laqueur, *The Work of the Dead: A Cultural History of Mortal Remains* (Princeton: Princeton University Press, 2015), 45–48.

5. John Pendleton Kennedy, "Address," in *The Dedication of Green Mount Cemetery, July 13, 1839* (Baltimore, 1839), 21.

6. Edward P. Humphrey, *An Address, Delivered on the Dedication of the Cave Hill Cemetery; Near Louisville: July 25, 1848* (Louisville, KY, 1848), 9.

7. "Population of the 100 Largest Urban Places: 1840," https://www2.census.gov /library/working-papers/1998/demographics/pop-twps0027/tab07.txt; "Population of the 100 Largest Urban Places: 1850," https://www2.census.gov/library/working-pa pers/1998/demographics/pop-twps0027/tab08.txt. Among the changes between the 1840 and 1850 census, Detroit rose from 40th to 30th most populous within a decade, and Chicago exploded in size, going from 92nd to 24th most populous during that period.

8. Blanche Linden-Ward and Alan Ward, "Spring Grove: The Role of the Rural Cemetery in American Landscape Design," *Landscape Architecture* 75, no. 5 (1985): 126.

9. *Magnolia Cemetery: The Proceedings at the Dedication of the Grounds: To Which Are Appended the Rules, Regulations and Charter of the Company* (Charleston, SC, 1851), 3.

10. Kent R. Lancaster, "Green Mount: The Introduction of the Rural Cemetery into Baltimore," *Maryland Historical Magazine* 74 (March 1979): 62; Samuel Moore, "Prospectus of the Green Mount Cemetery," in *Plan, Prospectus, and Terms, for the Establishment of a Public Cemetery, at the City of Baltimore, to Be Called the Green Mount Cemetery* (Baltimore 1838), 5.

11. "The Green Mount Cemetery," *The Sun* (Baltimore), June 22, 1838, 2.

12. "To the Public [prospectus of Green Mount Cemetery]," *The Sun* (Baltimore), January 12, 1839, 2–3; "Dedication of Green Mount Cemetery," *The Sun* (Baltimore), July 15, 1839, 2.

13. Dell Upton, "The Urban Cemetery and the Urban Community: The Origin of the New Orleans Cemetery," *Perspectives in Vernacular Architecture* 7 (1997): 137, 135. For an overall history of cemeteries and burial in New Orleans, see Paul Dedek, *The Cemeteries of New Orleans: A Cultural History* (Baton Rouge: Louisiana State University Press, 2017).

14. *Report of the Committee of the Firemen's Charitable Association, on the Cypress Grove Cemetery* (New Orleans, 1840), 4.

15. "Rural Cemetery at St. Louis," *Daily Picayune* (New Orleans), June 5, 1841, 1.

16. Dedek, *The Cemeteries of New Orleans*, 141.

17. These include, for example, the St. Louis Cemeteries Nos. 1, 2, and 3. See Robert Florence, *New Orleans Cemeteries: Life in the Cities of the Dead* (New Orleans: Batture Press, 1997), 50–73; Dedek, *The Cemeteries of New Orleans*.

18. "Magnolia Cemetery," *Charleston Courier*, July 20, 1850, 2.

19. Florence, *New Orleans Cemeteries*, 137.

20. A. D. G., "Rural Cemeteries," *The Horticulturalist and Journal of Rural Art and Rural Taste* 1, no. 6 (June 1855): 278–79. In *The Work of the Dead*, 217–22, Thomas Laqueur notes that attitudes toward the dead as dangerous to the living evolved during the eighteenth century in response to overcrowded church crypts and churchyards but also to the evolution in ways of thinking about smells and how the smell of corrupted flesh became synonymous with pollution.

21. As a rule, however, Catholics adhered to the requirement to be buried in Catholic cemeteries. Jewish populations also tended to have their own Hebrew burying grounds, usually associated with particular synagogues, although Jewish burials can be found throughout the country in non-Jewish cemeteries as well. In a number of cases, synagogues purchased sections within preexisting rural cemeteries or established Hebrew cemeteries adjacent to rural cemeteries as part of broader efforts to assimilate with mainstream Anglo-Protestant culture. See Allan Amanik, "'A Beautiful Garden Consecrated to the Lord': Marriage, Death, and Local Constructions of Citizenship in New York's Nineteenth-Century Jewish Rural Cemeteries," in Allan Amanik and Kami Fletcher, eds., *Till Death Do Us Part: American Ethnic Cemeteries as Borders Uncrossed* (Jackson: University Press of Mississippi, 2020), 15–34; Florence, *New Orleans Cemeteries*, 92–97; Solomon Breibart, "The Jewish Cemeteries of Charleston," *Catalogue: Bulletin of the South Carolina Historical Society* 9 (Summer 1993): 8–9, 14–16; Bobbie Malone, "New Orleans Uptown Jewish Immigrants: The Community of Congregation Gates of Prayer, 1850–1860," *Louisiana History* 32 (Summer 1991): 239–78; and B. H. Levy, "Savannah's Old Jewish Community Cemeteries," *Georgia Historical Quarterly* 66 (Spring 1982): 1–20.

22. Both Lebanon and Olive Cemeteries faced marginalization and destruction over the course of time, as was incredibly common with many Black burying grounds. Lebanon Cemetery especially was plagued by graverobbers during the second half of the nineteenth century and was closed by the city in 1899. Olive Cemetery was closed in 1923. Eden Cemetery, another Black-owned cemetery established in 1902, became the repository for the remains of those who had been buried originally at Lebanon and Olive. See "Lebanon Cemetery (Defunct)," https://www.findagrave.com/cemetery/2494796/lebanon-cemetery-(defunct); "Olive Cemetery (Defunct)," https://www.findagrave.com/cemetery/2672577/olive-cemetery; "Historic Eden Cemetery: Beginnings," https://www.edencemetery.org/beginnings

23. Angelika Krüger-Kahloula, "On the Wrong Side of the Fence: Racial Segregation in American Cemeteries," in Geneviève Fabre and Robert O'Meally, eds., *History*

and Memory in African-American Culture (New York: Oxford University Press, 1994), 130.

24. *Frankfort Cemetery in Kentucky* (Frankfort, KY: Kentucky Genealogical Society, 1988), 411.

25. *Elmwood: Charter, Rules, Regulations and By-Laws of Elmwood Cemetery Association of Memphis* (Memphis, 1874), 38.

26. Jeffrey E. Smith, "Till Death Keeps Us Apart: Segregated Cemeteries and Social Values in St. Louis, Missouri," in Amanik and Fletcher, *Till Death Do Us Part*, 157–82.

27. *Rules, Regulations, and By-Laws of Cave Hill Cemetery: With the Dedicatory Address and Topographical and Descriptive Notices* (Louisville, KY, 1860), 74–75; *Charter, By-Laws and Rules and Regulations of Cave Hill Cemetery Co. (Incorporated 1848) and Charter of Cave Hill Investment Co. (Incorporated 1882)* (Louisville, KY, 1901), 58.

28. Ryan K. Smith, *Death and Rebirth in a Southern City: Richmond's Historic Cemeteries* (Baltimore: Johns Hopkins University Press, 2020); Ryan K. Smith, "Richmond Cemeteries," www.richmondcemeteries.org; Veronica A. Davis, *Here I Lay My Burdens Down: A History of the Black Cemeteries of Richmond, Virginia* (Richmond, VA: Dietz Press, 2003), 7–31.

29. Like Philadelphia's Lebanon and Olive Cemeteries, Baltimore's Laurel Cemetery, once an elite Black burying ground, no longer exists. Urban development and marginalization eventually resulted in the displacement of some of the human remains to other burying grounds, and in the 1980s, "a Two Guys department store and parking lot was constructed on the site, over the remains of at least 2,000 of the people who had been buried there." See Ralph Clayton, *Black Baltimore, 1820–1870* (Bowie, MD: Heritage Books, 1987), 41–42.

30. "Local Matters," *The Sun* (Baltimore), July 12, 1852, 1. *The Sun* first reported on Laurel Cemetery in "New City of the Dead," *The Sun* (Baltimore), August 18, 1851, 1, in which it commented on the location and design of the new cemetery, including the planned architectural improvements that included two gateways, a keeper's lodge, a chapel, and a receiving vault.

31. *The Cemetery of Spring Grove* (Cincinnati, 1849), 6.

32. Today, Spring Grove Cemetery encompasses 733 acres and is the nation's third largest cemetery.

33. "Letter from Cincinnati," *Anti-Slavery Bugle* (Lisbon, OH), July 17, 1852, 2; Historical Currency Converter, https://futureboy.us/fsp/dollar.fsp?quantity=9000&currency=dollars&fromYear=1852

34. *The Cincinnati Cemetery of Spring Grove, Report for 1857* (Cincinnati: C. F. Bradley, 1857), 18.

35. Anne Marie Martin, "'In This City of the Dead': Charleston's Magnolia Cemetery and Middle-Class Aspiration," *Journal of Urban History* 47, no. 5 (September 2021): 1050.

36. "Intramural Interments," *Charleston Mercury*, January 17, 1859, 2.

37. *Magnolia Cemetery*, 85.

38. Thomas J. Brown, "Introduction," in Ted Ashton Phillips Jr., *City of the Silent: The Charlestonians of Magnolia Cemetery* (Columbia: University of South Carolina Press, 2010), xiii.

39. *Historical Sketch of Hollywood Cemetery, from the 3d of June, 1847, to 1st Nov., 1875* (Richmond, VA, 1875), 5, 30–32.

40. Mary H. Mitchell, *Hollywood Cemetery: The History of a Southern Shrine* (Richmond: Library of Virginia, 1999), 17.

41. *Hollywood Cemetery* (Richmond, VA, 1850), 3, 4, 11–13.

42. Mitchell, *Hollywood Cemetery*, 18.

43. Mitchell, *Hollywood Cemetery*, 22.

44. "Hollywood Cemetery," *Richmond Whig and Public Advertiser*, July 20, 1849, 4.

45. "Hollywood Cemetery," *Richmond Whig and Public Advertiser*, 4.

46. "The Hollywood Cemetery," *Richmond Whig and Public Advertiser*, March 26, 1850, 1.

47. "The Hollywood Cemetery," *Richmond Whig and Public Advertiser*, April 5, 1850, 1.

48. "The Beautiful Retreat," *Richmond Enquirer*, April 16, 1850, 2.

49. "The Hollywood Cemetery," *Richmond Enquirer*, April 16, 1850, 2.

50. "Hollywood Cemetery," *Richmond Whig and Public Advertiser*, April 19, 1850, 1.

51. *Richmond Enquirer*, March 16, 1852, 2.

52. Stanley French, "The Cemetery as Cultural Institution: The Establishment of Mount Auburn and the 'Rural Cemetery' Movement," *American Quarterly* 26 (March 1974): 40.

53. Humphrey, *An Address, Delivered on the Dedication of the Cave Hill Cemetery*, 9.

54. "Respect for the Dead—Elmwood Cemetery," *Memphis Daily Eagle and Enquirer*, June 17, 1854, 2.

55. "Memorials of the Dead," *Southern Literary Messenger* 19 (September 1853): 543–544.

56. *Historical Sketch of Hollywood Cemetery*, 34.

57. Samuel Moore, "Prospectus of the Green Mount Cemetery," in *Plan, Prospectus, and Terms, for the Establishment of a Public Cemetery, at the City of Baltimore, to Be Called the Green Mount Cemetery* (Baltimore, 1838), 8.

58. Kennedy, "Address," 29–30.

59. William Cronon, *Nature's Metropolis: Chicago and the Great West* (New York: W. W. Norton, 1991), 52, 91.

60. Rev. Noah Hunt Schenck, *Oration Delivered at the Opening Services of the Rosehill Cemetery Association, on Thursday, July 28, 1859* (Chicago: Rose Hill Cemetery Association, 1859), 13.

61. Gregg D. Kimball, *American City, Southern Place: A Cultural History of Antebellum Richmond* (Athens: University of Georgia Press, 2000), 56; *An Illustrated and Descriptive Catalogue of Manufactures of Tredegar Iron Works* (Richmond, VA, 1860), 94.

62. Oliver P. Baldwin, *Address Delivered at the Dedication of the Hollywood Cemetery, on Monday, the 25th June, 1849* (Richmond, VA, 1849), 13.

63. *Historical Sketch of Hollywood Cemetery*, 28.

64. "Two Parsons and Ne'er Church," *Southern Literary Messenger* 22 (April 1856): 271.

65. *Baltimore Clipper*, reprinted in "Green Mount Cemetery—Flowers," *Sentinel of Freedom* (Newark, NJ), May 25, 1841, 4.

66. "Green Mount Cemetery," *The Sun* (Baltimore), July 21, 1841, 2.

67. L. F. Johnson, *History of the Frankfort Cemetery* (Frankfort, KY, 1921), 6.

68. "Cincinnati and Covington Cemetery," *Cincinnati Enquirer*, July 9, 1842, 2.

69. "Elmwood Cemetery," *Detroit Free Press*, June 23, 1847, 2; *Detroit Free Press*, June 24, 1847, 2.

70. Wilson McCandless, *First Report of the Managers of the Allegheny Cemetery, Together with the Charter of the Corporation: Also a Funeral Address* (Pittsburgh, 1849), 21.

71. "Allegheny Cemetery," *Pittsburgh Gazette*, June 14, 1850, 2.

72. "Correspondence of the Courier," *Charleston Courier*, August 5, 1853, 2.

73. "Respect for the Dead—Elmwood Cemetery," *Memphis Daily Eagle and Enquirer*, June 17, 1854, 2.

74. Baldwin, *Address Delivered at the Dedication of the Hollywood Cemetery*, 14–15.

75. Fraser, *Address Delivered on the Dedication of Magnolia Cemetery*, 20.

76. *Dedication of the Bellefontaine Cemetery: Address of Professor Post, and Other Proceedings on That Occasion* (St. Louis, 1851), 31.

77. Humphrey, *An Address, Delivered on the Dedication of the Cave Hill Cemetery*, 17.

78. "The Dedication of Cave Hill Cemetery," *Louisville Morning Courier*, July 27, 1848, 2.

79. *Address Delivered on the Consecration of the Spring Grove Cemetery, Near Cincinnati, August 20th, 1845, by the Hon. John M'Lean* (Cincinnati, OH, 1845), 16–17.

80. *Second Report of the Board of Trustees of Elmwood Cemetery (from July 6, 1850, to October 9, 1857): Also, Rules, Regulations, and Suggestions: To Which Is Added the First Report of the Board* (Detroit: Geo. H. Fleming, 1858), 5.

81. "Akron Rural Cemetery," *Summit County Beacon* (Akron, OH), February 27, 1850, 1.

82. In my use of terminology, I am once again referring to Laqueur, *Work of the Dead*, 48.

83. Sarah J. Purcell, *Spectacle of Grief: Public Funerals and Memory in the Civil War Era* (Chapel Hill: University of North Carolina Press, 2022), 17–26 (quote on 18).

84. "Laying of the Corner-Stone of the Clay Monument," *Salem (MA) Register*, July 13, 1857, 2; John Winston Coleman, *Last Days, Death, and Funeral of Henry Clay: With Some Remarks on the Clay Monument in the Lexington Cemetery* (Ann Arbor: University of Michigan Press, 1951).

85. "Green Mount Cemetery," *The Sun* (Baltimore), January 16, 1839, 1.

86. "The Remains of Mr. Legare," *The Sun* (Baltimore), October 5, 1857, 1; "The Remains of Legaré," *Charleston Courier*, October 9, 1857, 2; "Removal of the Remains of Hugh Swinton Legare, Late Attorney General of the United States, from Mount Auburn to Magnolia Cemetery, Charleston, S.C.," *Charleston Courier*, November 2, 1857, 4.

87. Jennie C. Morton, "History of the Frankfort Cemetery," *Register of the Kentucky State Historical Society* 7 (January 1909): 26.

88. "Remains of Daniel Boone," *Alexandria (VA) Gazette*, August 7, 1845, 2.

89. "From the St. Louis New Erie," New York *Spectator*, August 9, 1845, 4.

90. *The Commonwealth* (Frankfort, KY), reprinted in "Remains of Daniel Boone," *Alexandria (VA) Gazette*, August 7, 1845, 2.

91. "Burial of Daniel Boon," *Albany (NY) Argus*, September 30, 1845, 1; Morton, "History of the Frankfort Cemetery," 26–27.

92. "Movements of General Scott," *Boston Daily Atlas*, October 4, 1852, 2; "Movements of Gen. Scott—Arrival at Lexington—Mrs. Clay," *New York Daily Times*, October 1, 1852, 1.

93. "Letter from St. Louis," *Evening Bulletin* (San Francisco), March 22, 1860, 1. For a history of the Boone reburial, see also Michael Kammen, *Digging Up the Dead: A History of Notable American Reburials* (Chicago: University of Chicago Press, 2010), 129–34.

94. On the Monroe reburial, see Kammen, *Digging Up the Dead*, 86–91.

95. Mitchell, *Hollywood Cemetery*, 35–45 (first quote on 36; second and fourth quotes on 39); "The Burial Place of Mr. Monroe," *Richmond Whig and Public Advertiser*, July 16, 1858 (third quote on 4); Kammen, *Digging Up the Dead*, 86–91.

96. "Interesting Ceremony," *Norwich (CT) Aurora*, July 10, 1858, 2; "Gov. Wise's Address at Hollywood Cemetery, on the Fifth of July," *Richmond Whig and Public Advertiser*, July 9, 1858, 1.

97. "The Burial Place of Mr. Monroe," *Richmond Whig and Public Advertiser*, July 16, 1858, 4.

98. "The Burial Place of Mr. Monroe," *Richmond Whig and Public Advertiser*, 4.

CHAPTER 5

1. Dolly Blount Lamar, *When All Is Said and Done* (Athens: University of Georgia Press, 1952), 35.

2. James R. Cothran and Erica Danylchak, *Grave Landscapes: The Nineteenth-Century Rural Cemetery Movement* (Columbia: University of South Carolina Press, 2018), 74.

3. "Rose Hill Cemetery," *Georgia Journal and Messenger* (Macon), March 26, 1856, 2.

4. "Who's to Blame?," *Macon Telegraph*, August 26, 1864, 2.

5. The most significant exception here would be Arlington National Cemetery,

which segregated the remains of African American servicemen and women until following President Truman's order to desegregate the military. See Micki McElya, *The Politics of Mourning: Death and Honor in Arlington National Cemetery* (Cambridge, MA: Harvard University Press, 2016).

6. For a broad treatment of the LMAs and their commemorative activities, see Caroline E. Janney, *Burying the Dead but Not the Past: Ladies' Memorial Associations & the Lost Cause* (Chapel Hill: University of North Carolina Press, 2008).

7. William Blair deftly illustrates the politicization of the cemetery landscape, particularly by ex-Confederates, in *Cities of the Dead: Contesting the Memory of the Civil War in the South, 1865–1914* (Chapel Hill: University of North Carolina Press, 2011).

8. I have previously written in detail about the case of Kentucky during and after the war. See Joy M. Giguere, "'Flaunting the Evidence of Treason in the Face of Loyalty': Funerals, Grave Decoration, and the Fashioning of Kentucky's Civil War Identity," *Ohio Valley History* 19, no. 4 (Winter 2019): 19–44.

9. G. William Beardslee, "The 1832 Cholera Epidemic in New York State: 19th Century Responses to *Cholerae Vibrio*," *Early America Review* 4, no. 1 (Fall 2000).

10. Amy S. Greenberg, *A Wicked War: Polk, Clay, Lincoln, and the 1846 U.S. Invasion of Mexico* (New York: Vintage Books, 2013), xvii.

11. J. David Hacker, "A Census-Based Count of the Civil War Dead," *Civil War History* 57, no. 4 (December 2011): 307–48.

12. David J. Eicher, *The Longest Night: A Military History of the Civil War* (New York: Simon & Schuster, 2001), 99.

13. "A Military Cemetery," *Charleston (SC) Daily Courier*, July 26, 1861, 1.

14. Thomas J. Brown, "Introduction," in Ted Ashton Phillips Jr., *City of the Silent: The Charlestonians of Magnolia Cemetery* (Columbia: University of South Carolina Press, 2010), xi–xiv.

15. "The Lamented Dead," *Charleston (SC) Daily Courier*, July 27, 1861, 1.

16. Drew Gilpin Faust, *This Republic of Suffering: Death and the American Civil War* (New York: Vintage Books, 2008), 154.

17. Judge Joseph Story, "An Address Delivered on the Dedication of the Cemetery at Mount Auburn, September 24th, 1831," in Jacob Bigelow, *A History of the Cemetery of Mount Auburn* (Boston: James Munroe, 1860), 148.

18. "Sesquicentennial Memorial Day Service," Magnolia Cemetery, http://www .magnoliacemetery.net; "As Confederate Symbols Come under Siege, Charleston Keeps Memorial Day Tradition," *Post and Courier*, May 12, 2016, https://www.postan dcourier.com/archives/as-confederate-symbols-come-under-siege-charleston-keeps -memorial-day/article_28624dbb-7e1c-59c1-b76f-f14b62bb53d8.html

19. Brown, "Introduction," xvii.

20. Magnolia Cemetery, http://www.magnoliacemetery.com/; on the renaming of Mobile's New Burying Ground to Magnolia Cemetery, see *Mobile Daily Tribune*, December 22, 1875, 3.

21. *Opelika (AL) Observer*, March 6, 1879, 2.

22. *Tuscaloosa (AL) News*, October 19, 1876, 2.

23. *Elmwood: Charter, Rules, Regulations and By-Laws of Elmwood Cemetery Association of Memphis. History of the Cemetery. Biographical Sketches. Attractive Monuments. Names of Proprietors* (Memphis, TN: Boyle & Chapman, 1874), 68.

24. "Grand Floral Ceremony," *Memphis Daily Argus*, April 25, 1866, 3.

25. T. Addison Richards, "The Rice Lands of the South," *Harper's New Monthly Magazine* 19, no. 114 (November 1859): 738.

26. Bonaventure Historical Society, https://www.bonaventurehistorical.org/must-see/

27. William D. Bryan, "Taming the Wild Side of Bonaventure: Tourism and the Contested Southern Landscape," *Southern Cultures* 23, no. 2 (Summer 2017): 59.

28. John Muir, *A Thousand Mile Walk to the Gulf* (Boston: Houghton Mifflin, 1916), 69.

29. Muir, *A Thousand Mile Walk to the Gulf*, 71–72.

30. *Atlanta Constitution*, May 13, 1875, 2.

31. Ryan K. Smith, *Death and Rebirth in a Southern City: Richmond's Historic Cemeteries* (Baltimore: Johns Hopkins University Press, 2020), 158.

32. "Graves of the Soldiers at Hollywood," *Richmond Dispatch*, August 20, 1861, 2.

33. "Burial of the Dead," *Richmond Dispatch*, July 12, 1862, 2; "A Journey Through the Confederacy," *Burlington (NC) Daily Times*, June 6, 1863, 1.

34. "Bury the Dead," *Richmond Dispatch*, July 12, 1862, 2.

35. "Fifteen Month at the South," *New York Times*, October 20, 1862, 2.

36. Ryan K. Smith, "Oakwood Cemetery" in Richmond Cemeteries: Exploring Richmond, Virginia's Historic Burial Grounds, https://www.richmondcemeteries.org/oakwood-cemetery/

37. "From Richmond—Funeral of Ex-President John Tyler," *Charleston (SC) Daily Courier*, January 22, 1862, 1.

38. Faust, *This Republic of Suffering*, 154.

39. Sarah J. Purcell, *Spectacle of Grief*, 90–91.

40. John Beauchamp Jones, *A Rebel War Clerk's Diary at the Confederate States Capital* (Philadelphia: J. B. Lippincott, 1866), 321.

41. "Burial Place of Gen. Jackson," *Daily Dispatch* (Richmond), May 13, 1863, 1.

42. *The Confederate* (Raleigh, NC), May 11, 1864, 1.

43. "General JEB Stuart Buried in Richmond," *Richmond Enquirer*, May 14, 1864.

44. Marta Lockett Avary, *A Virginia Girl in the Civil War: Being a Record of the Actual Experiences of the Wife of a Confederate Officer* (Santa Barbara, CA: Narrative Press, 2004), 208.

45. Regarding the reburial of Confederate soldiers killed at Gettysburg, see Mary H. Mitchell, *Hollywood Cemetery: The History of a Southern Shrine* (Richmond: Library of Virginia, 1999), 83–92; Caroline E. Janney, *Burying the Dead but Not the Past*, 119–27.

46. On the Confederate pyramid at Hollywood Cemetery, see Janney, *Burying the Dead but Not the Past*, 95–98.

47. Approximately ninety thousand loyal Kentuckians served in the Union army during the course of the war, and of these, a sizable number served in the USCT. Historians estimate that between twenty-five thousand and forty thousand Kentuckians fought for the Confederacy, either within the Confederate army and navy or as guerrillas in the state's "irregular war." See Anne Elizabeth Marshall, *Creating a Confederate Kentucky: The Lost Cause and Civil War Memory in a Border State* (Chapel Hill: University of North Carolina Press, 2013); Christopher Phillips, *The Rivers Ran Backward: The Civil War and the Remaking of the American Middle Border* (New York: Oxford University Press, 2016).

48. "Meeting of the Council," *Louisville Daily Democrat*, October 18, 1861.

49. Geoffrey R. Walden, *Confederate Soldiers and Civilians Buried in the Confederate Sections and National Cemetery, Cave Hill Cemetery, Louisville, Kentucky* (Louisville: G. R. Walden, 1996), i.

50. Burton Milward, *A History of the Lexington Cemetery* (Lexington: Lexington Cemetery Company, 1989), 44.

51. "Late Frankfort News," *Louisville Daily Democrat*, October 4, 1862.

52. *Commercial Tribune* (Cincinnati), July 3, 1861.

53. "Our Army Correspondence," *Wooster (OH) Republican*, January 2, 1862.

54. John David Smith and William Cooper, eds., *A Union Woman in Civil War Kentucky: The Diary of Frances Peter* (Lexington: University Press of Kentucky, 2000), 11–12.

55. Smith and Cooper, *A Union Woman in Civil War Kentucky*, 136.

56. "Yankee Rule in Maryland," *Richmond Dispatch*, August 12, 1863; *The Sun* (Baltimore), August 6, 1863; "News Brevities," *Daily True Delta* (New Orleans), August 18, 1863.

57. Giguere, "Flaunting the Evidence of Treason in the Face of Loyalty," 28–29.

58. On the popularity of floral iconography, see June Hadden Hobbs, "Say It with Flowers in the Victorian Cemetery," *Markers XIX* (2002): 240–71.

59. Kristen L. Streater, "'Not Much a Friend to Traiters No Matter How Beautiful': The Union Military and Confederate Women in Civil War Kentucky," in Kent T. Dollar, Larry H. Whiteaker, and W. Calvin Dickinson, eds., *Sister States, Enemy States: The Civil War in Kentucky and Tennessee* (Lexington: University Press of Kentucky, 2009), 249, 258.

60. Frances Peter, May 23, 1863, in Smith and Cooper, *A Union Woman in Civil War Kentucky*, 129, 131.

61. Anne E. Marshall, "A Sisters' War: Kentucky Women and Their Civil War Diaries," *Register of the Kentucky Historical Society* 110 (Summer–Autumn 2012): 484–85; G. Glenn Clift, ed., *The Private War of Lizzie Hardin: A Kentucky Confederate Girl's Diary of the Civil War in Kentucky, Virginia, Tennessee, Alabama, and Georgia* (Frankfort: Kentucky Historical Society, 1963), 82, 85–87.

62. "The Graves of Confederate Soldiers in Kentucky," *Daily Southern Crisis* (Jackson, MS), March 30, 1863.

63. "Our Dead Soldiers in New Orleans," *Shreveport (LA) Semi-Weekly News*, January 22, 1864.

64. "The Confederate Graves in New Orleans," *Yorkville (SC) Enquirer*, January 13, 1864.

65. "More Rebel Barbarity," *Portsmouth Journal of Literature and Politics*, April 30, 1864, 2.

66. "From Charleston," *New York Daily Tribune*, March 28, 1865, 5.

67. Friends of Mount Auburn, "The Civil War and Mount Auburn Cemetery," https://mountauburn.org/the-civil-war/; Erika Hayasaki, "Love Stories Buried No Longer," *Los Angeles Times*, February 14, 2008, provides the figure of forty Union generals buried at Laurel Hill Cemetery, including George G. Meade. The current figure of fifteen hundred Union burials at Laurel Hill is an approximate estimate given by the cemetery's staff, who noted in a phone call that "we're always coming across more Civil War burials" (September 6, 2022).

68. On embalming, see Drew Gilpin Faust, *This Republic of Suffering: Death and the American Civil War* (New York: Vintage Books, 2008), 92–98.

69. Blanche M. G. Linden, *Silent City on a Hill: Picturesque Landscapes of Memory and Boston's Mount Auburn Cemetery* (Amherst: University of Massachusetts Press, 2007), 324n81.

70. A cenotaph is a monument or marker, typically located in a cemetery, that functions as a grave marker for an individual whose physical remains are not present. We most often see cenotaphs being erected in the instances of death at sea or through warfare where the body does not return home.

71. Linden, *Silent City on a Hill*, 184; Friends of Mount Auburn, "Shaw Monument," https://mountauburn.org/shaw-monument-2/

72. I have written at greater length on Bigelow's Sphinx elsewhere. For a more comprehensive discussion of this topic, see Joy M. Giguere, "The Americanized Sphinx: Civil War Commemoration, Jacob Bigelow, and the Sphinx at Mount Auburn Cemetery," *Journal of the Civil War Era* 3, no. 1 (March 2013): 62–84; Joy Giguere, *Characteristically American: Memorial Architecture, National Identity, and the Egyptian Revival* (Knoxville: University of Tennessee Press, 2014), 127–62.

73. The purchase of the lot was made January 3, 1885 (cemetery staff, phone conversation, September 6, 2022).

74. "The Interment of Our Deceased Volunteers," *Brooklyn Daily Eagle*, June 7, 1862, 2.

75. Albany Rural Cemetery Soldiers' Lot, National Cemetery Administration, https://www.cem.va.gov/cems/lots/Albany_Rural.asp

76. *Semi-Weekly Wisconsin* (Milwaukee), May 1, 1863, 4.

77. Thomas J. Brown, *Civil War Monuments and the Militarization of America* (Chapel Hill: University of North Carolina Press, 2019).

78. Trudy Irene Scee, *Mount Hope Cemetery of Bangor, Maine: The Complete History* (Charleston, SC: History Press, 2012), 87–90; James R. Cothran and Erica Danylchak,

Grave Landscapes: The Nineteenth-Century Rural Cemetery Movement (Columbia: University of South Carolina Press, 2018), 60.

79. *Spring Grove Cemetery: Its History and Improvements, with Observations on Ancient and Modern Places of Sepulture* (Cincinnati: Robert Clarke, 1869), 55.

80. "The Interment of Our Deceased Volunteers," *Brooklyn Daily Eagle*, 2.

81. Jeffrey I. Richman, "Green-Wood Cemetery," *Military Images* 39, no. 4 (Autumn 2021): 60–66.

82. "Civil War Soldiers' Monument (1869)," https://www.green-wood.com/2010/civil-war-soldiers-monument-saved/

83. Albany Rural Cemetery Soldiers' Lot, National Cemetery Administration, https://www.cem.va.gov/cems/lots/Albany_Rural.asp

84. "Lion of Atlanta," *Atlanta Constitution*, April 27, 1894, 5.

85. Adeshina Emmanuel, "How the South Side Came to House a Not-So-Controversial Confederate Memorial," *Chicago Tribune*, September 21, 2017.

86. "Many Roads to Freedom: Abolitionist and Civil War Sites in Rochester," http://libraryweb.org/rochimag/roads/map14.htm

87. "The Rural Cemeteries of Massachusetts," *Boston Evening Transcript*, June 12, 1862, 2.

88. "Editorial Correspondence," *Muscatine (IA) Weekly Journal*, June 12, 1863, 1.

89. "Cave Hill Cemetery," *Louisville Daily Democrat*, May 17, 1863. Reporting on the damage at Cave Hill, the *New Albany Ledger* wrote, "These 'fortifications' run through Cave Hill Cemetery—the neighborhood of the city. In digging them the bodies of the dead have been disinterred in a number of instances, monuments and obelisks broken down or defaced, shrubbery destroyed, and other damage done" (October 3, 1862).

90. "General News Summary," *Charleston (SC) Mercury*, January 8, 1863, 2; *Weekly Mississippian* (Jackson), January 14, 1863.

91. "Cities of the Dead," *Times-Picayune* (New Orleans), October 30, 1864, 2.

92. Samuel Patton to Nelli Patton, October 27, 1862, Patton Family Papers, Filson Historical Society, Louisville, KY.

93. Jenkin Lloyd Jones, *An Artilleryman's Diary* (Madison: Wisconsin History Commission, 1914), 39.

94. "Mount Auburn Cemetery," *Pittston (PA) Gazette*, June 30, 1864, 2.

95. National Cemetery Administration, https://www.cem.va.gov/facts/NCA_History_and_Development_1.asp

96. Mitchell, *Hollywood Cemetery*, 91.

97. William Jonathan Davis to Francis Davis, May 22, 30, 1869, William Jonathan Davis Papers, 1857–1908, Filson Historical Society.

CHAPTER 6

1. George B. Tatum, "The Beautiful and the Picturesque," *American Quarterly* 3, no. 1 (Spring 1951): 42 (first quote); quoted in "Topeka Cemetery," *Weekly Commonwealth* (Topeka, KS), February 9, 1861, 7 (second quote).

2. In the Treaty of Guadalupe Hidalgo, the territories acquired from Mexico as a result of the Mexican-American War (1846–48) included California, Arizona, New Mexico, and what would become parts of Colorado, Utah, and Nevada. Already heavily populated by Native Americans and Mexicans of Spanish descent, these were regions where white settlers remained in the minority through much of the rest of the nineteenth century and, with the exception of California, urban development remained sparse for decades.

3. Salem Pioneer Cemetery, Summary History of the Cemetery, https://www.sa lempioneercemetery.org/history.php

4. "Topeka Cemetery," *Weekly Commonwealth* (Topeka, KS), 7.

5. "A Needed Enterprise," *Buchanan County Guardian* (Independence, IA), June 17, 1862, 3.

6. "Woodlawn Cemetery," *Winona (MN) Daily Republican*, June 19, 1863, 3.

7. *Vernon County Censor* (Viroqua, WI), November 11, 1863, 2.

8. "City and Rural Cemeteries," *Nashville Union and American*, May 12, 1866, 3.

9. "A 'Central Park' for Leavenworth!," *Leavenworth (KS) Bulletin*, August 27, 1863, 3.

10. Frederick Law Olmsted, "Parks: An Encyclopedic View," in Charles E. Beveridge, ed., *Frederick Law Olmsted: Writings on Landscape, Culture, and Society* (New York: Library of America, 2015), 158.

11. "A 'Central Park' for Leavenworth!," *Leavenworth (KS) Bulletin*, 3.

12. Prospect Park opened to the public in 1867. Olmsted was hired by the city of Boston in the 1870s to design the Emerald Necklace park system, which he completed in 1895.

13. Frederick Law Olmsted, "From Preface to the Plan for Mountain View Cemetery, Oakland, California," in Beveridge, ed., *Frederick Law Olmsted*, 299.

14. Olmsted, "From Preface to the Plan for Mountain View Cemetery," 297.

15. Blanche Linden-Ward and Alan Ward, "Spring Grove: The Role of the Rural Cemetery in American Landscape Design," *Landscape Architecture* 75, no. 5 (1985), 129.

16. Linden-Ward and Ward, "Spring Grove," 130.

17. "Visit to Spring Grove Cemetery, by Juliet M. Hirst," *Cincinnati Enquirer*, November 6, 1859, 1.

18. "Spring Grove Cemetery," *Cincinnati Daily Press*, November 6, 1860, 2.

19. *Spring Grove Cemetery: Its History and Improvements, with Observations on Ancient and Modern Places of Sepulture* (Cincinnati: Robert Clarke, 1869), 12.

20. Among the notable reported instances of misbehavior and transgressions committed during this period, the *Winona (MN) Daily Republican*, May 4, 1865, 3, reported that four large evergreens had been cut down and stolen from the cemetery, presumably to be used as Christmas trees, the prior winter. In Stockton, California, the *Daily Evening Herald*, July 6, 1866, 3, reported upon complaints about hunting in the local rural cemetery: "Parties are in the habit of shooting birds there. A buggy recently had its top sieved by bird shot passing through it. . . . Last Sunday a lot of Mexican boys were there hunting birds." At Albany Rural Cemetery in 1866, a man

identified as John Butler lured his twelve-year-old sister-in-law to the cemetery under the pretense of having a picnic, and then he proceeded to rape her in one of the more secluded sections. *Brooklyn Daily Eagle*, September 25, 1866, 1.

21. *Spring Grove Cemetery*, 6.

22. I would like to note here that in all of my research, I have never found an instance where an "offensive" monument was actually removed by a cemetery during the nineteenth century. The case of the refusal by Spring Grove under Strauch to erect the railroad steam engine monument is, as far as I can tell, a unique instance of extreme rigidity in what constituted an "appropriate" monument design. In more recent history, Spring Grove was once again the center of controversy concerning the placement on a burial lot of what the cemetery regarded as an inappropriate monument—in this case, it was a double monument that had been rendered as the cartoon character SpongeBob SquarePants to mark the grave of murdered Sgt. Kimberly Walker, who had, in life, been a huge fan of the cartoon character, and the future grave of her sister, who serves in the navy. See "Family, Cemetery Reinstall SpongeBob Headstones but with Changes," https://www.wlwt.com/article/family-ce metery-reinstall-spongebob-headstones-but-with-changes/3539583#

23. "Spring Grove Cemetery—A Breeze in the Vale of Jehoshaphat," *Cincinnati Daily Press*, October 1, 1860, 2.

24. "Mount Auburn Cemetery," *Boston Evening Transcript*, February 5, 1861, 4.

25. "Mount Auburn Cemetery," *Pittston (PA) Gazette*, June 30, 1864, 2.

26. *Annual Report of the Trustees of the Cemetery of Mount Auburn, Together with the Reports of the Treasurer and Superintendent, January, 1882* (Boston: Alfred Mudge & Son, 1882), 7.

27. "Cemeteries," *New Englander and Yale Review* 22 (October 1863): 606.

28. Verd Mont, "Greenwood Cemetery," *Vermont Journal* (Windsor), June 15, 1861, 3.

29. "Jottings by the Way," *National Republican* (Washington, DC), September 7, 1861, 2.

30. "Woodlawn Cemetery," *New York Times*, September 10, 1865, 8. It is unclear exactly who, at this time, served as secretary at Laurel Hill Cemetery. The minutes for the December 1865 board meeting list Benjamin Richards Jr. as just having been elevated to the role of treasurer, while John S. Smith, Lloyd Pearsall Smith, and Frederick Brown Jr. are listed as managers without specific titles. These minutes are the only ones available for 1865, and it would have been one of these men who visited Woodlawn in September.

31. "The Homes of the Dead—New-York City Cemeteries," *New York Times*, March 30, 1866, 2.

32. *The Woodlawn Cemetery, for the City of New York and Vicinity, Its Grounds, Provisions of the Statute, Rules and Regulations* (New York, 1864), 10.

33. *Boston Evening Transcript*, October 28, 1868, 3.

34. "A New Cemetery," *Evening Telegraph* (Philadelphia), November 22, 1869, 8.

35. Reprinted as "A Park Cemetery," *Philadelphia Inquirer*, April 28, 1870, 2.

36. *Reading (PA) Times*, December 23, 1870, 3.

37. "Comfort for Mourners," *San Francisco Chronicle*, May 26, 1871, 2.

38. "A Novelty," *Atchison (KS) Daily Champion*, June 4, 1871, 3.

39. "West Laurel Hill," *Philadelphia Inquirer*, June 19, 1877, 2.

40. *West Laurel Hill Cemetery* (Philadelphia: Office of the Company, 1907), 14; after Lebanon Cemetery was condemned in 1899, the bodies were relocated in 1903 to Eden Cemetery in Collingdale, Pennsylvania, and Lebanon Cemetery was formally closed in that year. "Lebanon Cemetery," https://www.findagrave.com/cemetery/2494796/lebanon-cemetery-(defunct)

41. Phone interview with Laurel Hill Cemetery staff, September 2022.

42. "Our Cemeteries, Old and New School," *Boston Evening Transcript*, August 19, 1873, 3.

43. "Cedar Grove Cemetery: A Brief History," https://www.cgcem.org/a-brief-history/

44. "Cemeteries. Old and New Plans of Laying Out and Ornamenting," *Pittsburgh Weekly Gazette*, January 7, 1873, 2; *Allegheny Cemetery: Historical Account of Incidents and Events Connected with its Establishment* (Pittsburgh: Bakewell & Marthens, 1873), 140, 144.

45. *Allegheny Cemetery*, 145.

46. *Allegheny Cemetery*, 146.

47. *Allegheny Cemetery*, 146–48.

48. "Cemeteries. Old and New Plans," *Pittsburgh Weekly Gazette*, 2.

49. *Homewood Cemetery, 1878–1905: Rules, Regulations and General Information* (Pittsburgh, 1905), 7–8.

50. *Homewood Cemetery*, 40.

51. *Homewood Cemetery*, 40–41.

52. *Homewood Cemetery*, 41.

53. *Homewood Cemetery*, 41–42.

54. *A Guide or Hand-Book for Mount Hope Cemetery, with Photo-Engravings and Diagram* (Rochester, NY: Democrat and Chronicle Book and Job Print, 1885), 12.

55. *West Laurel Hill Cemetery*, 16.

56. Gary Laderman, *The Sacred Remains: American Attitudes toward Death, 1799–1883* (New Haven: Yale University Press, 1996), 166–67.

57. Ann Douglas, "Heaven Our Home: Consolation Literature in the Northern United States, 1830–1880," *American Quarterly* 26, no. 5 (December 1974), 496–515; Sean A. Scott, "'Earth Has No Sorrow That Heaven Cannot Cure': Northern Civilian Perspectives on Death and Eternity during the Civil War," *Journal of Social History* 41, no. 4 (Summer 2008): 843–66.

58. Laderman, *The Sacred Remains*, 74–76.

59. Charles Rosenberg, *The Care of Strangers: The Rise of America's Hospital System* (Baltimore: Johns Hopkins University Press, 1987).

60. Laderman, *The Sacred Remains*, 167.

61. On the popularity of spiritualism, see Ronald Pearsall, *The Table-Rappers: The Victorians and the Occult* (Gloucestershire, UK: Sutton Publishing, 1972).

62. For an excellent source on postmortem material culture, see C. L. Miller, *Postmortem Collectibles* (Altglen, PA: Schiffer Publishing, 2001).

63. Joy M. Giguere, "'Palaces for the Dead': The Mausoleum Craze in Gilded Age America," *Markers XXXVII: The Annual Journal of the Association for Gravestone Studies* (2021): 120–60.

64. "Mount Auburn Cemetery," *Pittston (PA) Gazette*, June 30, 1864, 2.

65. Robert H. Wiebe, *The Search for Order, 1877–1920* (New York: Farrar, Straus and Giroux, 1967).

66. *King's Handbook of New York City* (Boston: Moses King, 1893), 520.

67. *Appleton's Dictionary of "Greater" New York and Its Vicinity* (New York: D. Appleton, 1898), 368.

68. Regarding the modern twentieth-century funeral industry, see Jessica Mitford, *The American Way of Death Revisited* (New York: Vintage, 2000); the comic novel *The Loved One*, by Evelyn Waugh, lampoons the modern cemetery and funeral industry of the early twentieth century.

69. "Druid Ridge Cemetery: Pretty Burial Ground at Pikesville Dedicated with Elaborate Exercises," *The Sun* (Baltimore), June 13, 1898, 7.

70. Regarding the stages of mourning, mourning attire, and expectations for length of bereavement for widows during the nineteenth century, see Lou Taylor, *Mourning Dress: A Costume and Social History* (London: G. Allen and Unwin, 1983).

71. Joseph Story, "An Address Delivered on the Dedication of the Cemetery at Mount Auburn, September 24th, 1831," https://mountauburn.org/joseph-storys-con secration-address/

72. "Caring for the Dead: Magnificent Cemetery to Be Dedicated at Somerton Hills," *Ocean Grove (NJ) Record*, May 24, 1899, 1.

73. "Our Cemeteries. Salient Features of Rosehill, Chicago's Beautiful 'City of the Dead,'" *Chicago Tribune*, September 19, 1886, 18.

74. "An Addition," *Statesman Journal* (Salem, OR), May 31, 1892.

75. "In Cave Hill: The Story of the Beautiful Cemetery," *Courier-Journal* (Louisville, KY), June 16, 1895, 17.

76. *Inter Ocean* (Chicago), January 29, 1898, 7.

77. Ryan K. Smith, *Death and Rebirth in a Southern City: Richmond's Historic Cemeteries* (Baltimore: Johns Hopkins University Press, 2020), 217–18.

78. Kami Fletcher, "Founding Baltimore's Mount Auburn Cemetery and Its Importance to Understanding African American Burial Rights," in Allan Amanik and Kami Fletcher, eds., *Till Death Do Us Part: American Ethnic Cemeteries as Borders Uncrossed* (Jackson: University Press of Mississippi, 2020), 129–56 (quote on 152).

79. *Oak Ridge Cemetery: Its History and Improvements, Rules and Regulations. National Lincoln Monument, and Other Monuments, Charter and Ordinances* (Springfield, IL: H. W. Rokker, 1879), 20.

CONCLUSION

1. "Half Million in Improvements at Cemetery," *Pasadena Post*, July 25, 1921, 5.

2. Forest Lawn—Glendale, https://forestlawn.com/parks/glendale/

3. Jessica Mitford, *The American Way of Death Revisited* (New York: Vintage, 1998), 105.

4. Philippe Ariès, *The Hour of Our Death* (New York: Alfred Knopf, 1981), 559–614; Shai Lavi, "How Dying Became a 'Life Crisis,'" *Daedalus* 137, no. 1 (Winter 2008): 57–65; Caitlin Doughty, *Smoke Gets In Your Eyes & Other Lessons from the Crematory* (New York: W. W. Norton, 2014).

5. Candi K. Cann, *Virtual Afterlives: Grieving the Dead in the Twenty-First Century* (Lexington: University Press of Kentucky, 2014), 13, 19–20. In the field of psychology, bereavement lasting more than a year for adults and six months for children accompanied by symptoms that disrupt normal daily life may be diagnosed as "prolonged grief disorder" according to the DSM-5. During the nineteenth century, by contrast, prolonged grief was a cultural expectation, especially for widows. Regarding the DSM-5 diagnosis, see https://www.psychiatry.org/patients-families/prolonged-grief -disorder

6. "Time to Grieve: Building Equitable Bereavement Guidelines," https://www .hrci.org/community/blogs-and-announcements/hr-leads-business-blog/hr-leads -business/2022/02/14/time-to-grieve-are-a-few-days-of-bereavement-leave-enough

7. David Charles Sloane, *Is the Cemetery Dead?* (Chicago: University of Chicago Press, 2018), 195; Kami Fletcher, "Long Live Chill: Exploring Grief, Memorial, and Ritual within African American R.I.P. T-shirt Culture," in Aubrey Thamann and Kalliopi M. Christodoulaki, eds., *Beyond the Veil: Reflexive Studies of Death and Dying* (New York: Berghahn Books, 2021), 209–34.

8. David Charles Sloane, *Is the Cemetery Dead?*, 191–212.

9. Lebanon Cemetery (Defunct), https://www.findagrave.com/cemetery/24947 96/lebanon-cemetery-(defunct); Erin McLeary, "The Curious Case of Body Snatching at Lebanon Cemetery," April 13, 2015, Hidden City: Exploring Philadelphia's Urban Landscape, https://hiddencityphila.org/2015/04/the-curious-case-of-body -snatching-at-lebanon-cemetery/

10. Mount Vernon Cemetery Conservation Company, https://www.mountverno ncemetery.org/; Friends of Mount Moriah Cemetery, https://friendsofmountmoriah cemetery.org/

11. Isaac Shearn and Elgin Klugh, eds., *A Place for Memory: Baltimore's Historic Laurel Cemetery* (New York: Rowman & Littlefield, 2023); History of Laurel Cemetery, https://laurelcemetery.omeka.net/history

12. Ed Snyder, "How Monument Cemetery Was Destroyed," *Cemetery Traveler*, May 6, 2011, http://thecemeterytraveler.blogspot.com/2011/05/how-monument-ce metery-was-destroyed.html; Ed Snyder, "The Watery Remains of Monument Cemetery," *Cemetery Traveler*, April 30, 2011, http://thecemeterytraveler.blogspot.com/20 11/04/watery-remains-of-monument-cemetery.html

13. Spring Grove—Locations, https://www.springgrove.org/locations/

14. Mount Hope Cemetery and Crematory Corporation—Services, https://mthop ebgr.com/services/

15. Mount Auburn Cemetery—Burial Space, https://www.mountauburn.org/ce metery/burial-space/

16. Green-Wood Cemetery—Full Price List, https://www.green-wood.com/full -price-list/

17. Mount Auburn Cemetery—Events Calendar, https://www.mountauburn.org /events/

18. Laurel Hill Cemetery—Annual Events, https://laurelhillphl.com/events/ann ual-events/

19. Official Run Like Hell 2021 Playlist, https://oaklandcemetery.com/official-run -like-hell-5k-2021-playlist/; Capturing the Spirit of Oakland Halloween Tour Info & FAQs, https://oaklandcemetery.com/cso-2022-faqs/

20. Cave Hill Heritage Foundation—Program Schedule, https://www.cavehillher itagefoundation.org/programs/public-tours/

21. "Louisville's Hidden Figures: Cave Hill Cemetery Offers Civil Rights Leaders Tour," https://www.whas11.com/article/news/local/louisvilles-hidden-figures-cave -hill-cemetery-offers-civil-rights-leaders-tour/417-454970423

22. Joseph Charap, Sara Evans, and Frank S. Rossi, "Confronting Climate Change at an Urban Grassland," *Arnoldia* 77, no. 3 (2020): 26–31.

23. Conversation with Jennie Benford, historian at the Homewood Cemetery Historical Fund, November 5, 2022.

24. Katie McClymont and Danielle Sinnett, "Planning Cemeteries: Their Potential Contribution to Green Infrastructure and Ecosystem Services," *Frontiers in Sustainable Cities*, December 16, 2021, https://doi.org/10.3389/frsc.2021.789925

Bibliography

PRIMARY SOURCES

Newspapers & Periodicals

Albany (NY) Argus, 1845
Alexandria (VA) Gazette, 1845
American Quarterly, 1834
American Quarterly Observer, 1834
American Traveller (Boston), 1834
Anti-Slavery Bugle (Lisbon, OH), 1852
Atchison (KS) Daily Champion, 1871
Atkinson's Casket, 1837
Atlanta Constitution, 1875–94
Atlantic Monthly, 1886
Baltimore Clipper, 1841
Baltimore Saturday Visiter, 1842
Bangor (ME) Daily Whig & Courier, 1836
Boston Daily Atlas, 1852
Boston Daily Evening Transcript, 1852–61
Boston Evening Transcript, 1862–73
Boston Medical & Surgical Journal, 1831
Boston Mercantile Journal, 1837
Boston Traveler, 1831
Brooklyn Daily Eagle, 1844–66
Buchanan County Guardian (Independence, IA), 1862
Burlington (NC) Daily Times, 1863
Centinel of Freedom (Newark, NJ), 1854
Charleston Courier, 1850–57
Charleston Daily Courier, 1861–62
Charleston Mercury, 1822–63
Chicago Tribune, 1886–2017
Christian Review, 1848

Cincinnati Daily Press, 1860
Cincinnati Enquirer, 1842–59
Columbus (MS) Democrat, 1837
Columbus (OH) Democrat, 1837
Commercial Tribune (Cincinnati), 1861
The Commonwealth (Frankfort, KY), 1845
The Confederate (Raleigh, NC), 1864
Courier-Journal (Louisville), 1895
Daily Dispatch (Richmond), 1863
Daily Evening Herald (Stockton, CA), 1866
Daily Picayune (New Orleans), 1841
Daily Southern Crisis (Jackson, MS), 1863
Daily True Delta (New Orleans), 1863
Detroit Free Press, 1847
Evening Bulletin (San Francisco), 1860
Evening Post (New York), 1822–47
Evening Telegraph (Philadelphia), 1869
Fall River (MA) Monitor, 1836
Georgia Journal and Messenger (Macon), 1856
Gloucester (MA) Telegraph, 1838
Harper's New Monthly Magazine, 1859
Horticulturalist and Journal of Rural Art and Rural Taste, 1848–55
Inter-Ocean (Chicago), 1898
*Ladies' Garland and Family Wreath Embracing Tales, Sketches, Incidents,
    History, Poetry, Music, etc.*, 1838–39
Leavenworth (KS) Bulletin, 1863
Liberator (Boston), 1833
Long-Island Star (Brooklyn), 1840
Los Angeles Times, 2008
Louisville Daily Democrat, 1861–63
Louisville Morning Courier, 1848
Lowell Offering, 1840
Macon (GA) Telegraph, 1864
*Magazine of Horticulture, Botany, and All Useful Discoveries and Improvements
    in Rural Affairs*, 1853
Mechanics' Magazine & Register of Inventions & Improvements, 1833
Memphis Daily Argus, 1866
Memphis Daily Eagle and Enquirer, 1854
Mobile Daily Tribune, 1875
Muscatine (IA) Weekly Journal, 1863
Nashville Union and American, 1866
National Advocate (New York), 1822

National Aegis (Worcester, MA), 1842–43

National Gazette (Philadelphia), 1826–37

National Republican (Washington, DC), 1861

New Albany (IN) Ledger, 1862

New Bedford (MA) Register, 1843

New England Farmer (Boston), 1831–36

New England Farmer & Horticultural Journal, 1829–31

New-England Magazine, 1832–34

New Englander, 1849

New Englander and Yale Review, 1863

New York American, 1833

New-York American for the Country, 1822

New York Commercial Advertiser, 1845–46

New York Daily Times, 1852

New York Daily Tribune, 1865

New-York Farmer & Horticultural Repository, 1831

New York Spectator, 1822–45

New York Times, 1862–66

Norfolk Democrat (Dedham, MA), 1845

North American Review, 1831–85

Norwich (CT) Aurora, 1858

Ocean Grove (NJ) Record, 1899

Opelika (AL) Observer, 1879

Parley's Magazine, 1835

Pasadena Post, 1921

Philadelphia Inquirer, 1870–1957

Pittsburgh Gazette, 1850

Pittsburgh Weekly Gazette, 1873

Pittston (PA) Gazette, 1864

Portsmouth Journal of Literature and Politics, 1864

Post and Courier (Charleston, SC), 2016

Reading (PA) Times, 1870

Richmond Dispatch, 1861–63

Richmond Enquirer, 1850–64

Richmond Whig and Public Advertiser, 1849–58

Salem (MA) Gazette, 1838

Salem (MA) Register, 1857

San Francisco Chronicle, 1871

Saturday Morning Transcript (Boston), 1833–39

Semi-Weekly Wisconsin (Milwaukee), 1863

Sentinel of Freedom (Newark, NJ), 1841

Shreveport (LA) Semi-Weekly News, 1864

Southern Literary Messenger, 1853–56
Southern Patriot (Charleston), 1845
The Statesman (New York), 1822
Statesman Journal (Salem, OR), 1892
Summit County Beacon (Akron, OH), 1850
The Sun (Baltimore), 1838–98
Taunton Whig and Courier, 1836
Times-Picayune (New Orleans), 1864
Tuscaloosa (AL) News, 1876
Vermont Journal (Windsor), 1861
Vernon County Censor (Viroqua, WI), 1863
Washington (PA) Reporter, 1849
Weekly Commonwealth (Topeka, KS), 1861
Weekly Mississippian (Jackson), 1863
Winona (MN) Daily Republican, 1863–65
Wooster (OH) Republican, 1862
Yorkville (SC) Enquirer, 1864

Archives

Patton Family Papers, Filson Historical Society, Louisville, KY
William Jonathan Davis Papers, 1856–1908, Filson Historical Society, Louisville, KY

Pamphlets, Guidebooks, Essays, Reports, Diaries, Books

Albany Rural Cemetery Association: Its Rules, Regulations, &c. with An Appendix. Albany, NY, 1846.
Allegheny Cemetery: Historical Account of Incidents and Events Connected with Its Establishment. Pittsburgh: Bakewell & Marthens, 1873.
Allen, Francis D. *Documents and Facts Showing the Fatal Effects of Interments in Populous Cities.* New York, 1822.
Annual Report of the Trustees of the Cemetery of Mount Auburn, Together with the Reports of the Treasurer and Superintendent, January, 1882. Boston: Alfred Mudge & Son, 1882.
Appleton's Dictionary of "Greater" New York and Its Vicinity. New York: D. Appleton, 1898.
Avary, Marta Lockett. *A Virginia Girl in the Civil War: Being a Record of the Actual Experiences of the Wife of a Confederate Officer.* Santa Barbara, CA: Narrative Press, 2004.
Baldwin, Oliver P. *Address Delivered at the Dedication of the Hollywood Cemetery, on Monday, the 25th June, 1849.* Richmond, VA, 1849.
Bigelow, Jacob. *Elements of Technology, Taken Chiefly from a Course of Lectures Delivered at Cambridge, on the Application of the Sciences to the Useful Arts, Now Published for the Use of Seminaries and Students.* Boston: Hilliard, Gray, Little and Wilkins, 1829.
Bigelow, Jacob. *A History of the Cemetery of Mount Auburn.* Boston: James Munroe, 1859.

Bigelow, Jacob. *The Useful Arts, Considered in Connexion with the Applications of Science, with Numerous Engravings*, 2nd ed. New York: Harper & Brothers, 1863.

Brewer, William A. *Recreations of a Merchant, or the Christian Sketch-Book.* 1836.

Browning, George. "On Yellow Fever." *British Medical Journal* 1, no. 168 (March 17, 1860): 208–10.

The Cemetery of Spring Grove. Cincinnati, 1849.

The Charter, By-Laws and Regulations of the Woodlands Cemetery Company, with a List of the Lot Holders, to August 1857. Philadelphia: James B. Chandler, 1857.

Charter, By-Laws and Rules and Regulations of Cave Hill Cemetery Co. (Incorporated 1848) and Charter of Cave Hill Investment Co. (Incorporated 1882). Louisville, KY, 1901.

Church, Rev. Pharcellus. *An Address Delivered at the Dedication of Mount Hope Cemetery, Rochester, Oct. 2, 1838; And Repeated, By Request, Before the Rochester Athenaeum and Young Men's Association.* Rochester, 1839.

The Cincinnati Cemetery of Spring Grove, Report for 1857. Cincinnati: C. F. Bradley, 1857.

Cleaveland, Nehemiah. *Green-Wood Illustrated, in Highly Finished Line Engraving, from Drawings Taken on the Spot by James Smillie.* New York: R. Martin, 1847.

Clift, G. Glenn, editor. *The Private War of Lizzie Hardin: A Kentucky Confederate Girl's Diary of the Civil War in Kentucky, Virginia, Tennessee, Alabama, and Georgia.* Frankfort: Kentucky Historical Society, 1963.

Coffin, John Gorham. *Remarks on the Dangers and Duties of Sepulture: Or, Security for the Living, with Respect and Repose for the Dead.* Boston: Phelps and Farnham, 1823.

Cushing, Caroline Elizabeth Wilde. *Letters, Descriptive of Public Monuments, Scenery, and Manners in France and Spain, Vol. I.* Newburyport, MA: E. W. Allen, 1832.

Davison, Gideon Miner. *The Traveller's Guide through the Middle and Northern States, and Provinces of Canada.* Saratoga Springs, NY, 1834.

Dearborn, Nathaniel. *A Concise History of, and Guide through Mount Auburn.* Boston: Nathaniel Dearborn, 1843.

Dedication of the Bellefontaine Cemetery: Address of Professor Post, and Other Proceedings on That Occasion. St. Louis, MO, 1851.

The Dedication of Green Mount Cemetery, July 13, 1839. Baltimore, 1839.

Downing, Andrew Jackson. "Public Cemeteries and Public Gardens." In *Rural Essays*, edited by George William Curtis. New York, 1853, 154–59.

Duncan, John M. *Travels through Part of the United States and Canada in 1818 and 1819.* New York: W. B. Gilley, 1823.

Dwight, Theodore. *Things as They Are: Or, Notes of a Traveller through Some of the Middle and Northern States.* New York: Harper & Brothers, 1834.

Dwight, Timothy. *A Statistical Account of the Towns and Parishes in the State of Connecticut, Published by the Connecticut Academy of Arts and Sciences.* New Haven: Walter and Steele, 1811.

Elmwood: Charter, Rules, Regulations and By-Laws of Elmwood Cemetery Association of Memphis. Memphis, TN, 1874.

Emery, Samuel Hopkins. *History of Taunton, Massachusetts: From Its Settlement to the Present Time.* Syracuse, NY: D. Mason, 1893.

Exposition of the Plan and Objects of the Green-Wood Cemetery. An Incorporated Trust Chartered by the Legislature of the State of New York. New York: 1839.

Fraser, Charles. *Address Delivered on the Dedication of Magnolia Cemetery, on the 19th of November, 1850.* Charleston, SC, 1850.

A Guide or Hand-Book for Mount Hope Cemetery, with Photo-Engravings and Diagram. Rochester, NY: Democrat and Chronicle Book and Job Print, 1885.

Guide to Laurel Hill Cemetery, Near Philadelphia. C. Sherman, 1847.

Haliburton, Thomas Chandler. *The Clockmaker: The Sayings and Doings of Samuel Slick of Slickville.* Paris, 1841.

Hardie, James. *An Account of the Yellow Fever, Which Occurred in the City of New-York, in the Year 1822, to Which Is Prefixed a Brief Sketch of the Different Pestilential Diseases, with Which This City Was Afflicted, in the Years 1798, 1799, 1803 & 1805, with the Opinion of Several of Our Most Eminent Physicians, Respecting the Origin of the Disease, Its Prevention and Cure, to Which is Added, a Correct List of All the Deaths by Yellow Fever during the Late Season, Taken from Official Documents.* New York: Samuel Marks, 1822.

Harris, Thaddeus William. *Discourse Delivered before the Massachusetts Horticultural Society, on the Celebration of its Fourth Anniversary, October 3, 1832.* Cambridge: E. W. Metcalf, 1832.

Hayward, John. *A Gazetteer of the United States of America: Comprising a Concise General View of the United States; Also, Its Mineral Springs, Waterfalls, Caves, Beaches, and Other Fashionable Resorts.* Philadelphia, 1854.

Historical Sketch of Hollywood Cemetery, from the 3d of June, 1847, to 1st Nov., 1875. Richmond, VA, 1875.

A History of the Proceedings of the Board of Health, of the City of New-York, in the Summer and Fall of 1822; Together with an Account of the Rise and Progress of the Yellow Fever, Which Appeared during That Season, and the Several Documents in Relation to It, Which Were Laid before the Board. New York: Board of Health, 1823.

Hollywood Cemetery. Richmond, VA, 1850.

Homewood Cemetery, 1878–1905: Rules, Regulations and General Information. Pittsburgh, 1905.

Humphrey, Edward P. *An Address Delivered on the Dedication of the Cave Hill Cemetery Near Louisville, July 25, 1848.* Louisville, KY, 1848.

An Illustrated and Descriptive Catalogue of Manufactures of Tredegar Iron Works. Richmond, VA, 1860.

Johnson, L. F. *History of the Frankfort Cemetery.* Frankfort, KY, 1921.

Jones, Jenkin Lloyd. *An Artilleryman's Diary.* Madison: Wisconsin History Commission, 1914.

Jones, John Beauchamp. *A Rebel War Clerk's Diary at the Confederate States Capital.* Philadelphia: J. B. Lippincott, 1866.

King's Handbook of New York City. Boston: Moses King, 1893.

Lamar, Dolly Blount. *When All Is Said and Done.* Athens: University of Georgia Press, 1952.

Lawrence, Robert Means. *Old Park Street and Its Vicinity*. Boston, 1922.

Laws of the General Assembly of the Commonwealth of Pennsylvania. Harrisburg: J. M. G. Lescure, 1848.

Lincoln, Levi. *An Address Delivered on the Consecration of the Worcester Rural Cemetery, September 8, 1838, by Levi Lincoln*. Boston, 1838.

Magnolia Cemetery: The Proceedings at the Dedication of the Grounds: To Which Are Appended the Rules, Regulations and Charter of the Company. Charleston, SC, 1851.

Martineau, Harriet. *Retrospect of Western Travel, Vol. 3*. London, 1838.

McCandless, Wilson. *First Report of the Managers of the Allegheny Cemetery, Together with the Charter of the Corporation: Also a Funeral Address*. Pittsburgh, 1849.

McLean, Hon. John. *Address Delivered on the Consecration of the Spring Grove Cemetery, Near Cincinnati, August 20th, 1845, by the Hon. John M'Lean*. Cincinnati, 1845.

Muir, John. *A Thousand Mile Walk to the Gulf*. Boston: Houghton Mifflin, 1916.

Oak Ridge Cemetery: Its History and Improvements, Rules and Regulations. National Lincoln Monument, and Other Monuments, Charter and Ordinances. Springfield, IL: H. W. Rokker, 1879.

Pascalis-Ouvrière, F. *Exposition of the Dangers of Interments in Cities*. New York, 1823.

The Picturesque Pocket Companion, and Visitor's Guide, through Mount Auburn: Illustrated with Upwards of Sixty Engravings on Wood. Boston: Otis, Broaders, 1839.

Plan, Prospectus, and Terms, for the Establishment of a Public Cemetery, at the City of Baltimore, to Be Called the Green Mount Cemetery. Baltimore, 1838.

Regulations of the Laurel Hill Cemetery, on the River Schuylkill, near Philadelphia. 1837.

Report of the Board of Managers to the Proprietors and Lot-Holders of Green Mount Cemetery. Baltimore, 1840.

Report of the Committee of the Firemen's Charitable Association, on the Cypress Grove Cemetery. New Orleans, 1840.

Report of the Select Committee in Relation to the Quarantine Laws of the Port of New York. New York State Legislature, 1846.

Romaine, Benjamin. *Observations, Reasons and Facts, Disproving Importation: And Also, All Specific Personal Contagion in Yellow Fever, from Any Local Origin, Except That Which Arises from the Common Changes of the Atmosphere*. New York: J. C. Spear, 1823.

Rules, Regulations, and By-Laws of Cave Hill Cemetery: With the Dedicatory Address and Topographical and Descriptive Notices. Louisville, KY, 1860.

Rules and Regulations of the Green-Wood Cemetery; with a Catalogue of Proprietors, and Mr. Cleaveland's Descriptive Notices of Green-Wood Illustrated. New York, 1851.

Schenck, Rev. Noah Hunt. *Oration Delivered at the Opening Services of the Rosehill Cemetery Association, on Thursday, July 28, 1859*. Chicago: Rose Hill Cemetery Association, 1859.

Second Report of the Board of Trustees of Elmwood Cemetery (from July 6, 1850, to October 9, 1857): Also, Rules, Regulations, and Suggestions: To Which Is Added the First Report of the Board. Detroit: Geo. H. Fleming, 1858.

Smith, John David, and William Cooper, editors. *A Union Woman in Civil War Kentucky: The Diary of Frances Peter*. Lexington: University Press of Kentucky, 2000.

Spring Grove Cemetery: Its History and Improvements, with Observations on Ancient and Modern Places of Sepulture. Cincinnati: Robert Clarke, 1869.

Stiles, Ezra. *The Literary Diary of Ezra Stiles, Edited under the Authority of the Corporation of Yale University.* New York: C. Scribner's Sons, 1901.

Story, Joseph. "An Address Delivered on the Dedication of the Cemetery at Mount Auburn, September 24th, 1831." https://mountauburn.org/joseph-storys-consec ration-address/

Stuart, James. *Three Years in North America, Volume I.* Edinburgh: John Stark, 1833.

Trollope, Frances. *Domestic Manners of the Americans.* London, 1832.

Walter, Cornelia. *Mount Auburn Illustrated in Highly Finished Line Engraving, from Drawings Taken on the Spot, by James Smillie. With Descriptive Notices by Cornelia W. Walter.* New York: Robert Martin, 1847.

West Laurel Hill Cemetery. Philadelphia: Office of the Company, 1907.

Willard, Emma Hart. *Journal and Letters from France and Great Britain.* Troy, NY: N. Tuttle, 1833.

The Woodlawn Cemetery, for the City of New York and Vicinity, Its Grounds, Provisions of the Statute, Rules and Regulations. New York, 1864.

"Yellow Fever and Mosquitoes." *Science* 12, no. 305 (November 2, 1900): 692–93.

SECONDARY SOURCES

Books

Amanik, Allan, and Kami Fletcher, editors. *Till Death Do Us Part: American Ethnic Cemeteries as Borders Uncrossed.* Jackson: University Press of Mississippi, 2020.

Apel, Thomas A. *Feverish Bodies, Enlightened Minds: Science and the Yellow Fever Controversy in the Early American Republic.* Stanford: Stanford University Press, 2016.

Ariès, Philippe. *The Hour of Our Death.* New York: Alfred Knopf, 1981.

Benes, Peter, editor. *Puritan Gravestone Art: The Dublin Seminar for New England Folklife Annual Proceedings, 1976.* Boston: Boston University Press, 1977.

Berry, Daina Ramey. *The Price for Their Pound of Flesh: The Values of the Enslaved, from Womb to Grave, in the Building of a Nation.* Boston: Beacon Press, 2017.

Beveridge, Charles E., editor. *Frederick Law Olmsted: Writings on Landscape, Culture, and Society.* New York: Library of America, 2015.

Binski, Paul. *Medieval Death.* London: British Museum Press, 1996.

Blair William. *Cities of the Dead: Contesting the Memory of the Civil War in the South, 1865–1914.* Chapel Hill: University of North Carolina Press, 2011.

Brown, Thomas J. *Civil War Monuments and the Militarization of America.* Chapel Hill: University of North Carolina Press, 2019.

Bynum, Helen. *Spitting Blood: The History of Tuberculosis.* London: Oxford University Press, 2015.

Cann, Candi K. *Virtual Afterlives: Grieving the Dead in the Twenty-First Century.* Lexington: University Press of Kentucky, 2014.

Chaffee, Linda Smith, John B. Coduri, and Ellen L. Madison. *Built from Stone: The Westerly Granite Story*. Westerly, RI: Babcock-Smith House Museum, 2011.

Chase, Theodore, and Laurel K. Gabel. *Gravestone Chronicles I*. Boston: New England Historic Genealogical Society, 1997.

Chase, Theodore, and Laurel K. Gabel. *Gravestone Chronicles II*. Boston: New England Historic Genealogical Society, 1997.

Clayton, Ralph. *Black Baltimore, 1820–1870*. Bowie, MD: Heritage Books, 1987.

Coleman, John Winston. *Last Days, Death, and Funeral of Henry Clay: With Some Remarks on the Clay Monument in the Lexington Cemetery*. Ann Arbor: University of Michigan Press, 1951.

Costello, Matthew R. *The Property of the Nation: George Washington's Tomb, Mount Vernon, and the Memory of the First President*. Lawrence: University Press of Kansas, 2019.

Cothran, James R., and Erica Danylchak. *Grave Landscapes: The Nineteenth-Century Rural Cemetery Movement*. Charleston: University of South Carolina Press, 2018.

Cronon, William. *Nature's Metropolis: Chicago and the Great West*. New York: W. W. Norton, 1991.

Davis, Ren, and Helen Davis. *Atlanta's Oakland Cemetery: An Illustrated History and Guide*. Athens: University of Georgia Press, 2012.

Davis, Veronica A. *Here I Lay My Burdens Down: A History of the Black Cemeteries of Richmond, Virginia*. Richmond, VA: Dietz Press, 2003.

Dedek, Paul. *The Cemeteries of New Orleans: A Cultural History*. Baton Rouge: Louisiana State University Press, 2017.

Deetz, James. *In Small Things Forgotten: An Archaeology of Early American Life*. New York: Anchor Books, 1996.

De Jong, Mary, editor. *Sentimentalism in Nineteenth-Century America: Literary and Cultural Practices*. Madison, NJ: Farleigh Dickinson University Press, 2013.

Doughty, Caitlin. *Smoke Gets In Your Eyes & Other Lessons from the Crematory*. New York: W. W. Norton, 2014.

Ehrenpreis, Anne Henry, editor. *Happy Country This America: The Travel Diary of Henry Arthur Bright*. Columbus: Ohio State University Press, 1978.

Eicher, David J. *The Longest Night: A Military History of the Civil War*. New York: Simon & Schuster, 2001.

Fabre, Geneviève, and Robert O'Meally, editors. *History and Memory in African-American Culture*. New York: Oxford University Press, 1994.

Faust, Drew Gilpin. *This Republic of Suffering: Death and the American Civil War*. New York: Vintage Books, 2008.

Florence, Robert. *New Orleans Cemeteries: Life in the Cities of the Dead*. New Orleans: Batture Press, 1997.

Forbes, Harriet Merrifield. *Gravestones of Early New England and the Men Who Made Them, 1653–1800*. Boston: Houghton Mifflin, 1927.

Frankfort Cemetery in Kentucky. Frankfort, KY: The Kentucky Genealogical Society, 1988.

Giguere, Joy M. *Characteristically American: Memorial Architecture, National Identity, and the Egyptian Revival.* Knoxville: University of Tennessee Press, 2014.

Greenberg, Amy S. *A Wicked War: Polk, Clay, Lincoln, and the 1846 U.S. Invasion of Mexico.* New York: Vintage Books, 2013.

Grimsted, David. *Melodrama Unveiled: American Theater and Culture, 1800–1850.* Chicago: University of Chicago Press, 1968.

Howe, Daniel Walker. *What Hath God Wrought: The Transformation of America, 1815–1848.* New York: Oxford University Press, 2007.

Janney, Caroline E. *Burying the Dead but Not the Past: Ladies' Memorial Associations & the Lost Cause.* Chapel Hill: University of North Carolina Press, 2008.

Johnson, Paul E. *Sam Patch, the Famous Jumper.* New York: Hill & Wang, 2004.

Joyce, J. St. George. *Story of Philadelphia.* Philadelphia, 1919.

Jupp, Peter C., and Clare Gittings, editors. *Death in England: An Illustrated History.* New Brunswick, NJ: Rutgers University Press, 1999.

Kammen, Michael. *Digging Up the Dead: A History of Notable American Reburials.* Chicago: University of Chicago Press, 2010.

Kasson, John F. *Rudeness & Civility: Manners in Nineteenth-Century Urban America.* New York: Hill & Wang, 1990.

Kelly, Catherine E. *Republic of Taste: Art, Politics, and Everyday Life in Early America.* Philadelphia: University of Pennsylvania Press, 2016.

Kete, Mary Louise. *Sentimental Collaborations: Mourning and Middle-Class Identity in Nineteenth-Century America.* Durham: Duke University Press, 2000.

Kimball, Gregg D. *American City, Southern Place: A Cultural History of Antebellum Richmond.* Athens: University of Georgia Press, 2000.

Laderman, Gary. *The Sacred Remains: American Attitudes Toward Death, 1799–1883.* New Haven: Yale University Press, 1996.

Laqueur, Thomas W. *The Work of the Dead: A Cultural History of Mortal Remains.* Princeton: Princeton University Press, 2015.

Lears, T. J. Jackson. *No Place of Grace: Antimodernism and the Transformation of American Culture, 1880–1920.* Chicago: University of Chicago Press, 1994.

Levine, Lawrence W. *Highbrow Lowbrow: The Emergence of Cultural Hierarchy in America.* Cambridge, MA: Harvard University Press, 1988.

Linden, Blanche M. G. *Silent City on a Hill: Picturesque Landscapes of Memory and Boston's Mount Auburn Cemetery.* Amherst: University of Massachusetts Press, 2007.

Ludwig, Allan. *Graven Images: New England Stonecarving and Its Symbols, 1650–1815.* Hanover, NH: University Press of New England, 1966.

Marshall, Anne Elizabeth. *Creating a Confederate Kentucky: The Lost Cause and Civil War Memory in a Border State.* Chapel Hill: University of North Carolina Press, 2013.

Masur, Louis P. *1831: Year of Eclipse.* New York: Hill and Wang, 2001.

Matthews, Glenna. *The Rise of Public Woman: Woman's Power and Woman's Place in the United States, 1630–1970.* New York: Oxford University Press, 1992.

McConachie, Bruce A., and Daniel Friedman, editors. *Theater for the Working-Class Audiences in the United States, 1830–1980*. Westport, CT: Praeger, 1985.

McDannell, Colleen. *Material Christianity: Religion and Popular Culture in America*. New Haven: Yale University Press, 1995.

McDowell, Peggy, and Richard E. Meyer. *The Revival Styles in American Memorial Art*. Bowling Green, OH: Bowling Green State University Popular Press, 1994.

McElya, Micki. *The Politics of Mourning: Death and Honor in Arlington National Cemetery*. Cambridge, MA: Harvard University Press, 2016.

McNeur, Catherine. *Taming Manhattan: Environmental Battles in the Antebellum City*. Cambridge, MA: Harvard University Press, 2014.

Miller, C. L. *Postmortem Collectibles*. Altglen, PA: Schiffer Publishing, 2001.

Milward, Burton. *A History of the Lexington Cemetery*. Lexington: Lexington Cemetery Company, 1989.

Mitchell, Mary H. *Hollywood Cemetery: The History of a Southern Shrine*. Richmond, VA: Library of Virginia, 1999.

Mitford, Jessica. *The American Way of Death Revisited*. New York: Vintage, 2000.

Pearsall, Ronald. *The Table-Rappers: The Victorians and the Occult*. Gloucestershire, UK: Sutton Publishing, 1972.

Phillips, Christopher. *The Rivers Ran Backward: The Civil War and the Remaking of the American Middle Border*. New York: Oxford University Press, 2016.

Phillips, Ted. *City of the Silent: The Charlestonians of Magnolia Cemetery*. Columbia: University of South Carolina Press, 2010.

Purcell, Sarah J. *Spectacle of Grief: Public Funerals and Memory in the Civil War Era*. Chapel Hill: University of North Carolina Press, 2022.

Reynolds, David S. *Waking Giant: America in the Age of Jackson*. New York: Harper Collins, 2008.

Rosenberg, Charles. *The Care of Strangers: The Rise of America's Hospital System*. Baltimore: Johns Hopkins University Press, 1987.

Rosenzweig, Roy, and Elizabeth Blackmar. *The Park and the People: A History of Central Park*. Ithaca: Cornell University Press, 1992.

Sachs, Aaron. *Arcadian America: The Death and Life of an Environmental Tradition*. New Haven: Yale University Press, 2013.

Sayre, Gordon M. *Les Sauvages Américains: Representations of Native Americans in French and English Colonial Literature*. Chapel Hill: University of North Carolina Press, 2000.

Scee, Trudy Irene. *Mount Hope Cemetery of Bangor, Maine: The Complete History*. Charleston, SC: History Press, 2012.

Seeman, Erik R. *Death in the New World: Cross-Cultural Encounters, 1492–1800*. Philadelphia: University of Pennsylvania Press, 2010.

Seeman, Erik R. *Speaking with the Dead in Early America*. Philadelphia: University of Pennsylvania Press, 2019.

Sellers, Charles. *The Market Revolution: Jacksonian America, 1815–1846*. New York: Oxford University Press, 1991.

Shearn, Isaac, and Elgin Klugh, editors. *A Place for Memory: Baltimore's Historic Laurel Cemetery*. Lanham, MD: Rowman & Littlefield, 2023.

Sloane, David Charles. *Is the Cemetery Dead?* Chicago: University of Chicago Press, 2018.

Sloane, David Charles. *The Last Great Necessity: Cemeteries in American History*. Baltimore: Johns Hopkins University Press, 1991.

Smith, Jeffrey. *The Rural Cemetery Movement: Places of Paradox in Nineteenth-Century America*. Lanham, MD: Lexington Books, 2017.

Smith, Ryan K. *Death and Rebirth in a Southern City: Richmond's Historic Cemeteries*. Baltimore: Johns Hopkins University Press, 2020.

Stannard, David. *The Puritan Way of Death: A Study in Religion, Culture, and Social Change*. New York: Oxford University Press, 1977.

Swedlund, Alan C. *Shadows in the Valley: A Cultural History of Illness, Death, and Loss in New England, 1840–1916*. Amherst: University of Massachusetts Press, 2010.

Tashjian, Dickran, and Ann Tashjian. *Memorials for Children of Change: The Art of Early New England Stonecarving*. Middletown, CT: Wesleyan University Press, 1974.

Taylor, Lou. *Mourning Dress: A Costume and Social History*. London: G. Allen and Unwin, 1983.

Thamann, Aubrey, and Kalliopi M. Christodoulaki, editors. *Beyond the Veil: Reflexive Studies of Death and Dying*. New York: Berghahn Books, 2021.

Townshend, Henry H. *The Grove Street Cemetery: A Paper Read before the New Haven Colony Historical Society, October 27, 1947*. Printed for the Society, 1948.

Upton, Dell. *Another City: Urban Life and Urban Spaces in the New American Republic*. New Haven: Yale University Press, 2008.

Walden, Geoffrey R. *Confederate Soldiers and Civilians Buried in the Confederate Sections and National Cemetery, Cave Hill Cemetery, Louisville, Kentucky*. Louisville: G. R. Walden, 1996.

Wiebe, Robert H. *The Search for Order, 1877–1920*. New York: Farrar, Straus, and Giroux, 1967.

Wilson, Susan. *Garden of Memories: A Guide to Historic Forest Hills*. Boston: Forest Hill Educational Trust, 1998.

Articles, Papers, and Book Chapters

Amanik, Allan. "'A Beautiful Garden Consecrated to the Lord': Marriage, Death, and Local Constructions of Citizenship in New York's Nineteenth-Century Jewish Rural Cemeteries." In Allan Amanik and Kami Fletcher, editors, *Till Death Do Us Part: American Ethnic Cemeteries as Borders Uncrossed*, 15–34. Jackson: University Press of Mississippi, 2020.

Bachand, Marise. "Gendered Mobility and the Geography of Respectability in Charleston and New Orleans, 1790–1861." *Journal of Southern History* 81 (February 2015): 41–78.

Beardslee, G. William. "The 1832 Cholera Epidemic in New York State: 19th Century

Responses to *Cholerae Vibrio*." *Early America Review* 3, no. 2 (Fall 2000). Available at https://web.archive.org/web/20100502025213/http://www.earlyamerica.com/review/2000_fall/1832_cholera_part1.html

Bender, Thomas. "The 'Rural' Cemetery Movement: Urban Travail and the Appeal of Nature." *New England Quarterly* 47, no. 2 (June 1974): 196–211.

Bluestone, Daniel M. "From Promenade to Park: The Gregarious Origins of Brooklyn's Park Movement." *American Quarterly* 39 (Winter 1987): 529–50.

Bohan, Ruth L. "A Home Away from Home: Bellefontaine Cemetery, St. Louis, and the Rural Cemetery Movement." *Prospects* 13 (October 1988): 135–79.

Breibart, Solomon. "The Jewish Cemeteries of Charleston." *Catalogue: Bulletin of the South Carolina Historical Society* 9 (Summer 1993): 8–9, 14–16.

Bryan, William D. "Taming the Wild Side of Bonaventure: Tourism and the Contested Southern Landscape." *Southern Cultures* 23, no. 2 (Summer 2017): 49–74.

Butsch, Richard. "Bowery B'hoys and Matinee Ladies: The Re-Gendering of Nineteenth-Century American Theater Audiences." *American Quarterly* 46 (September 1994): 374–405.

Charap, Joseph, Sara Evans, and Frank S. Rossi. "Confronting Climate Change at an Urban Grassland." *Arnoldia* 77, no. 3 (2020): 26–31.

Ciregna, Elise Madeleine. "Museum in the Garden: Mount Auburn Cemetery and American Sculpture, 1840–1860." *Markers XXI* (2004): 100–147.

Darnell, Margaretta J. "The American Cemetery as Picturesque Landscape: Bellefontaine Cemetery, St. Louis." *Winterthur Portfolio* 18 (Winter 1983): 249–69.

Deetz, James, and Edwin Dethlefsen. "Death's Head, Cherub, Urn and Willow." *Natural History* 76, no. 3 (1967): 29–37.

Deetz, James, and Edwin Dethlefsen. "Death's Heads, Cherubs, and Willow Trees: Experimental Archaeology in Colonial Cemeteries." *American Antiquity* 31, no. 4 (April 1966): 502–10.

Domosh, Mona. "Those 'Gorgeous Incongruities': Polite Politics and Public Space on the Streets of Nineteenth-Century New York City." *Annals of the Association of American Geographers* 88 (June 1998): 209–26.

Douglas, Ann. "Heaven Our Home: Consolation Literature in the Northern United States, 1830–1880." *American Quarterly* 26, no. 5 (December 1974): 496–515.

Fletcher, Kami. "Founding Baltimore's Mount Auburn Cemetery and Its Importance to Understanding African American Burial Rights." In Allan Amanik and Kami Fletcher, editors, *Till Death Do Us Part: American Ethnic Cemeteries as Borders Uncrossed*, 129–56. Jackson: University Press of Mississippi, 2020.

Fletcher, Kami. "Long Live Chill: Exploring Grief, Memorial, and Ritual within African American R.I.P. T-shirt Culture." In Aubrey Thamann and Kalliopi M. Christodoulaki, editors, *Beyond the Veil: Reflexive Studies of Death and Dying*, 209–34. New York: Berghahn Books, 2021.

Francaviglia, Richard V. "The Cemetery as an Evolving Cultural Landscape." *Annals of the Association of American Geographers* 61 (September 1971): 501–9.

French, Stanley. "The Cemetery as Cultural Institution: The Establishment of Mount Auburn and the 'Rural Cemetery' Movement." *American Quarterly* 26, no. 1 (March 1974): 37–59.

Giguere, Joy M. "The Americanized Sphinx: Civil War Commemoration, Jacob Bigelow, and the *Sphinx* at Mount Auburn Cemetery." *Journal of the Civil War Era* 3, no. 1 (Spring 2013): 62–84.

Giguere, Joy M. "'Flaunting the Evidence of Treason in the Face of Loyalty': Funerals, Grave Decoration, and the Fashioning of Kentucky's Civil War Identity." *Ohio Valley History* 19, no. 4 (Winter 2019): 19–44.

Giguere, Joy M. "'Palaces for the Dead': The Mausoleum Craze in Gilded Age America." *Markers XXXVII: The Annual Journal of the Association for Gravestone Studies* (2021): 120–60.

Giguere, Joy M. "Variety There Must Be: Eclecticism, Taste and the Nineteenth-Century Rural Cemetery Landscape." *Markers XXXIII* (2017): 82–104.

Hacker, J. David. "A Census-Based Count of the Civil War Dead." *Civil War History* 57, no. 4 (December 2011): 307–48.

Hijiya, James. "American Gravestones and Attitudes toward Death: A Brief History." *Proceedings of the American Philosophical Society* 127, no. 5 (October 14, 1983): 339–63.

Hobbs, June Hadden. "Say It with Flowers in the Victorian Cemetery." *Markers XVIIII* (2002): 240–71.

Horrocks, Krista. "Burials under the Pavement: The History of Columbus, Ohio's North Graveyard and the 2023 Excavations at the North Market Parking Lot." Annual Meeting of the Association for Gravestone Studies, University of Denver, June 20–25, 2023.

Krüger-Kahloula, Angelika. "On the Wrong Side of the Fence: Racial Segregation in American Cemeteries." In Geneviève Fabre and Robert O'Meally, editors, *History and Memory in African-American Culture*, 130–49. New York: Oxford University Press, 1994.

La Roche, Cheryl J., and Michael L. Blakey. "Seizing Intellectual Power: The Dialogue at the New York African Burial Ground." *Historical Archaeology* 31, no. 3 (1997): 84–106.

Lancaster, R. Kent. "Green Mount: The Introduction of the Rural Cemetery into Baltimore." *Maryland Historical Magazine* 74 (March 1978): 62–79.

Lavi, Shai. "How Dying Became a 'Life Crisis.'" *Daedalus* 137, no. 1 (Winter 2008): 57–65.

Levy, B. H. "Savannah's Old Jewish Community Cemeteries." *Georgia Historical Quarterly* 66 (Spring 1982): 1–20.

Linden-Ward, Blanche. "'The Fencing Mania': The Rise and Fall of Nineteenth-Century Funerary Enclosures." *Markers VII* (1990): 34–58.

Linden-Ward, Blanche. "Strange but Genteel Pleasure Grounds: Tourist and Leisure Uses of Nineteenth Century Rural Cemeteries." In Richard E. Meyer, editor,

Cemeteries & Gravemarkers: Voices of American Culture, 293–328. Logan: Utah State University Press, 1989.

Linden-Ward, Blanche, and Alan Ward. "Spring Grove: The Role of the Rural Cemetery in American Landscape Design." *Landscape Architecture* 75 (September/October 1985): 126–31.

Malone, Bobbie. "New Orleans Uptown Jewish Immigrants: The Community of Congregation Gates of Prayer, 1850–1860." *Louisiana History* 32 (Summer 1991): 239–78.

Malone, Patrick M., and Charles A. Parrott. "Greenways in the Industrial City: Parks and Promenades along the Lowell Canals." *IA: The Journal of the Society for Industrial Archaeology* 24, no. 1 (1998): 19–40.

Marshall, Anne E. "A Sisters' War: Kentucky Women and Their Civil War Diaries." *Register of the Kentucky Historical Society* 110 (Summer–Autumn 2012): 481–502.

Martin, Anne Marie. "'In This City of the Dead': Charleston's Magnolia Cemetery and Middle-Class Aspiration." *Journal of Urban History* 47, no. 5 (September 2021): 1050–66.

McClymont, Katie, and Danielle Sinnett. "Planning Cemeteries: Their Potential Contribution to Green Infrastructure and Ecosystem Services." *Frontiers in Sustainable Cities* (December 16, 2021). https://doi.org/10.3389/frsc.2021.789925

Meeks, C. L. V. "Picturesque Eclecticism." *Art Bulletin* 32, no. 3 (September 1950): 226–35.

Morton, Jennie C. "History of the Frankfort Cemetery." *Register of the Kentucky State Historical Society* 7 (January 1909): 23, 25–34.

Nystrom, Kenneth C. "The Bioarchaeology of Structural Violence and Dissection in the 19th-Century United States." *American Anthropologist* 116, no. 4 (December 2014): 765–79.

Patterson, K. David. "Yellow Fever Epidemics and Mortality in the United States, 1693–1905." *Social Science & Medicine* 34, no. 8 (1992): 855–65.

Richman, Jeffrey I. "Green-Wood Cemetery." *Military Images* 39, no. 4 (Autumn 2021): 60–66.

Roark, Elisabeth L. "Embodying Immortality: Angels in America's Rural Cemeteries, 1850–1900." *Markers XXIV* (2007): 56–111.

Rotundo, Barbara. "Mount Auburn Cemetery: A Proper Boston Institution." *Harvard Library Bulletin* 22 (July 1974): 268–79.

Rotundo, Barbara. "Mount Auburn: Fortunate Coincidences and an Ideal Solution." *Journal of Garden History* 4 (July–September 1984): 255–67.

Sachs, Aaron. "American Arcadia: Mount Auburn Cemetery and the Nineteenth-Century Landscape Tradition." *Environmental History* 15 (April 2010): 206–35.

Schuyler, David. "The Evolution of the Anglo-American Rural Cemetery: Landscape Architecture as Social and Cultural History." *Journal of Garden History* 4 (July–September 1984): 291–304.

Scobey, David. "Anatomy of the Promenade: The Politics of Bourgeois Sociability in Nineteenth-Century New York." *Social History* 17 (May 1992): 203–27.

Scott, Sean A. "'Earth Has No Sorrow That Heaven Cannot Cure': Northern Civilian Perspectives on Death and Eternity during the Civil War." *Journal of Social History* 41, no. 4 (Summer 2008): 843–66.

Smith, Jeffrey. "Till Death Keeps Us Apart: Segregated Cemeteries and Social Values in St. Louis, Missouri." In Allan Amanik and Kami Fletcher, editors, *Till Death Do Us Part: American Ethnic Cemeteries as Borders Uncrossed*, 157–82. Jackson: University Press of Mississippi, 2020.

Story, Ronald. "Class and Culture in Boston: The Athenaeum, 1807–1860." *American Quarterly* 27, no. 2 (May 1875): 178–99.

Streater, Kristen L. "'Not Much a Friend to Traiters No Matter How Beautiful': The Union Military and Confederate Women in Civil War Kentucky." In Kent T. Dollar, Larry H. Whiteaker, and W. Calvin Dickinson, editors, *Sister States, Enemy States: The Civil War in Kentucky and Tennessee*, 245–66. Lexington: University Press of Kentucky, 2009.

Tatum, George B. "The Beautiful and the Picturesque." *American Quarterly* 3, no. 1 (Spring 1951): 36–51.

Taylor, Dorceta E. "Central Park as a Model for Social Control: Urban Parks, Social Class and Leisure Behavior in Nineteenth-Century America." *Journal of Leisure Research* 31, no. 4 (1999): 420–77.

Upton, Dell. "The Urban Cemetery and the Urban Community: The Origin of the New Orleans Cemetery." *Perspectives in Vernacular Architecture* 7 (1997): 131–45.

Wall, David. "Andrew Jackson Downing and the Tyranny of Taste." *American Nineteenth Century History* 8 (June 2007): 187–203.

Websites

Albany Rural Cemetery Soldiers' Lot. National Cemetery Administration. https://www.cem.va.gov/cems/lots/Albany_Rural.asp

Bonaventure Historical Society. https://www.bonaventurehistorical.org/must-see/

Capturing the Spirit of Oakland Halloween Tour Info & FAQs. https://oaklandcemetery.com/cso-2022-faqs/

Cave Hill Heritage Foundation—Program Schedule. https://www.cavehillheritagefoundation.org/programs/public-tours/

"Cedar Grove Cemetery: A Brief History." https://www.cgcem.org/a-brief-history/

"Celebrating Indiana's Limestone History." https://www.visitbloomington.com/limestone/

"Civil War Soldiers' Monument (1869)." https://www.green-wood.com/2010/civil-war-soldiers-monument-saved/

"Family, Cemetery Reinstall SpongeBob Headstones but with Changes." https://www.wlwt.com/article/family-cemetery-reinstall-spongebob-headstones-but-with-changes/3539583#

Forest Lawn—Glendale. https://forestlawn.com/parks/glendale/

"The Freedom Lots." https://green-wood.maps.arcgis.com/apps/MapJournal/index.html?appid=b550a7818cbd408d812755c5183bd619

French, Mary. New York City Cemetery Project: Public Burial Ground, Bryant Park. https://nycemetery.wordpress.com/2019/05/30/public-burial-ground-bryant-park/

Friends of Mount Auburn. "The Civil War and Mount Auburn Cemetery." https://mountauburn.org/the-civil-war/

Friends of Mount Auburn. "Shaw Monument." https://mountauburn.org/shaw-monument-2/

Friends of Mount Moriah Cemetery. https://friendsofmountmoriahcemetery.org/

Green Mount Cemetery: Architecture. https://www.greenmountcemetery.com/greenmount-cemetery-features-architecture.html

Green-Wood Cemetery—Full Price List. https://www.green-wood.com/full-price-list/

"Henry Toland, Jr." https://www.findagrave.com/memorial/73102918/henry-toland

"Historic Eden Cemetery: Beginnings." https://www.edencemetery.org/beginnings

Historical Currency Converter. https://futureboy.us/fsp/dollar.fsp

History of Laurel Cemetery. https://laurelcemetery.omeka.net/history

Laurel Hill Cemetery—Annual Events. https://laurelhillphl.com/events/annual-events/

"Lebanon Cemetery (Defunct)." https://www.findagrave.com/cemetery/2494796/lebanon-cemetery-(defunct)

"Louisville's Hidden Figures: Cave Hill Cemetery Offers Civil Rights Leaders Tour." https://www.whas11.com/article/news/local/louisvilles-hidden-figures-cave-hill-cemetery-offers-civil-rights-leaders-tour/417-454970423

Magnolia Cemetery. http://www.magnoliacemetery.com/

"Many Roads to Freedom: Abolitionist and Civil War Sites in Rochester." http://libraryweb.org/rochimag/roads/map14.htm

McLeary, Erin. "The Curious Case of Body Snatching at Lebanon Cemetery." April 13, 2015, Hidden City: Exploring Philadelphia's Urban Landscape. https://hiddencityphila.org/2015/04/the-curious-case-of-body-snatching-at-lebanon-cemetery/

Mount Auburn Cemetery—Burial Space. https://www.mountauburn.org/cemetery/burial-space/

Mount Auburn Cemetery—Events Calendar. https://www.mountauburn.org/events/

Mount Hope Cemetery and Crematory Corporation—Services. https://mthopebgr.com/services/

Mount Vernon Cemetery Conservation Company. https://www.mountvernoncemetery.org/

"Nathan Dunn and His Museum of '10,000 Chinese Things.'" https://blogs.harvard.edu/preserving/2015/06/03/nathan-dunn-and-his-museum-of-10000-chinese-things/

National Cemetery Administration. https://www.cem.va.gov/facts/NCA_History_and_Development_1.asp

Official Run Like Hell 2021 Playlist. https://oaklandcemetery.com/official-run-like-hell-5k-2021-playlist/

"Olive Cemetery (Defunct)." https://www.findagrave.com/cemetery/2672577/olive-cemetery

"Population of the 61 Urban Places: 1820." https://www.census.gov/population/www/documentation/twps0027/tab05.txt

"Population of the 100 Largest Urban Places: 1840." https://www2.census.gov/library/working-papers/1998/demographics/pop-twps0027/tab07.txt

"Population of the 100 Largest Urban Places: 1850." https://www2.census.gov/library/working-papers/1998/demographics/pop-twps0027/tab08.txt

Prolonged Grief Disorder. DSM-5. https://www.psychiatry.org/patients-families/prolonged-grief-disorder

Salem Pioneer Cemetery, Summary History of the Cemetery. https://www.salempioneercemetery.org/history.php

"Sesquicentennial Memorial Day Service." Magnolia Cemetery. http://www.magnoliacemetery.net

Smith, Ryan K. "Richmond Cemeteries." www.richmondcemeteries.org

Snyder, Ed. "How Monument Cemetery Was Destroyed." *Cemetery Traveler*, May 6, 2011. http://thecemeterytraveler.blogspot.com/2011/05/how-monument-cemetery-was-destroyed.html

Snyder, Ed. "The Watery Remains of Monument Cemetery." *Cemetery Traveler*, April 30, 2011. http://thecemeterytraveler.blogspot.com/2011/04/watery-remains-of-monument-cemetery.html

Spring Grove—Locations. https://www.springgrove.org/locations/

"The State Street Burying Grounds." *The Church Grounds—Albany Rural Cemetery*. https://albanychurchgrounds.wordpress.com/the-state-street-burying-grounds/

"Time to Grieve: Building Equitable Bereavement Guidelines." https://www.hrci.org/community/blogs-and-announcements/hr-leads-business-blog/hr-leads-business/2022/02/14/time-to-grieve-are-a-few-days-of-bereavement-leave-enough

"Who's Buried in Laurel Hill Cemetery? PCP Luminaries." https://usciencesblogs.typepad.com/experts/2011/04/whose-buried-in-laurel-hill-cemetery-pcp-luminaries.html

World Health Organization: Yellow Fever. https://www.who.int/news-room/fact-sheets/detail/yellow-fever

Index

Abolitionism, 42, 240n
African American cemeteries, 90,
  118–19, 169, 220n; East End Cem-
  etery (Richmond, VA), 200; Eden
  Cemetery (Philadelphia, PA), 204,
  231n, 243n; Evergreen Cemetery
  (Richmond, VA), 118, 200; Laurel
  Cemetery (Baltimore), 6, 118–19, 120–
  21, 204–5, 212n, 232n, 245n; Lebanon
  Cemetery (Philadelphia), 61, 116–17,
  185–86, 204, 231n, 243n, 245n; Mount
  Auburn Cemetery (Baltimore, MD),
  200, 244n; Olive Cemetery (Philadelphia), 116–17, 231n
African (Negroes') Burial Ground (New
  York City), 22, 214n
African Americans, 117, 148; burial of,
  27, 28–29, 85, 116–17, 147, 185–86, 215;
  burial societies, 118, 200; emancipa-
  tion of, 142; establishment of Black
  cemeteries, 6, 118, 200, 231n; funerals,
  118; United States Colored Troops,
  141, 204, 238n
Akron, OH, 112
Akron Rural Cemetery (Akron, OH),
  42, 133–34, 234n. See also Glendale
  Cemetery
Albany, NY, 26, 161–62, 215n
Albany Rural Cemetery (Albany, NY),
  6, 110, 116, 215n, 225n, 241–42n; Civil
  War soldiers' lot and monument, 159,
  161–62, 164, 239n, 240n
Ali, Muhammad, 207

All Saints' Day, 157
Allegheny Cemetery (Pittsburgh, PA),
  ix, 6, 68, 70, 110, 116, 131, 187–89,
  208, 234n, 243n; Winter mausoleum,
  208–9
Allen, Francis D., 24–25, 29, 215n
Allen, Stephen, 23
American Quarterly Observer, 51–52, 80,
  219n, 224n
Antiquity, 64, 67, 133, 158
Appleton, Samuel, 35, 103
Appleton's Dictionary of New York, 197,
  244n
Architectural eclecticism. See architec-
  tural revivalism
Architectural revivalism, 99; criticisms
  of, 69, 99, 102, 222n; Egyptian revival,
  2, 17, 32, 54, 66–69, 100, 102, 134, 208,
  214n, 222n, 227–29n, 239n; Gothic
  revival, 32, 67–70, 102, 208, 228–29n;
  Neoclassicism, 4, 14, 17, 44–45, 68,
  98–100, 102, 195
Arlington National Cemetery, 235–36n
Association for the Benefit of Colored
  Orphans, 85
Association for Gravestone Studies, 10,
  208–9, 220–21n, 244n, 260n
Austin, Henry, 67–68
Austin, James T., 35
Avary, Marta Lockett, 150, 237n

Baker, George N., 60
Baldwin, Oliver P., 130–31, 234n